International studies in the history of sport
series editor J. A. Mangan

Sport, politics and the working class

Sport, politics
and the working class

Organised labour and sport
in inter-war Britain

Stephen G. Jones

Manchester University Press

Manchester and New York

Distributed exclusively in the USA and Canada
by St. Martin's Press

Published by Manchester University Press
Oxford Road, Manchester M13 9PL, UK
and Room 400, 175 Fifth Avenue, New York, NY 10010, USA

Distributed exclusively in the USA and Canada
by St. Martin's Press, Inc.,
175 Fifth Avenue, New York, NY 10010, USA

British Library cataloguing in publication data

Jones, Stephen G. (Stephen Glyn), *1957–1987*.
  Sport, politics and the working class:
  a study of organised labour and sport
  in inter-war Britain.—(Studies in the history of sport series).
  1. Great Britain. Leisure activities,
  1919–1939
  I. Title   II. Series
  306′.48′0941

Library of Congress cataloging in publication data

Jones, Stephen G.
  Sport, politics, and the working class : a study of organised
  labour and sport in inter-war Britain/Stephen G. Jones.
    p. cm. — (Studies in the history of sport series)
  Bibliography: p. 201.
  Includes index.
  ISBN 0-7190-2616-4 : $35.00 (est.)
    1. Sports—Great Britain—History—20th century. 2. Labor and
  laboring classes—Great Britain—Recreation—History—20th century.
  3. Sports and state—Great Britain—History—20th century. 4. Great Britain—
  Politics and government—1918-1936.   I. Title.
  II. Series.
  GV605.J6 1988
  796′.0941—dc19

Typeset by Witwell Limited, Southport
Printed in Great Britain
by Billing & Sons Limited, Worcester

ISBN 0-7190-2616-4 *hardback*

Contents

		page
Acknowledgements		viii
Series editor's foreword		ix
List of abbreviations		xi
Chapter 1	Introduction	1
2	Sport and the working class in the late nineteenth century	15
3	Working-class sport in the years of peace, 1918–39	42
4	'Up the Reds': workers, socialists and sport	73
5	The Labour Party, the unions and sport in the 1930s	104
6	The State, working-class politics and sport	129
7	'Sport under red flags': the working class and international sport	164
8	Conclusion	196
Select bibliography		201
Index		217

Dedicated to the memory of
STEPHEN GLYN JONES (1957–87)
from his wife, Kathryn.

I loved him as a man,
admired him as a scholar
and shall always miss him
as my friend.

Acknowledgements

Tragically, my husband was killed in a road accident very shortly after producing the typescript for this book. Although he may have been intending a few minor revisions, I believe that it is essentially complete. Unfortunately, however, he never wrote his acknowledgements, so on his, and indeed on my own, behalf, I wish to thank everyone who has been instrumental in the birth of this text. In this respect, I would like to thank his friends and colleagues in the Department of Economics and Economic History at Manchester Polytechnic, in particular Neville Kirk and Terry Wyke for reading drafts, and the latter for the task (an onerous one, I know) of producing an index. Also, I wish it to be known that I am forever appreciative of the unstinting support of Mr George Zis, Head of Department at the Polytechnic, whom Stephen always regarded as a respected mentor. Lastly, for myself, I wish to acknowledge the immense debt I owe to all my friends and family for their support through this terrible time.

Kathryn Jones, December 1987

Series editor's foreword

This series is the first of its kind in the academic world. It is surely timely. Frederick Boas, the distinguished American anthropologist, once remarked that to have an understanding of a complex phenomenon, it is necessary not only to know what it is, but how it came into being. In the modern world sport is both complex and extensive. It is a major social phenomenon of this century, with political, cultural, economic, spiritual and aesthetic dimensions. E. J. Hobsbawm has called it one of the most significant of the new social practices of late nineteenth-century Europe. Its significance has clearly increased in the twentieth. Its late nineteenth-century international institutionalisation, Hobsbawm suggests, had three facets: it was an extended form of conspicuous consumption, it provided a means of uniting members of the same class and it offered liberalising opportunities for bourgeois women. Considered simply in these restricted terms and within this short time scale it is a fit and proper subject of study for historians. There can be little danger here of the social historical heresy Walvin has warned against, that of 'elevating minutiae to the level of social significance'. Rather, the question should be asked as to why such an important aspect of modern society has been so inexcusably neglected. The wonder is that professional myopia has lasted for so long. The reason is not hard to find. To extend the argument of Bryan Turner regarding a sociology of the body, to sport, history like sociology is still essentially Cartesian in implicitly accepting a rigid mind/body dichotomy when philosophy has dismissed the distinction as invalid. And to extend Turner's argument still further, it is time that sport, like the body, was incorporated within conventional historical debate about ideologies, control, organisation, stratification and mobility.

This series, it is hoped, will reduce academic shortsightedness. Among its early publications will be studies of English social life and association football by N. B. F. Fishwick, English society and cricket between the wars by Jack Williams, women, medicine and exercise in the nineteenth century by Patricia Vertinsky, the role of sport in the evolution of soviet society by James Riordan and the hotrod culture and American society by H. F. Moorhouse.

One point should be laboured at the outset. These studies will attempt to set sport in its full cultural context. Its relationship to society will be the concern of the authors. The case for the history of sport as a self-contained specialism will not be argued or advanced in this series. Furthermore, the contributors may be considered *historiens–sociologues* rather than *historiens–historisantes*. They are interested in sequences, tendencies, outcomes and change within specific cultural contexts.

It is with a mixture of pleasure and sadness that I introduce the first volume in the series. Stephen Jones (tragically killed shortly after completing this book) is in no doubt about his fundamental purpose. His study of sport, politics and the working class is solidly located 'in the broader political economy, the ensemble of economic and social relationships and the values' of British society during the inter-war years.

Jones focuses on the role of the British labour movement in the development of sport between 1918 and 1940. In essence, he presents a case study of the subtle interaction between political structure and human response, and documents the limits imposed on the British working class by the historical and contemporary 'contradictions and tensions of capitalist society' – deep divisions of class and gender and widespread middle-class male control. At the same time, he reveals the gains made by the workers, through both the process of 'asymmetrical' negotiation between proletariat and bourgeoisie and Labour's challenge of orthodox views about the relationship of sport to society. In abstract terms this resulted in partial autonomy and complicated association; in concrete terms it resulted in changed views on access to the countryside, improved sports facilities and opposition to continental fascism. Jones makes it clear that sport was 'but one of the many sites of struggle which involved socialist intervention,' and a site on which the working class were far from impotent, gained access to the decision-making structure of society and influenced events. He integrates sport into the full set of aspirations and efforts of the proletariat to change its life for the better in the period between the First and Second World Wars.

Nothing could illustrate more appropriately the fact, as Walvin has suggested, that the historical study of sport will flourish most successfully within the complex, diverse and sympathetic habitat of social history rather than in artificial isolation.

J. A. Mangan

Abbreviations

AAA	Amateur Athletic Association
BBC	British Broadcasting Corporation
BWSF	Britsh Workers' Sports Federation
CCC	Clarion Cycling Club
CGT	Confédération Générale du Travail
CP	Communist Party
CWS	Co-operative Wholesale Society
FCSDA	Fine Cotton Spinners' and Doublers' Association
FSGT	Fédération Sportive et Gymnique du Travail
ILP	Independent Labour Party
NMM	National Minority Movement
NPFA	National Playing Fields Association
NUWM	National Unemployed Workers' Movement
NWSA	National Workers' Sports Association
RSI	Red Sports International
SDF	Social Democratic Federation
SWSI	Socialist Workers' Sports International
TUC	Trades Union Congress
WTA	Workers' Travel Association
YCL	Young Communist League

Chapter 1

Introduction

This book focuses on the relationship between the labour movement and sport in inter-war Britain. At the outset, though, the meanings and study of sport in society have to be considered. Obviously, sport includes a diversity of activities from cricket and croquet to horse-racing and rugby. If anything, sport is fundamentally about play, fun and amusement. It is also often about contests between participants, as in team sports or athletics. And again, sports may be organised, as in professional soccer, or more spontaneous, as in children's games. Sport therefore operates on a multiplicity of levels: professional and amateur, participation and spectatorship, elite sports and sports for all, the production and consumption of sports manufactures and services. Needless to say, as the opening section of the next chapter will suggest, the social position of sport changes over time. In essence, the pervasive influence of sport needs to be placed firmly within the overall socio-economic formation of work, politics and community.

The differences between sport and such related social categories as recreation and leisure are not easy to delineate, though leisure in a generic sense encompasses a much wider variety of spare-time activities like film-going and music. This is not the place to rehearse the semantics of the question, and throughout the book the terms sport, recreation, games and play are used interchangeably. More importantly, the starting point for this study is at the macro-level, namely sport and the working class in society. The theoretical and historical perspectives brought to the study will thus reflect the nature of the subject matter, and cannot hope to be specific to the variety and diversity of all sports at the micro-level.

In a similar vein, it should be emphasised that the sociological and historical analysis of sport is still in its infancy. After all, notwithstanding the tradition of British 'community studies' and the 'cultural criticism' of Richard Hoggart and Raymond Williams, it was not until the 1970s, with the publication of Kenneth Roberts' *Leisure* (1970), that a British sociology of leisure truly emerged. As Jennifer Hargreaves has maintained, serious academic treatment of sport has its roots in the physical education community and the explosion of sociology in the 1950s and 1960s.[1] Much of this work was concerned with policy questions and often lacked sustained critical analysis. At the same time, however, cultural studies and a broadly conceived Marxian social theory were beginning to make their mark. Here was a salutary attempt to analyse the social significance of culture and place it in a wider societal context. Arguably, a new school of social historians was influenced by the Marxian paradigm, as represented so powerfully in E. P. Thompson's seminal book, *The Making of the English Working Class* (1963). And most relevant for this study, sports history in Britain developed out of the rise of modern social history in the last twenty-five years or so. Sports history began to move beyond the anecdotal, the commemorative study or the statistical compendium to show the ways in which sport was historically constituted, and shaped by socio-economic, political and ideological forces. In the 1970s and early 1980s, the first serious historical studies of horse-racing, association football, rugby union and the rest began to appear.

Sport as a serious academic subject has flourished in recent years. Scholars drawn from a range of disciplines have in various ways exposed sport to rigorous inquiry. No doubt this reflects the fact that sport in industrial societies is an important economic, social and political activity in its own right, able to provide the specialist with vital evidence about labour markets, capital investment, class, gender and even international relations. Growing interest is to some extent demonstrated in that sports history is now establishing itself as an important substratum of the historical sciences, a sign of which was the launch in 1984 by Dr. J. A. Mangan of the *British Journal of Sports History* (now *The International Journal of the History of Sport*). However, as James Walvin suggested in the journal's first number, there are dangers in advancing sports history as a specialist discipline, inasmuch as this can create 'among its proponents a form of intellectual "tunnel vision" which shuts out the broader perspective'. Here Walvin is surely right to warn sports historians that 'in seeking to stake out an autonomous historical empire, it is all too easy to wrench sports history from its determining social and economic context'.[2] Serious historians of leisure, sport and recreation would find it difficult to refute such a view. Indeed, given the multidisciplinary nature of sports studies and the fact that sociological and historical approaches to sport have had similar foundations in cultural studies and modern social history, it is appropriate for the historian to relate sport to wider socio-economic trends and influences.

It is thus a fundamental proposition of this study of sport and organised labour in inter-war Britain that games and play have to be located in the broader political economy, the *ensemble* of economic and social relationships and values of a particular society. After all, sports are '"determined" forms of conduct', shaped by, amongst other things, a society's ownership patterns, power networks and ideologies.[3] Leisure and sports history cannot be studied in isolation or divorced from what is happening in the world outside. A framework for analysing the historical development of sport must be firmly based on the socio-economic totality, and the various categories which make up that totality. Moreover, though writing as an historian rather than a social theorist, it is useful for the narrative to embrace elements of theory and concept, and to blend them in with the historical evidence. At least in more general terms, the attempt to link history with sociology, in what some have called historical sociology – a 'cumulative movement on both sides towards a sensible intellectual pluralism in which theory and narrative cease to stand over against one another as principled alternatives and are instead locked together in a unified project of explanation' – has been the subject of much debate in recent years.[4] The purpose of this opening chapter is therefore to provide a general theoretical underpinning for the historical analysis of sport and the wider society of which it is a part.

Theoretical approaches to sport

This brief opening section cannot hope to provide a detailed or systematic critique of sport and society, or to show the ways in which the various sociological approaches share common trait nd weaknesses; rather, the aim is to draw the reader's attention to th   ents of an emerging sports sociology. Clearly there are problems i   st the difficulty of following up the introductory comments in   the text. Yet, given limitations of space, the section c   the history of sport must be engaged in dialogue wit notably those which focus on the relation betwee

Theories of sport have of late been the subject   ion and debate. Though this is not the place to reflect on the   -ranging nature of the debate, it can be noted that social theorists have been drawn in from a number of schools of thought. In particular, ideas and concepts based upon social formalism, figurational sociology and Marxism have been applied fruitfully to leisure and sport.[5] This section will now outline briefly the main alternative approaches to sport, and then set out the particular approach taken in this study.

The first approach, that of social formalism, is linked to a scientific evaluation of society and functionalist theory. Quantification is stressed in both theory and research, and survey methods – specifically the collection of hard data – underpin the research programme. At the top of the social formalist agenda is the need for scientific definitions. Sport may be classified in terms of, say, the rules and regulations specific to individual games, the degree of organisation and the element of competition. From this, sport can be contrasted with other kinds of activities such as work and politics. Once sport has been rigorously defined it is then possible to quantify, for example, the opportunities for sport amongst discrete social groupings such as the skilled working class, women or the aged. After the 'hard' facts have been revealed it is then possible to take these into account in policy formation and action.

From functionalist theory sport is then viewed as having a functional position in the wider society, reinforcing dominant mores and conventions, and enabling people to adapt to new economic and social pressures such as the requirements of work, the bureaucracy and urban living. Put simply, sport is one way in which groups adapt to changes in the social order. It is one means of socialisation and integration. Furthermore, from this perspective, sport is sometimes seen as a kind of *voluntary* forum in which social actors are able to exercise a degree of choice, flexibility and self-determination often denied them by the inevitable disappointments and 'compulsory' character of modern living.

David Aspin's recent work on rowing seems to fit in with this pattern. Professor Aspin suggests that rowing 'consists in and is exhibited by a pattern of movements engaged in, voluntarily and with complete consciousness of what they are about, by human agents possessed of intelligence and doing what they do with reference to some ends that they value'. Hence the definition, but what about the meanings of sport? Though political and social forces are pervasive, the chief value surrounding sport is that of 'personal autonomy', and the most important principle is the morality of 'choice and freewill':

> In the final analysis engagement in sports and games is an activity of the free choice of free men and women who are masters (sic) of their own situation and determiners of their own ends. By the exercise and on the basis of their autonomy they express their will to succeed in overcoming both the efforts of other competitors and the obstacles of Nature.[6]

Quite rightly, in focusing on definitional issues, Aspin and others have observed that sport in all its disparate forms is a unique social activity, providing particular opportunities for physical self-expression – such as contests between human beings, and struggles against nature and the elements. Yet, as John Hargreaves and Chris Rojek have cogently argued, functionalist approaches are defective insomuch as they tend to isolate and separate sport from wider societal pressures and conditions which are constituted over time. After all, sport is limited by its relationship with economic and political forces. In particular, the functionalist position is insensitive to the subtle interdependence between sport and such variables as power and conflict. In capitalist society, where social divisions are so apparent, it is relevant to pose the question: for whom is sport functional – society as a whole, the nation state, the ruling elite, workers, women? Social formalism therefore tends to be rather static, failing to emphasise class power, economic inequalities, and the way in which the position of sport in society is a process contingent upon particular *historical* circumstances.

On the other hand, figurational sociology accepts that sport is produced historically within structures of 'mutually oriented and dependent people', social bonding and webs of interdependence. At root, it is the concept of interdependence which lies behind the figurational approach. This core concept stresses that bonds or relationships between people and, in turn, social networks shape development in unanticipated and anti-reductionist ways. For Norbert Elias, as the leading practitioner of the figurational approach, sport cannot be reduced to some *a priori* social or economic category, such as the material base. Thus it is singularly inappropriate for analyses of sport to be premised by teleological explanations of, say, the fate of the capitalist economic system. Rather, it is appropriate to view sport as bounded by the specific relations between people based on forms and degrees of power, whether economic, political or emotional. Most importantly, the ways in which these relations are composed and lead to changes in the 'figurations' which actually constitute society are an open-ended process; they are not static, but fluid patterns whose development can be, and must be, delineated by empirical study.

More specifically, this is to say, sport has developed in a complex and ambiguous way alongside the special figurations formed by, and interactions between, class structures, education, bureaucracy, the family and the rest. Eric Dunning's and Kenneth Sheard's excellent *Barbarians, Gentlemen and Players* is a figurational approach to sports history *par excellence*. Here it is assumed that rugby football developed in line with such figurations as the British class system and the position of the public school within that system, the civilising process, the gradual establishment of more open channels of democracy, and the friction between professional and amateur ideals. Very briefly, the pre-industrial game of boisterous village football was modified, indeed civilised, by the public school system in the second half of the nineteenth century. Given the ideological sway of public school masters, they were able to codify the game with new rules and regulations and effectively turn it into an organised and disciplined amateur activity. Yet this did not happen in isolation, for it interacted with other social changes, such as the apparent diminution of violence. At the same time, commerecial pressures, together with the demands of the working class, led to tensions and frictions over who controlled the sport. Hence the bifurcation of football into the two codes of rugby union and soccer. To be sure, the argument is far more complex than is indicated here. But for our purposes the point to note is that Dunning and Sheard are at pains to stress rugby's development as a process 'determined by the structure and dynamics of the overall social context within which at any given time, the game was played'; a context of 'incipient modernisation', the division of labour, urban change, democratisation, state formation and other interrelated social phenomena.[7]

Figurational sociology is to be welcomed for its historical emphasis, and also the way it suggests that human agents can intervene in social processes and transform them. Even so, it must be added that the ways in which individuals seek change are seen as essentially pluralistic; the character and dynamics of human figurations are reduced to power struggles between groups of like-minded individuals, rather than circumscribed by the profound inequalities of capitalist society. There is an implicit functionalism here, at least in the focus on the particular roles or functions of sport for people in figurations. As in social formalism, sport is often perceived as a specific kind of counterbalance to the 'stress-tensions of people's non-leisure life', or a compensation for the multiple constraints imposed on human development by industrialisation, urbanisation and the civilising process. Elias puts it thus:

> Whether it is the mimetic battle of a soccer game, a baseball game, a tennis tournament, an ice-hockey match, a bicycle race, a boxing match, a ski race or any other variety of the sports contests which abound in our world, and in spite of all the excesses and distortions, one can observe, again and again, the liberating effect, the release from stress-tensions that is provided, first, by the spectacle of the mock-battle, and then by its tension-relieving climax, the victory of one side or the other.[8]

Indeed, Dunning and Sheard even suggest at one point that sport functions as a medium of social integration through its role in group identification.[9]

Finally, cruder versions of Marxism suggest that sport is conditioned by the economic structures of capitalism, specifically preparing the way for capital accumulation, reproduction and legitimation. From this perspective, modern sport is an historically specific social institution which emerged with the birth of the capitalist mode of production. Sport mirrors those determining socio-economic conditions which surround it – 'an exact reflection of capitalist categories'. It is yet another means by which capitalist owners extract surplus value from the proletariat, realise profits on the market, and underwrite the accumulation process. Sport helps to reproduce a labour force which is healthy, disciplined and efficient – machine-like – as well as being ideal for inculcating such capitalist values as competitiveness, hierarchy and chauvinism; it 'is part and parcel of ruling bourgeois ideology'. And not only this, sport becomes part of capitalist commodity production in its own right, a virgin territory for the extraction of surplus value and a means of celebrating commercialism. Furthermore, the dominant class which controls sport connives with the State to enhance nationalist and imperialist ambitions.[10] Essentially then, within this unconvincing reflection thesis, sport is a mere epiphenomenon of deep-rooted materialist and infrastructural forces.

It is important to note, however, that there are contrasting approaches to sport within the Marxian tradition. Some interpretations propose that, due to the alienation of work, leisure and sport are an opportunity for relative freedom and happiness, whilst for those aligned to the Frankfurt school of critical social theory, sport, as part of the so-called 'culture industry', is seen as a means whereby capital structures leisure relations to deceive the working class. This version of the classic 'bread and circuses' idea provides little room for sport to be used creatively by the subordinate classes. Even when sport is viewed as relatively autonomous from the mode of production, it is still said to function in the last instance as an integral aspect of class domination and exploitation, insomuch as it secures a tractable labour force, often imbued with a strong sense of individualism, sexism and nationalism.[11]

From yet another Marxian position, it is true that David Whitson, John Hargreaves and others have applied the Gramscian concept of hegemony to sport and society in a more refined way. Here the crude concept of social control is rejected, though the 'economic', or the ethos of production, is still omnipresent. Hargreaves stresses that sport is neither a form of human freedom nor structural enslavement, but rather an historical process of contestation between and among social classes, by which dominant groups have to continually win over subordinate groups by means of concessions and compromises, accompanied at times by coercion:

> Sporting activity, we contend, can never be adequately explained purely as an instrument of social harmony, or as a means of self-expression, or as a vehicle for satisfying individual needs; for this ignores the divisions and conflicts, and the inequalities of power in societies, which if we care to look more closely, register themselves in sports. Nor can their social role be explained simply as a means whereby the masses are manipulated into conformity with the social order, capitalist or otherwise, for to do so is to regard people as passive dupes, and it ignores their capacity to resist control and to stamp sports with their own culture.[12]

To be sure, Hargreaves's sociological and historical analysis is extremely sensitive to the complex personality of sport in modern capitalist societies. In the last resort, however, sport is again characterised as perpetuating ruling-class hegemony through, for example, the media effect, despite promises that it can evoke opposition, change and freedom.[13]

Having outlined three main perspectives in the sociology of sport, it must be repeated that for reasons of space they have not been exposed to detailed treatment. Nonetheless, there has been some indication that they all suffer from certain flaws, some of which are common to all three. In particular, social formalism, figurational sociology and vulgar Marxism often resort to functionalist explanations. In social formalism the function of sport is posed in terms of social integration, in figurational sociology in terms of the place of individuals in figurations, and in Marxism in terms of bourgeois class rule and domination. By the same token, all three schools of thought have in places perceived sport as a compensation for the rigours of an increasingly monotonous working environment. Yet the most obvious weakness of these approaches is their failure to develop concepts which deal adequately with the position of women and ethnic minorities. Excepting the work of feminist scholars and the excellent ongoing research of H. F. Moorhouse,[14] analyses of gender and ethnicity in sociological studies of sport and leisure have often been conspicuous by their absence. And it must be stressed that this is as true of Marxism as it is of alternative traditions. Classical Marxist terms have tended to regard gender and ethnicity as secondary aspects of social class relationships. However, in placing sports in an overall social formation stratified on many levels, gender, ethnic background and nationalism have a complex and ambiguous relation to class, and cannot be reduced to a simple side-effect of capitalist exploitation. A balanced discussion of sport must be sensitive to women's limited role in sport, the symbolic nationalism demonstrated in, say, the Scotland versus England soccer match, or the exclusion of Jews and Blacks from certain voluntary organisations. This is not to argue, of course, that women and ethnic communities have been unable to find spaces for sporting initiatives of their own.

The point has now been reached to state that this study will borrow from one particular theoretical approach which has much in common with neo-Marxist political economy and cultural analysis.[15] Such an approach has been developed most recently and explicitly by Richard Gruneau in his thought-provoking *Class, Sports and Social Development*. Here there is an attempt to sustain a critique of those theoretical approaches which perceive sport simply in terms of unremitting capitalist domination on the one hand and human freedom on the other. At least by implication, Gruneau provides a form of dialogue between Marxism and social formalism, albeit by focusing on the sensitive relationship between structure and agency. But most of all, he is at pains to bind theory to detailed historical investigation. He attempts, quite brilliantly, to bring the role of sports alive by placing it in a historically specific context. Sports, so it is asserted, are 'distinctly social practices existing in, and constitutive of, historically shifting limits and possibilities that specify the range of powers available to human agents at different historical moments'.[16]

Gruneau's starting point is to see sport as limited by the kind of society in which it exists; that is, modern sports are contoured by those structural limitations which have surfaced during capitalist industrialisation. But what are these structural limitations? Though Gruneau is not particularly explicit on this, above all the central force behind capitalism is the accumulation of profit, secured by the buying and selling of labour power. From this, a complex set of class relationships, institutions and values emerge around the buyers of labour, the bourgeoisie and the sellers, the proletariat. For certain, there is no identical relationship between the dominant bourgeoisie and the subordinate proletariat, due to internal fragmentation within these two classes: different forms of waged (and domestic) labour based on, say, gender, ethnicity and skill have different relations to capital, which itself is divided along the lines of age, size, sector and spatial range. We would therefore expect, say, working-class males, women, ethnic minorities, industrialists, landowners, merchants and the rest to face sports with varying opportunities and preoccupations. Thus, as already intimated, the so-called 'under-classes', like women in the home, have had least access to sport due to their underprivileged social position. Fundamentally, any historical analysis of sport must be sensitive to the role played by class inequality, and in turn political power, state intervention and so on. For, as Gruneau argues, 'play, games, and sports are influenced by differential resources that people can bring to bear on their life situation, as a result of class differences in social life'.[17] Additionally, there may be a reciprocal relationship between class and sport: leisure and sport actually play a part in the formation and reproduction of class structures; or, at least, to borrow from R. S. Neale, the notion of a 'dialectical image' can help to demonstrate that the relationship of culture (including sport) to the wider capitalist economy is ultimately about the determination of class relations.[18]

Notwithstanding the point that dominant bourgeois or ruling groups have greater collective strength and influence, subordinate groups have still been able to 'make their own history', though not necessarily 'under conditions of their own choosing'.[19] Of course choices do exist, but these choices are limited by forces like the pattern of work, often beyond the control of the individual. Nonetheless, dominant modes of production, culture and ideology have certainly not exhausted some of the people's desire for greater autonomy and control over their own lives. In other words, the ability of people to constitute their own history is what we mean by the term *agency*. Human agents from ruling cliques such as landowners, amateur gentlemen and churchmen to organised labour movements, spontaneous crowds, and players and athletes themselves have been able to bring their own meaning, culture, concerns and emotions to sport. Once again it should be recognised that certain agents have greater leverage over the structures they have created: football chairmen have had more influence over the game than the average, individual supporter. Also here, the notion of social agency needs to be fragmented to take into account the diversity of interests from class to age and gender, the plurality of issues, and the level of agency – public or private, national or local.

Sport in capitalist society was, and is, therefore bounded by a dialectical relationship between socio-economic structures and human agency. Of course, approaches to structure and agency within English Marxism have been the site of much, and sometimes heated, discussion for a number of years. The structuralists have lined up against the culturalists, Louis Althusser against E. P. Thompson, or, as Susan Magarey has put it in an entertaining contribution, 'That hoary old chestnut, free will and determinism: culture vs. structure, or history vs. theory'.[20] Moreover, the opposition between structuralism and culturalism has now moved towards some kind of resolution in which 'structuring tendencies' are said to be reciprocated in all actions. Even so, historians should still be sensitised to this duality of structures and agencies, and the way in which groups are able to develop and transform sports against the background of objective material and social conditions. What this means is that the place of sport in capitalist society is inherently contradictory. Sport is never simply an 'instrument of domination', though ruling groups may use it as 'an access to domination', appropriating it as 'raw materials' for the expression of capitalist principles.[21] In fact, even in periods where there are profound economic and political inequalities, there is still scope to resist ruling interests and needs. In brief, it can be argued that the working class influence the constitution of sports on many levels.

This is central to the main theme of this study, for it will be maintained that in inter-war Britain sports were not sacrificial lambs to capitalist enterprise and domination. By focusing on the position of the British working-class movement – socialist political and cultural bodies, trade unions, co-operative societies – it can be shown that forms of collective self-determination have been evident in sport. True, the labour movement in Britain did not pay anywhere near as much attention to sport as its Continental counterpart. Yet to suggest that British labour made no initiatives or 'had little influence on sports overall', as Hargreaves does, is an oversimplification.[22] If Hargreaves had carried out research into the broad labour movement he would have found a great deal of evidence to refute his contention. Indeed, as one editorial in *History Workshop Journal* (no. 12) recognised, the inter-war labour movement had a rich cultural life which embraced drama, education, film and music. It is only due to 'the paucity of primary research upon the local culture between the wars' that commentators are able to perpetuate the myth that socialists neglected the cultural sphere. Not only did labour organisations spawn recreational offspring, but they also helped to modify the nature and character of the British sporting tradition.

Moreover, despite the fact that the socialist or workers' sports movement was on the margins of official sport and politics, the failure to focus on its activities, contributions and potential has the debilitating effect of, to use Dominick La Capra's words, 'depriving historiography of the need to recover significant aspects of the past that may have "lost out"'.[23] Expressed in slightly different terms, Stephen Yeo is justified in arguing that a failure to interest ourselves in change or in history 'is to conceal alternative latent potentials and achievements, in the interests of existing, manifest facts and ideologies'. For, as he continues in eloquent prose, even in the late nineteenth century, as a determined, structured, monstrous 'system' was growing up – evidenced in Empire as well as in entertainment, linked through capitalist uses of communication – and even as the eye was being battered by more and more appearances in commodity form; human efforts to comprehend and resist were (are) being made and it was becoming materially possible to supersede such a system in a way never before possible in human history.[24]

Indeed, an historical study of the British working-class movement and inter-war sport indicates that Yeo, Gruneau and a number of other commentators are quite right in pointing to the 'historical reality of resistance' and the fact that challenges to, and changes in, the dominant order have been, and can be, achieved.

This study will therefore suggest that inter-war sport was a site of class struggle and continuous debate, in which the working classes were not without an effective voice. Though working-class activists were often isolated, they evidently had influence and at one level were a force in the formal politicisation of leisure. As a study which touches on aspects of both 'labour' and 'sports' history, subsequent chapters will attempt to demonstrate that working people played an active, rather than passive, role in those dynamic economic, social, political, cultural and intellectual processes which often imposed limits on, and sometimes offered possibilities for the transformation of, sport. As such, the relationship between the working class and sport will be viewed against particular elements in the overall inter-war capitalist formation: labour movements, commerce, politics, ideologies, the State, and the international situation.

The opening chapter has provided a brief overview of certain theoretical approaches to sport. Hopefully it will enable the reader to situate the historical discussion in the remaining chapters in a theoretical framework which is attuned to the relationship between structure and social agency. Chapter 2 seeks to outline the main developments in sport in the late nineteeth century, and particularly the role played by labour groups and the Clarion movement. Chapter 3 focuses on the main trends in inter-war working-class sport, and stresses the dynamic effects of commercialisation and commodity production in the sporting domain. Chapters 4 and 5 explore Marxian and Labour–Socialist initiatives in sport, with reference to ideas, institutions and policy. The final chapters, 6 and 7, examine the political aspects of the socialist intervention. In chapter 6, the relationship between working-class politics, the State and sporting reforms is investigated, and, in chapter 7, we turn our attention to British participation in European workers' sport.

Introduction

Notes

(all books are published in London unless otherwise stated)

1 J. A. Hargreaves (ed.), *Sport, culture and ideology* (1982), ch. 1.
2 J. Walvin, 'Sport, social history and the historian', *British Journal of Sports History*, vol. 1 (1984), pp. 7,13.
3 R. W. Malcolmson, 'Sports in society: a historical perspective', *British Journal of Sports History*, vol. 1 (1984), p. 60.
4 P. Abrams, 'History, sociology, historical sociology', *Past and Present*, no. 87 (1980), p.11.
5 See the critical comments in Hargreaves, *Sport, culture and ideology*. H. Cantelon and R. Gruneau (eds), *Sport, Culture and the Modern State* (Toronto, 1982). J. M. Hoberman, *Sport and Political Ideology* (1984). J. Clarke and C. Critcher, *The Devil Makes Work: Leisure in Capitalist Britain* (1985). C. Rojek, *Capitalism and Leisure Theory* (1985). J. Horne, D. Jary and A. Tomlinson (eds), *Sports, Leisure and Social Relations* (1987).
6 D. Aspin, 'On the nature and purpose of a sporting activity: the connection between sport, life and politics', *Physical Education Review*, vol. 9 (1986), pp. 5,9.
7 E. Dunning and K. Sheard, *Barbarians, Gentlemen and Players: A Sociological Study of the Development of Rugby Football* (1979).
8 N. Elias and E. Dunning, *Quest for Excitement: Sport and Leisure in the Civilizing Process* (Oxford, 1986), p. 60.
9 Dunning and Sheard, *Barbarians*, pp. 281-2.
10 J. M. Brohm, *Sport – A Prison of Measured Time* (1978).
11 See L. Althusser, 'Ideology and ideological state apparatuses (notes towards an investigation)', in *Lenin and Philosophy and other essays* (1971).
12 J. Hargreaves, *Sport, Power and Culture: A Social and Historical Analysis of Popular Sports in Britain* (Cambridge, 1986), p. 3. See also D. J. Whitson, 'Sport and hegemony: on the construction of the dominant culture', *Sociology of Sport Journal*, vol. 1 (1984).
13 See L. Haywood, 'Hegemony – another blind alley for the study of sport', in J. A. Mangan and R. B. Small (eds), *Sport, Culture and Society: International historical and sociological perspectives* (1986).
14 See R. Deem, *All Work and No Play? The Sociology of Women and Leisure* (Milton Keynes, 1986). H. F. Moorhouse, 'Scotland against England: football and popular culture', *International Journal of the History of Sport*, vol. 4 (1987).
15 For Different Marxist approaches to cultural studies, see S. Hall, 'Cultural studies: two paradigms', in R. Collins *et al.* (eds), *Media, Culture and Society: A Critical Reader* (1986). R. Williams, *Marxism and Literature* (Oxford, 1977). R. S. Neale, 'Cultural materialism: a critique', *Social History*, vo. 9 (1984).
16 R. Gruneau, *Class, Sports and Social Development* (Amherst, 1983), p. 140.
17 *Ibid.*, p. 53.
18 D. Dawson, 'Leisure and social class: some neglected theoretical considerations', *Leisure Sciences*, vol. 8 (1986). Neale, 'Cultural materialism', p. 212.
19 Gruneau, *Class*, p. 55.
20 S. Magarey, 'That hoary old chestnut, free will and determinism: culture vs. structure, or history vs. theory in Britain', *Comparative Studies in Society and History*, vol. 29 (1987).

13

21 These terms have been borrowed from L. Kipnis, "Refunctioning" reconsidered: towards a left popular culture', in C. MacCabe (ed.), *High Theory/Low Culture: Analysing popular television and film* (Manchester, 1986), pp. 31-2.
22 Hargreaves, *Sport, Power and Culture*, p. 213. See also S. Hall, 'Notes on deconstructing "the popular" ', in R. Samuel (ed), *People's History and Socialist Theory* (1981), p. 231.
23 D. La Capra, *Rethinking Intellectual History: Texts, Contexts, Language* (Ithaca, 1983), p. 35.
24 S. Yeo, 'State and anti-state: reflections on social forms and struggles from 1850', in P. Corrigan (ed.), *Capitalism, State Formation and Marxist Theory: Historical Investigations* (1980), pp. 113, 122.

Chapter 2

Sport and the working class in the late nineteenth century

Introduction

Sport as a social phenomenon has, of course, changed over time. Put simply, sport is not the same kind of activity in the advanced capitalist societies of the late twentieth century as it was in the pre-capitalist societies of the seventeenth century. A turn to the *Oxford English Dictionary* is revealing. In 1653, we are told that sport was a 'Pastime afforded by the endeavour to kill wild animals, game, or fish', and by 1671 jesting, mirth and merriment had been added to the catalogue. In the early stages of industrialisation sports were a 'diversion', but more than that, they were linked to the rules and hierarchies of a traditional social order, and often a release from them. Sports were taken in the public domain at carnivals, festivities and parish celebrations, whilst ritual played an important role. Even the puritan reformers failed to destroy public merriment overnight. In short, the society underpinning sport was very different from today's democratic welfare state (just), commercialised lifestyle, and so on. Hence, in the seventeenth century, folk football gathered around it large numbers of active participants, and varied significantly in rules, organisation and regularity from locality to locality.[1] By the twentieth century football had been systematised and pacified, notwithstanding the hooligan element. It had become a spectator sport, organised on a national basis, and was an integral aspect of consumer culture.

The historical personality of sport needs to be recognised. It is therefore incumbent on the historian of sport to focus on the dynamics of change. This chapter will explain briefly the salient developments in working-class sport to the Victorian and Edwardian era. This will provide an essential backdrop to our discussion of the place occupied by the labour movement in late nineteenth-century sport.

The evolution of modern sports

During the course of industrialisation in the eighteenth and nineteenth centuries the sports of the British people were slowly but surely transformed. Arguably, in pre-industrial societies there was little division between work and leisure, and sports were largely determined by the rhythm of the agricultural cycle. Indeed, blood sports, field sports and those pastimes associated with the annual parish feast, market or fair were closely related to wider rural and farming influences. To take but one example: 'At fairs up and down the country, after the trading had been done and the labourers had been hired for the season, there would be athletic competitions of various kinds for young men and women.'[2] Needless to say, notwithstanding such non-violent activities as running, stoolball and climbing the greasy pole, many rural sports were rugged and very boisterous. Though the enjoyment of popular sports – those most associated with the working classes – gave the oligarchy and the gentry the opportunity to cement social bonds with the local populace, the multi-layered nature of controls made it difficult for them to impose themselves on the culture of the lower orders.[3] Even with proto-industrialisation, the modern working day had barely evolved, subject as it was to seasonal fluctuations, rural traditions, customary leisure, wakes, absenteeism, and so on.

With the advent of industrial capitalism and urban society, however, there gradually emerged a clearer separation between the quite distinct spheres of work and leisure. To be sure, capitalist modes of factory organisation, though developing unevenly over space and time, meant that the new proletariat was constrained by the exigencies of work and time discipline – the division of labour, the wage nexus, the activities of the time-keeper and informer, the face of the clock and whistle of the hooter.[4] This is not to deny, however, that workers had the capacity to control time in both work and community. Also significant is the likelihood that demands on women in the home increased as they became responsible for the reproduction of labour power. Male labour was differentiated from the female sphere in pre-capitalist societies and there is a good deal of evidence to suggest that women were especially dependent on their menfolk during menstruation, childbearing, and so on. Women's oppression was not therefore new under capitalism. Yet for certain, capitalist relations of production changed the social position of women in a qualitative sense. Though many women were wage labourers themselves, many were not, and their realm became domestic work, producing and maintaining the material needs of the family. Also, there is a further class dimension to this, for as the nineteenth century progressed more and more working-class women became domestic servants to their middle-class sisters, releasing the latter to experiment in sport and leisure.

As working time became regularised, leisure was increasingly perceived as that free time left over after work had been completed. In turn popular sports slowly became linked (at least indirectly) to the needs of capitalist masters. In accordance with market orders and delivery dates, employers required a disciplined, temperate and reliable workforce. Blood sports and other rowdy pursuits which went against this objective and led to a fall in labour productivity were countered. For as James Walvin has argued: 'The new urban society required new games for a new type of people, just as it needed new attitudes to work.'[5] One reflection of this new regime is the fact that by 1834 there were only eight statutory half-day holidays in England, whereas before there had been many more. In the following year, bull-baiting was prohibited by the Cruelty to Animals Act. And at local level, Anthony Delves has shown the way in which street football was suppressed in Derby.[6] In their place, masters, supported by religious interests, temperance advocates, the new police and even professional labour leaders, sponsored rational recreation in the form of organised sport, regulated amusement and public provision.[7] Thus, accepting the need for more local studies, over the period 1700 to 1850 the division and supervision of labour, the introduction of bells, clocks and rational financial incentives, the diminution of recreational space and suppression of sports, and the proselytism of the middle classes had helped to form new labour and leisure habits and a new time-discipline.

Having said all this, it must be added that employers and like-minded groups were not always successful in fashioning working-class behaviour. In the first place, there were differences of opinion and position among the dominant classes so that ruling factions such as bohemian aristocrats, Tory-Anglican employers, the drink trade and entertainment interests often sought to defend traditional, rougher sports.[8] Furthermore, 'historians eager to identify major changes in leisure activities have probably tended to underplay the strong elements of continuity'.[9] Robert Storch and others have shown that pre-industrial cultural practices were remarkably durable, and many 'irrational' sports survived until the late nineteenth century and beyond.[10] As is now well established, the customary holiday of St. Monday continued to be celebrated in certain regions, even after 1850.[11] Similarly, in Southern English villages much of the old rural culture was maintained up to 1914.[12] After all, despite galloping urbanisation, a substantial minority of the population were rural based, and even in the cities 'rural' values were not entirely suffocated. Hugh Cunningham is therefore surely right to claim that people defended and even 'clung to customs whose original meaning had been lost'.[13] Also interesting is the fact that the working class was often resentful of patronage, and in turn was able to re-shape middle-class provision to meet their own needs and tastes. Particularly interesting in the context of this study is that not only did working-class methodism spawn its own cultural outlets, but so too did working-class radicalism. Owenism, Chartism, Co-operation and even New-Model Unionism were more than political or industrial movements pure and simple, they also had a radical culture of their own.[14] Moreover, in the various working-men's clubs which were established at mid-century, political activity was an integral aspect of club affairs, a minority of members wishing to understand 'socialist' theory and promote the radical message. There were even verbal attacks on the institutions of the Victorian establishment: the Church of England, monarchy, Tory Party and the representatives of capital.[15] Given that sections of the dominant classes wished to control popular sports, whilst sections of the subordinate classes wished to express themselves through sports, there has been some debate between historians as to whether leisure was a means of bourgeois social control or working-class expression.[16] Either way, most historians agree that a new world of sport and leisure had broken through by the late Victorian period. But what did this new leisure world consist of?

First of all it must be stressed that by the 1870s Britain had established itself as the premier capitalist nation, with an important manufacturing base, towns and cities, a national transport and communications network, class relations, a central state and, of course, the strings of Empire. In the period 1850-73 – the so-called Great Victorian Boom – Britain undoubtedly benefited from a remarkable expansion of overseas trade, and was able to exert economic and indeed political influence in most corners of the globe. Inevitably, the rise of new industrial powers and centres of political and cultural influence in America, the Far East and most of all, the Continent, must have, to say the least, upset the susceptibilities of the Victorians. Yet somewhat paradoxically, it was during the period of the Great Depression in the 1870s and 1880s when growth rates were decelerating that modern sports emerged. Though some sports failed to become popular, football, horse-racing and cricket were well received. Indeed, according to Vamplew, 'sport for the masses was one of the economic success stories of late Victorian Britain'.[17] Such a success story was underpinned by four main factors: first, the consolidation of the new work regime; second, the penetration of market forces into the sports domain; third, new codes of regulated and organised recreation; and fourth, the formation of an essentially working-class culture. Each of these will now be examined in a little more detail.

As already noted, by about the 1850s the leisure opportunities of the British working class were clearly constricted by the length and character of work. Long arduous labour in the workplace or the home placed limits on the openings for sport. Even so, to some extent the constraints of work were mitigated during the second half of the nineteenth century by reductions in working hours. The fifty-four-hour week norm had been introduced in the 1870s for certain relatively privileged groups of workers, but there were many exceptions to the rule – agricultural labourers, shop assistants, domestic servants and women in the home. Extensions were also being made to unpaid free time as legislation in 1871 and 1875 brought in the bank holiday. Most of all, though, a longer weekend evolved with the establishment of the Saturday afternoon holiday, which enabled male workers to occupy their time with sports, be it as participants or spectators. For urban male workers, Saturday afternoons in 1850 were very different from those in 1900.

As far as spectator sport is concerned, growth was stimulated by a rise in purchasing power. Notwithstanding the fact that poverty continued to be a major social problem, it is generally agreed that wages began to rise from the 1850s. Estimates show that real wages increased by about one third between 1875 and 1900, falling off slightly until the First World War. Unfortunately there is a lack of evidence as to expenditure patterns and family budgets, though it is likely that there was greater outlay on sport. Further, presumably the decline in beer consumption starting in the 1870s freed resources into sport and entertainment. Certainly, impressionistic evidence suggests that more money was being spent at football matches, race courses and cycling shops.[18] This points to the second major feature of sport in the late Victorian period, namely its commercial basis.

Secondly then, sport had been gradually commercialised since the eighteenth century, but it was only from about 1870 that the working class began to spend significant amounts at the turnstile or retail outlet. For instance, association football had become, in Walvin's words, 'a highly commercialised weekly ritual'.[19] Thus by the 1908-09 season six million people watched First Division games in England, producing an average crowd per game of approximately 16,000. Similar crowds were recorded at horse-races, rising to perhaps 80,000 at bank holiday events. The enclosed gate money meeting itself stands out as the major agent of change: by the early 1880s football clubs such as Blackburn Rovers, Darwen and Preston North End had improved their grounds, whilst in horse-racing Sandown Park had opened its turnstiles as an enclosed course in 1875, soon to be followed by Kempton Park, Derby racecourse and the rest. Other sports such as cricket and rugby league also began to attract large attendances.[20]

It also has to be remembered that commercialised sport was becoming an industry in its own right with significant capital investment, the entry of entrepreneurs and a professional structure. Perhaps sport was regarded as a potential avenue for surplus funds generated in the older sectors of the economy. Without question, the opportunities for sport were widened by the development of the nation's economic infrastructure. The spread of railways stimulated sport, as did new technology and financial institutions. There was much capital outlay on athletics, boxing, cricket, cycling, football, horse-racing and rugby as grounds were enclosed, stadia built and facilities brought up to date. Equally, technology was applied to a range of sports. Cycling benefited from increasingly sophisticated pneumatic tyres, lightweight frames, gears and other accessories, while cricket was at least partially modified by the use of the lawn-mower and heavy roller on pitches, more elaborate gloves and pads, and even the 'development of bowling machines, practice nets, and indoor coconut matting pitches'.[21] Overall, sports were revolutionised by new production processes in the rubber and metal trades. Undoubtedly investment in stadia and technique was made somewhat more secure by the limited liability laws of 1862, though, as Mason has argued for football clubs, investors in sport were motivated by a number of factors, not just the scramble for profit.[22] Sport also became something of a profession, so that by about 1910 there were 200 first-class professional cricketers and many more league professionals, some 400 jockeys and apprentices, and a total of 6,800 registered paid footballers. Interestingly enough, there were attempts to form trade unions, leading one historian to ruminate about the 'class' struggle between football players and directors.[23]

Lastly here, an ancillary sports industry was developing rapidly by the end of the century. Without entering into the minutiae, such occupations as gambling (football-coupon betting originated in the 1890s), the manufacture of sports goods and garments, and even the filming of events like the Derby, the Boat Race and Henley Regatta were of growing importance. No doubt strong drink also had a close connection with some sports. Particularly interesting was the establishment of a specialist sports literature. The weekly *Bell's Life in London and Sporting Chronicle* began in 1820, and this was joined in the 1860s by such papers as *Sporting Life* (1859), *Sporting Gazette* (1862), *Sporting Opinion* (1864), *Sporting Times* (1865) and the

Athlete (1866). By the following decade, according to the *Waterloo Directory of Victorian Periodicals*, publications began to appear catering for individual sports as represented by *John Wisden's Cricketers Almanack* (1870), the *Football Annual* (1873) and the *Rugby Union Football Annual* (1874). At the turn of the century there was a surfeit of specialist magazines, including the *Cyclist* (1879), the pigeon *Fancier's Guide and Homing World* (1886), the boxers' *Mirror of Life* (1886) and *Hockey* (1897). In addition, we must not forget the Saturday football specials which sprang up in many towns in the eighties and nineties, and the general coverage in the national press. For sure, there is much research to be carried out on the origins, economics and functions of the nineteenth-century sporting press.

Thirdly, by late century both professional and amateur sport had been codified with a set of rules and regulations administered by hierarchical national organisations. It is true that certain ruling groups, variously described as 'barbarians' and the 'leisure class', hoped for status, exclusivity, security, power and, of course, pleasure in their sports.[24] And as such they were staunchly independent, reluctant to concede the need for the organisation and democratisation of sport. However, as Eric Hobsbawm has claimed in a splendid paper, by the end of the century new traditions had been invented; most of all, sports had been extended from the aristocracy and rich bourgeoisie to other social classes, and institutionalised on a national, even international, scale.[25] It is therefore salutary to recall that by 1900 numerous national sporting organisations had been formed: for example, the Football Association in 1863, Amateur Metropolitan Swimming Association in 1869, Rugby Football Union in 1871, Amateur Athletic Association in 1880, Amateur Boxing Association in 1884 and Badminton Association in 1895. As governing bodies it was their responsibility to see that rules were laid down, and abided by, and if not, to ensure that effective action was taken. Organised competitions such as the FA Cup, county cricket championship, Wimbledon and Davis Cup could thus be 'invented'. In addition, sports run from national headquarters in London were also exported abroad through the energies of British businessmen, educators, army personnel and empire-builders, as the final chapter of this study notes. England was presumed to be, in Mandell's phrase, the 'Land of Sport'.[26]

The way in which organised sport established itself is not easy to trace, though it had something to do with the influence of local employers, athletic churchmen, social reformers and officials of the state. Intellectuals drawn from the ruling elites became involved in sport, not simply at the level of ideas but also, to apply Gramsci's revealing terms, 'in active participation ... as conductor, organiser, "permanent persuader"'.[27] Thus, for the Carnegie Trust to achieve its ideological goal of elevating the moral, social and cultural senses of the people, it had to get involved, organise, and, as in Dunfermline, provide baths, gyms, men's clubs and parks.[28] More generally, certain football clubs originated in the activities of paternalistic employers, uniformed youth movements or muscular Christians – twenty five of the 112 teams in Liverpool in 1885 had religious affiliations – whilst the state provided the essential means of regulation: legislation, provision of amenities like parks and swimming baths, and control agencies in the guise of board schools, the police and the courts. But above all, the prompting of the public schools should be noted.

It is clear from J. A. Mangan's eloquent and widely acclaimed study of athleticism in six different types of Victorian and Edwardian public schools, that gradually over the second half of the nineteenth century 'a new era of games regimentation had arrived'.[29] Before 1845 the leisure time of the boys was generally spent in an ill-disciplined manner, stone-throwing, fighting, poaching, trespassing, and the like. However, the decision was soon taken to use organised games and physical exercise as a form of social control. Athleticism was perceived as 'a highly effective means of inculcating valuable instrumental and impressive educational goals: physical and moral courage, loyalty and co-operation, the capacity to act fairly and take defeat well, the ability to both command and obey'.[30] In building up athleticism as both an educational theory and a practical discipline, the public schools helped to diffuse a new approach to sport, which stressed order, restraint, manliness and character. This was reinforced to a greater rather than lesser extent by its symbolic power and links with Oxbridge and the Empire.[31] In short, athleticism as constructed by the public school gave further momentum to the codification and standardisation of national sports. The extent to which workers were influenced by public school forms of athleticism, or for that matter the clubs established by muscular Christians and amateur gentlemen, is a more problematical area, especially as some ruling bodies like the Amateur Rowing Association and the Bicycle Union were hostile to the working class. In any case, rulers found it difficult to manipulate the ruled, for as the final part of this section will discuss, the culture of the working class was very different from that of the middle or ruling class.

The final feature of late Victorian sport was its class nature. True, modern forms of sport were being established, albeit sometimes faltering and with many gaps. Yet, this should not lead us to believe that the 'leisure revolution' was received in the same way through all levels of society. As in general areas of life, there was inequality in sport and significant differences in experience according to social class and other divisions. Despite the development of an all-pervasive mass sporting culture which had consequences for everyone, certain sports such as badminton, golf, hockey and tennis were ostensibly for the middle classes. There was segregation and distinctions between classes in their sports, as was also the case at seaside resorts and in the music hall. Income was clearly a crucial factor – for the poor many leisure products were beyond their reach – as was gender. For women, it appears that the cricket ground, football stadium and racecourse were mainly male preserves, and, of course, not everybody returned to work on Mondays and discussed sport. For working-class women, and mothers in particular, leisure was essentially a domestic and private affair spent in the home. As one Preston woman remarked, 'It was all bed and work'.[32] Victorian notions of femininity, sexual decorum and dress were also powerful inhibiting forces. It is important to add that access to sport was similarly the function of age, ethnic background and region. But most of all, class differentiation in sport was an outcome of different cultures, value systems and conventions.

British working-class culture had been shaped by capitalist political economy – especially the wage nexus – serving as a form of defence against an exploitative material environment of low wages, long hours, poverty, poor housing and political inequality. The first industrial nation produced a proletariat which, though internally stratified along the lines of occupation, gender and the like, was tough and resilient with a 'collective self-consciousness' set apart from other social classes. Class-consciousness, for Eric Hobsbawm, is found 'everywhere' in a deep-rooted feeling of 'us' and 'them'. But there were three main features of working-class consciousness in Britain: 'a profound sense of separateness of manual labour, an unformulated but powerful moral code based on solidarity, "fairness", mutual aid and cooperation, and the readiness to fight for just treatment'.[33] Certainly, by the 1880s 'an increasingly self-contained working-class culture, sharply distinguished from bourgeois society by its own patterns of housing, consumption and recreation' had taken root in the context of a mature industrial economy.[34] This could be seen in the institutions and community of the working class, as well as in powerful ideological notions of sociability, association and sharing. Arguably, the working classes were not politically conscious in the sense that they sought to oppose capitalism and the wage form and fight for revolutionary change. Rather, working-class culture was simply an alternative to bourgeois society, seeking to work and adapt within it, but not overthrow it. For Tom Nairn, the working class

> was, so to speak, forced into a *corporative* mode of existence and consciousness, a class in and for itself, within but not of society, generating its own values, organizations, and manner of life in conscious distinction from the whole civilization round about it. Everywhere, the conditions of capitalism made of the worker something of an exile inside the society he (sic) supported. Only English conditions could bring about such total exile.[35]

This said, it is evident that sport was an integral aspect of workers' culture. Indeed, following Nairn, Gareth Stedman Jones sought to explain a London working-class 'culture of consolation' with reference to the development of sport. Stedman Jones views the decline of an older independent artisanal culture and the remaking of the working class in the late Victorian era as enfolded by structural changes in the material environment and the rise of a new popular culture. Though the working class may have been apart from the dominant society – 'middle-class evangelism failed to recreate a working class in its own image' – Stedman Jones argues that sport, together with the music hall and pub, were socially conservative and politically disabling.[36] Even so, the fact is that sport became, to use Hobsbawm's terms once again, 'a mass proletarian cult'.

Precisely how the working class adopted sports is still relatively obscure. Obviously, commercial and bourgeois sports and the activities of middle-class didacts must have had some impact. However, the revealing fact is that sections of the working class were able to appropriate some of the sports and games governed within bourgeois society and incorporate them with their own culture. Significantly, the workers may have accepted middle-class sponsorship, but not its ideology.[37] Certain sports which had been reconstructed and codified by the middle classes were taken over by the proletariat who impressed their own culture on them:

> Working-class people stamped sports like association football and rugby league with their own character and transformed them in some ways into a means of expression for values opposed to the bourgeois athleticist tradition: vociferous partisanship, a premium on victory, a suspicion of and often a disdain for, constituted authority, a lack of veneration for official rules, mutual solidarity as the basis of team-work, a preference for tangible monetary rewards for effort and a hedonistic 'vulgar' festive element, were all brought to sports.[38]

Eric Dunning and Kenneth Sheard have thus shown that the working class in South Wales was able to gain effective control over rugby union by the late nineteenth century. Seemingly this was linked to the unique class structure of South Wales society. Though the 'old boy' public school influence can be discerned in the early stages of the game's development, due to the lack of an indigenous aristocracy, the migration of the Welsh middle classes to England, and also the fact that those 'native' bourgeois elements who remained were largely apathetic to administrative requirements, the proletariat dominated rugby at all its levels. Out of pit villages and valleys sprang not only the majority of the players and spectators, but also the officials of the game too. In the characteristic jargon of the school of figurational sociology, Dunning and Sheard thus postulate that the dominant 'social configuration' in South Wales 'was evidently conducive to the emergence of playing, spectating and even administrative dominance by working men'.[39] A similar situation arose in Northern rugby league, though having different roots – professional ones at that.

The social and cultural milieu associated with spectatorship was also far from conducive to the bourgeois world-view. Recent research has confirmed that in the three and a half decades before the Great War spectator misconduct at football occurred on a substantial scale: there were over 2,000 cases of disorderliness in the English game in the years 1908-14.[40] As Vamplew has found, there were riots, vandalism, assaults (including some on the referee) and confrontations between rival supporters with missiles thrown, pitches invaded and matches abandoned.[41] At the time, Charles Edwardes thus protested that 'The new football is a far more effectual arouser of the ungenerate passions of mankind than either a political gathering or a race meeting.'[42] Six years later, in 1898, Ernest Ensor wrote that 'The effect of League matches and cup ties is thoroughly evil ... The excitement during the match is epidemic, and twenty thousand people, torn by emotions of rage and pleasure roaring condemnation and applause, make an alarming spectacle ... That the tendency of it all towards brutality cannot be doubted.'[43]

Questions remain, and indisputably there is a need for further research on the political economy of sport in the urban and rural settings of pre-war Britain, research which will involve a fair degree of historical reconstruction and theoretical speculation, due to limited sources. But, arguably, the working class was able to take out of games those elements, rituals and values which fitted into their own culture. Bourgeois control within governing bodies did not necessarily mean that sport was a vehicle of assimilation, whereby canons of decorum, order and sportsmanship were simply refracted downwards into the working class. The comments of Alan Ingham and Stephen Hardy are relevant here: 'we need to be sensitive to the fact that institutionalisation takes place over contested terrain. Thus the historical constitution of an institutionalised game dramatises not only the nature of class relations but also the complex interlocking of political, social, and cultural forces that occurs in hegemonic and counterhegemonic activities.'[44] Sport was far more entangled and contradictory than any simple model of social control would credit. The proletariat, in brief, discovered in modern sports *possibilities* for the articulation and advancement of their own interests.

Workers not only inhabited those sports sponsored by commerce and amateur gentlemen, but also produced sporting organisations and traditions of their own. Hence, in Crewe, autonomous worker sports were a pervasive element in local society, literally stunting the growth of commercialised leisure.[45] Elsewhere, as Richard Holt has recently speculated, a myriad of small amateur teams sprang up in working-class districts in the late nineteenth century – perhaps 10,000 or more football clubs by the Edwardian years. Sport became integrated into the closely-knit life of neighbourhood and community. Team sports like football and cricket were intimately related to the concerns of local society, perhaps organised at the local chapel, pub and workplace or springing up spontaneously in the informal activities of the street.[46] Boxing in Bermondsey, angling in Sheffield (there were some 200,000 anglers nationally by 1914) and rugby union in South Wales were all similarly linked to class needs and preoccupations, offering males the opportunity to shine within their respective communities.[47] By the same token, in various parts of the country, local working-class organisations, trade unions and socialist societies catered for the recreational interests of their members. This is an important point, for working-class culture is very much diluted if organised labour is left out. Therefore in the final section of this chapter the recreational life of the labour movement will be discussed.

Socialists, sport and the 'new life'

Late Victorian Britain represented a new dawn in the history of the labour movement. Craft unions covering skilled workers had, of course, existed since mid-century. These were joined in the late 1880s and 1890s by unions seeking to organise the unskilled. The formation in 1887 of Ben Tillett's Tea Operatives and General Labourers' Association, consisting of dock workers at the port of London, is just one instance of unions emerging all over the country to represent dockers, match-girls, gas workers, labourers, firemen, and shop assistants. By 1892 trade union membership stood at approximately 1.6 million. Significantly, a number of socialist groups had posed industrial action in class and political terms. Indeed, the 1880s witnessed the beginnings of independent labour politics: the Marxist Social Democratic Federation (SDF) had first been launched in 1881, the Socialist League in 1884, the Fabian Society also in 1884, the Independent Labour Party (ILP) in 1893, culminating in the foundation of the Labour Representation Committee (later the Labour Party) in 1900. Additionally, there was a strong co-operative movement which included some 1,439 societies and 1.7 million members by the turn of the century. It was this growth of industrial, political and co-operative organisations which lay behind the rise of a diverse 'socialist' cultural formation.

In a stimulating paper, Stephen Yeo has argued that the period from the mid-1880s to the mid-1890s saw the emergence of a 'religion of socialism'. During this period the socialist movement was apparently characterised by 'the sheer pleasure of fraternity'; that is, a number of unities between different sections of the movement, between means and ends – the agencies of political change prefiguring the kind of society desired – and between activities usually held separate in the movement. This meant, for example, that there was a kind of unity between socialist politics and leisure.[48] Though Yeo is sensitive to the transient nature of, and opposition to, these *particular* unities, there certainly is evidence that socialists appreciated the importance of sport and leisure.

In the first instance, the labour movement was fighting for greater leisure opportunities in the form of the shorter working week. Harold Cox, H. H. Champion (the maverick upper-class socialist), and J. A. Murray MacDonald were all making out a case for the eight-hour day in the columns of the *Nineteenth Century*, whilst Tom Mann was performing a similar function in pit, forge and workshop through the Eight-Hours League – an organisation which attempted to bring trade unionists and socialists together.[49] Fundamentally, the hours campaign was a demand for cultivated and refined recreation – to increase the possibility of self-improvement and political awareness, rather than hedonistic pleasure. As the engineers' leader, J. T. Brownlie, wrote on the eve of the First World War:

> A shorter working day means a real and permanent gain to Labour – less sickness, fewer accidents, longer lives, more leisure to the individual toiler, greater opportunities for self-improvement, increased facilities to appreciate the beauties of culture and the wonders of science, and more time to devote to

the consideration of great public questions: unemployment, education, housing, temperance – thus become more conscious agents to assist in the unfolding of history.[50]

It is true, as Brownlie acknowledged, that the hours campaign had not been won.[51] Yet by the 1890s it is apparent that organised labour was aware of the importance of leisure. The *Labour Annual* proclaimed that 'The Great Leisure Problem is almost as great an issue as the Labour Problem itself', and Alfred Salter, a London socialist, contended that the 'right to leisure' was as real and significant as the 'right to work'.[52] *Justice*, the organ of the SDF, believed that even the agitation for making the Royal marriage of 1893 a holiday could be used to further the hours campaign.[53] Seemingly, if the working class was wedded to sport, then the policies and actions of the labour movement reflected this.

At this point it should be stressed that there was more than one socialist approach to sport. Some socialists were, of course, indifferent to sport, and others were downright hostile – as in the case of Bruce Glasier, an architect and founding member of the ILP, who became chairman of the Party, editor of the *Labour Leader*, and a close political friend of his fellow Scot, Keir Hardie. For Glasier and other leading figures in the ILP, sport was perceived as politically debilitating, drawing workers away from the socialist cause: 'cycling, football, and other forms of personal recreation have cost us the zealous services of many admirable propagandists'.[54] The decision to dispense with the 'athletics' column of the Party's paper, however, did not stop some workers from abandoning ILP branch work – in 1909 socialist meetings in the West Riding had to be cancelled because socialists preferred to attend local football matches.[55] And even Keir Hardie's son signed professional forms with Sunderland FC. Additionally, it was quite commonly believed that sport, especially the passive spectator variety – 'football was becoming a "performance" rather than a "sport," a "passion" rather than a "recreation," and a spectacle that "is not sport, nor exercise, nor recreation"' – was alienating workers from socialist ideas. Such a perspective was articulated by Matt Simm, chairman of the North East Federation of the ILP:

> I do not suggest there is anything wrong with football, but there does seem something wrong with the majority of people who habitually attend football matches and fill their minds with things that don't matter ... Difficult though the task may be to push football out of heads and push Socialism in, the task must be undertaken, for just as surely as football doesn't matter, Socialism matters a very great deal.[56]

From a slightly different perspective, sections of the Fabian Society, with their asceticism, utilitarianism and generally elitist outlook, were intolerant of those sports inimical to refinement.[57] This said, an association of junior Fabians, the Fabian Nursery, did organise recreational and cultural activities, and was still functioning in the late 1930s.[58] In fact, just before the Great War broke out, one contributor to the *Fabian News* called for trade union athletic clubs.[59] And, of course, Fabians had been the pioneers of the municipalisation of leisure as an integral aspect of gas and water socialism, and an alternative to consumer capitalism.

Socialist critiques of sport could be mere copies of bourgeois thought and sentiment, similar in content to the position taken by rational recreationists and philanthropists. Yet occasionally they could also be inspired by a more systematic and materialist view of the world. The fact that sport was commercialised, professionalised and in turn competitive was viewed with considerable antipathy. Apparently sport was becoming like any other consumer product, manufactured, commodified and sold in the market for profit. In an article appearing in *Justice* in 1891, entitled 'Socialism and Sport', H. Stratton provided a notable overview: 'The truth is that sport, like every other thing, is demoralised and damned by capitalism. All the race-horses, greyhounds and means of providing sport are the property now of the capitalist classes, who exhibit, purchase, or sell their sporting animals, human and otherwise, on purely profit-mongering principles.'[60] In further suggesting that working-class boxers were 'forced to become the paid nominee of a sporting monopolist' and the athlete 'his wage-slave', Stratton concluded: 'Until capitalism is dead no real sport can have life. Sport in its present aspect must go too.'[61] However, it should not be construed that socialists were necessarily hostile to the idea of sport: capitalism was the problem, not sport.

Socialist opinion was not uniform, and for every socialist opposed to sport there was sure to be one firmly in favour. According to the Yeos, the *Clarion* was even putting forward and debating the socialist case for the professionalisation and capitalisation of sport.[62] Stratton himself believed 'That a love of sport is consistent with and necessary to the intellect and moral development of human character'.[63] Equally, one of the leading socialists of the time, Robert Blatchford, included such 'pleasures' as walking, rowing, swimming, football and cricket among the 'mental needs of life'.[64] Further, it is likely that socialists who were also temperance advocates saw in sport and healthy recreation a means to wean workers away from the dreaded intoxicant. The ILP, in particular, as 'the most militantly teetotal of all socialist sects', used a variety of strategies to counter the demoralising influence of the 'strolling potman'.[65]

At local level there were many instances of labour organisations catering for sport. Here there certainly was an emphasis on those unities already referred to. Workers drawn from different economic and political communities came together to enjoy those sports which were linked to wider concerns about life and society, and acted as models for a socialist future. Hence, socially progressive but non-aligned groupings like the Ancoats Recreation Movement in Manchester used non-competitive sports as a vehicle for social reform and the diffusion of the brotherhood ideal – a rambling club was formed in 1886, a cycling club in 1895-96, and the first athletic sports were organised in the late nineties, soon followed by continental tours and weekend parties to the Lake District. The close contact with socialism is evidenced by the fact that before 1914 the Movement's recreation hall was visited by such labour speakers as J. R. Clynes, Will Crooks, Tom Mann, Philip Snowden, and Ben Tillett.[66] The Labour Club movement was also the centre of culture and brotherhood. Though John Taylor has lamented that by the 1890s entertainment had replaced socialist politics as the main function of clubs, contrary evidence suggests that many clubs retained their earlier intellectual and cultural vitality.[67] As Rowbotham and Weeks claim: 'The importance of the club, the stress on fellowship, the bicycle outings, the songs, poems, music and love, the everyday culture which bound men and women to the movement continued ... to be a living force certainly until the 1920s.'[68] Arguably, the Colne Valley Labour Union was to be the genesis of a whole counter-culture; that is, a socially self-contained community with its sports, tea-parties, socials, bazaars, education, and its socialist fellowship.[69] Similar experiences came the way of the Newcastle Socialist Society, Sheffield Socialist Society, Chopwell Communist Club, the Comrades' circles of the co-operative movement, and even union branches like the Crewe Amalgamated Society of Railway Servants.

Clearly politics was a joint part of this cultural formation. The activities of the Glasgow Socialist Rambling Club were said to *unite* 'the pleasure of a summer Saturday's country ramble and the dull slogging work of Socialist propaganda'; armed with socialist song books, photographic apparatus, a ramblers' banner and a fair amount of literature, Glasgow socialists would tramp the countryside campaigning for the time 'When leisure and pleasure shall be free'.[70] The link between recreation and socialist politics could occasionally spill over into political action. Allen Clarke, the socialist editor of the *Northern Weekly*, which had sales of about 30,000 at its peak in 1902-03, was responsible for the organisation of cycling, rambling and picnics, including one which attracted some 10,000 people. Given this commitment to the outdoors, the question of the land was a recurring theme, leading the Bolton SDF to organise a series of mass demonstrations over Winter Hill in 1896 in defence of an old right of way.[71]

It is also significant that the ILP scouts not only 'went out cycling with other bodies in the name of Socialist unity', but also tied recreation to 'propaganda work in the outlying and rural districts'.[72] Leaders such as Bruce Glasier may have been antagonistic towards sport, but indoor and outdoor recreation remained popular. The Halifax ILP had a swimming club and organised annual sports days which in 1899 generated one-third of all reported income that year, the Bolton ILP had a cricket club, the Sheffield Party gardening and rambling sections, and the ILP in Leicester was attractive to those 'working class families who sought social outlets, but who could not afford other forms of recreation'.[73] Unsurprisingly perhaps, in stressing that 'It is the duty of Social Secretaries to provide for the fellowship needs of the Branch', the ILP leadership eventually came round to acknowledging the need for such activities as sports, rambles, garden meetings in summer and annual entertainments.[74] The ILP, and incidentally Bruce Glasier himself, also had a close attachment to the Socialist Sunday Schools which happily sponsored country rambles and games competitions, even having religious lessons on gambling, sports and pastimes. Founded out of the Labour Church movement in the early 1890s to spread a love of humanity, a sense of service to others and a resistance to oppression, there were some 120 schools with a congregation of 8,000 in 1911.[75]

There was evidently a multiplicity of socialist agencies catering for recreation, but at the apex of them all was of course the Clarion movement, which provided cultural support for socialists in much the same way as the Primrose League did for the Conservatives. In 1891 Robert Blatchford founded a socialist paper, the *Clarion*, and around this were grouped Cinderella Clubs to provide meals and entertainment for poor children, Clarion Scouts and Clarion Vans to disseminate the socialist message throughout the country, and a wide array of societies catering for cycling, rambling and camping. Such clubs as the Sheffield Clarion Ramblers (1900) were particularly strong, as was the Clarion Cycling Club (CCC).[76]

The socialist character of the CCC was clear from the inception of the first club in February 1894 at the Birmingham Labour Church. Not only did the club co-operate 'harmoniously' with the Labour Church, but also was 'empowered to vote any surplus cash to the Labour Movement'.[77] Though Tom Groom later recalled that there was never much surplus money, in fact the Birmingham section contributed £15 towards the engineers' strike fund in December 1897.[78] In April 1895, the National Clarion Cycling Club was established, and with eighty affiliated clubs by the end of the year its object was 'To propagate Socialism and Good Fellowship'. Membership slowly increased to reach 230 clubs with over 6,000 members in 1909, and 8,000 members in 1913. For certain, they received publicity in the cycling column of the *Clarion*, as well as in susidiary journals like the *Scout* (1895-96), *King of the Road* (1897), and the Manchester-based *Clarion Cyclists' Journal* (1896-98).[79] There was, however, some unease within the Birmingham section about cycling coverage in the *Clarion*: 'The want of literary ability, the prosy stories and the uninteresting information given, combine to mark the cycling column the least pleasing feature of The Clarion.'[80] No doubt this is why alternative papers – *Sport and Play, Cycling*, the *Cycle*, as well as the *Clarion Cyclists' Journal* – were purchased for the club room.[81]

The sporting activities of the CCC appear to have been wide-ranging. The annual Clarion Easter Weekend Meet, the first of which was held at Ashbourne, Derbyshire, in 1895, were at first rather sober, even drab, affairs. In 1902, the Stafford Meet consisted simply of two smoking concerts, a handicraft exhibition and a fellowship conference. In contrast, as the Clarion branched out, the Meet became more vibrant, so that in 1912 at Buxton, aside from smoking concerts and conferences, there were lantern displays, a visit to Poole's cavern, football, swimming, cycling, dances, socials, whist drives and a number of meetings. This merely reflected the fact that there was quite comprehensive provision. A National Clarion Swimming Club was inaugurated in 1905, and by 1913 this had been joined by football, rambling, cricket and hockey clubs, and even a Motor Cycle Union – all were well served by clubhouses and camps in the vicinity of London, Manchester, Nottingham and Sheffield.[82] Needless to say, however, cycling reigned supreme.

Lack of evidence precludes an analysis of the class or occupation composition of Clarion membership. Presumably, the costs of subscription, together with the purchase of bicycles, equipment, club badges and the rest, excluded many unskilled workers. Even so, it is a safe bet that members were drawn from the working class, albeit labour aristocrats and white-collar workers. As Judith Fincher has asserted: 'The Clarion movement was a working-class organization in the main.'[83] Notwithstanding Blatchford's anti-feminist stand and the fact that women were often responsible for non-cycling duties – 'lady' members of the Birmingham section made costumes for the Walsall cycle parade – there seem to have been many female cyclists.[84] After all, the *Clarion* journalist, Julia Dawson (the pen-name of Mrs D. J. Myddleton-Worrall), Enid Stacey from Bristol, Ada Nield from Crewe, and their 'sisters' were leading lights in the Clarion Van Movement.

As to the politics of the CCC, recreation and socialism seemed to have been closely connected. In the first place, cycling was to be a non-competitive socialist sport, as indicated by the decision of the Birmingham section to protest 'against the large amount of attention paid by (the National Cyclists' Union) to racing matters against purely road matters'.[85] On the other hand, the CCC was not averse to co-operating with 'bourgeois' cycling organisations when the rights of cyclists were infringed. Hence the decision to support the National Cyclists' Union and the Cyclists' Touring Club in their campaign to gain travel concessions from the railway companies.[86] In the end, though, the CCC needs to be judged on its socialist commitment and propaganda.

Judith Fincher is probably correct in claiming that 'the movement had its greatest impact as a political force during the 1890's when it played an important role in the formation and direction of an independent labour party'.[87] Even so, in spite of Blatchford's reluctance to use recreation for propaganda purposes, Clarion cyclists continued to spread socialist thought and policy during their trips into towns and rural retreats.[88] In 1911, the CCC was involved in the movement for socialist unity with its clear belief 'that the socialisation of the instruments of production, distribution and exchange can alone put a stop to the class struggle existing in our capitalist society to-day, and that independent political action on Socialist lines is necessary as a means to an end'.[89] Though the National Committee was against a merger with the newly formed British Socialist Party, this did not dilute its commitment to the co-operative commonwealth.[90]

With the exception of Denis Pye's recent work on Bolton, there is little published material on the local politics of the Clarion.[91] Nonetheless, teasing out points from the available evidence, it does seem that by 1913 the CCC was strongest in the North-West, with thirty-three sections in the Manchester Union, thirteen in north Lancashire and ten in south-west Lancashire and Cheshire.[92] Even then, Tom Stephenson could recall that the Blackburn branch did not have much success in its socialist propaganda activities: 'It was very often the case of talking to a couple of men and a dog and a couple of kids.'[93]

This said, the Clarion movement was very much part of the socialist offensive in the Edwardian period, and as such it is hardly surprising that the CCC was approached by workers' sports organisations from the Continent. As will be discussed in the final chapter, the CCC participated in the founding conference of the Socialist International for Physical Education in 1913. This is testimony enough to the advances made by the Clarion movement. By 1914, the CCC was truly on the sporting and political maps, with sections throughout the British Isles from London to Halifax, the Isle of Man to Scotland. Henry Pelling is surely right to refer to the CCC as 'the rage in the North of England', and Geoffrey Pearson to call it 'enormously popular'.[94]

Conclusion

Modern sports in Britain before the First World War developed in the context of capitalist political economy and class inequality. As Gruneau has theorised, industrial capitalism as a social formation meant that structural limitations were placed in the way of the working class as they came to sport and, of course, the wider society. The fact that workers had to sell their labour power in order to gain the means of survival was perhaps the major limitation. But there was also an unequal distribution of political and cultural resources. This meant that the bourgeois classes were in a commanding position to shape the development of both professional and amateur sports, as witnessed in the energy of captains of industry, muscular Christians, officials of the state and public school masters. After all, it was usually they who controlled the capital invested in commercialised sports or pulled the strings on the governing bodies of national voluntary organisations. It was they who reconstructed sport into its modern organised form. Yet there were contradictory forces and tensions at play between, say, commerce and amateurism. Moreover, in spite of the inegalitarian structure of late Victorian society, there were possibilities for working-class agencies to imprint their own culture on sports. Arguably, the working classes colonised various commercial sports, and installed autonomous sports clubs in their own respective communities. The recreational activities of the labour movement fell into this latter pattern. Throughout Britain there were many socialist bodies, some linked to the SDF, ILP, trade union branch or co-operative society, others relatively independent, which attempted to combine socialist politics with a cultural and recreational creativity. Though never able to compete with commercialised spectator sport, the pub or the music hall, the Clarion movement in particular, with its myriad of cycling, rambling and political interests and links with the broader labour movement, made an impact on sport and politics.

In his excellent discussion of the politics of popular culture in the late Victorian and Edwardian period, however, Chris Waters has questioned the originality of socialist initiatives in the recreational sphere and the vitality and impact of the religion of socialism. In particular, Waters is correct to argue that there was little by way of a socialist or Marxist critique of leisure, merely a sterile borrowing from rational recreationists who viewed workers' interests in the pub, music hall or football stadium as unedifying, even morally bankrupt. Further, the fact that 'new life' socialists were not particularly keen on competitive sport meant that their mainstream recreational projects were similar in content to those provided by the Pleasant Sunday Afternoon Brotherhood, chapels and other groups of social and religious reformers. Thus because there were complicated links and relationships between the alternative, possibly oppositional, nature of 'new life' socialism and the dominant culture, at least at the level of ideas and social criticism, it was not possible to break free from the wider assumptions of the established order. In any case, the leaders of the religion of socialism set themselves up as superior to the working class, and hence failed to reach many workers. This is not to deny, however, that the labour movement was embroiled in the leisure question, or that there were occasional socialist and materialist interventions. Waters also proposes that with the triumph of labourism, as enclosed by the institutionalisation of labour politics and the growth of mass consumer culture, socialists became less sanguine about transforming class recreation.[95] Significantly, it is this interpretation which is now becoming something of an orthodoxy among labour and social historians. Thus, for Fincher, the First World War signalled the Clarion's 'virtual disintegration as a politically organised effort'.[96] By the same token, Stanley Pierson has claimed that by the 1920s the ethical basis and utopian versions of socialism, which had emerged in the nineteenth century, had lost credence as organised labour adapted to the political and industrial realities of power.[97] Moreover, Stephen Yeo argues that as the labour movement became increasingly bureaucratised, committed to expensive electioneering, involved with the State, wedded to the ideologies of administrative and academic 'social engineers' and constrained by the influence of the Soviet Union, the religion of socialism and the 'new life' declined. Most importantly here, the unity between socialism and recreation was seemingly eclipsed by the development of a mass leisure industry.[98] Indeed, in another contribution we are further informed that 'Rather than challenging dominant capitalist leisure modes ... social democratic leaders have always tended to use the images which those modes project of "most people" (the masses) as justifications for their own retreats from radicalism.'[99]

However, there are problems with this interpretation. As David Clark has pointed out, labour organisation and electioneering in Colne Valley was the *raison d'être* for socialist cultural initiatives – specifically the labour club movement – helping to sustain ethical socialism.[100] More to the point, as subsequent chapters will show, the pull of the leisure industry failed to destroy the link between socialism and recreation which, if anything, was stronger in the inter-war period. Of course, the socialist approach to sport and leisure in the inter-war years was different to the religion of socialism. Yet to argue, or at least imply, that socialists vacated this arena to capital shows the lack of serious historical research on the post-First World War years. There may well be evidence that the links between socialism and recreation were breaking up in the early twentieth century, but such links could be recast again in the changed economic, political and cultural landscape of the 1920s and 1930s.

Notes

1 See R. Malcolmson, *Popular Recreations in English Society 1700-1850* (Cambridge, 1973), pp. 34-40.
2 P. McIntosh, *Sport in Society* (1963), p. 61
3 J. Hargreaves, *Sport, Power and Culture: A Social and Historical Analysis of Sports in Britain* (Cambridge, 1986), pp. 19-20.
4 E. P. Thompson, 'Time, work-discipline, and industrial capitalism', *Past and Present*, no. 38 (1967). Cf. R. Whipp, '"A time to every purpose", an essay on time and work', in P. Joyce (ed.), *The historical meanings of work* (Cambridge, 1987).
5 Quoted in D. Reid, 'Leisure and recreation', *History*, vol, 65 (1980), p. 54.
6 A. Delves, 'Popular recreation and social conflict in Derby 1800-1850', in E. and S. Yeo (eds), *Popular Culture and Class Conflict 1590-1914: Explorations in the History of Labour and Leisure* (Brighton, 1981).
7 See R. D. Storch, 'The problem of working-class leisure. Some roots of middle-class moral reform in the industrial North: 1825-50', in A. P. Donajgrodzki (ed.), *Social Control in Nineteenth-Century Britain* (1977); P. Bailey, *Leisure and Class in Victorian England: Rational recreation and the contest for control* (1978), ch. 2.
8 Hargreaves, *Sport, Power and Culture*, p. 35.
9 J. K. Walton and J. Walvin, 'Introduction', in J. K. Walton and J. Walvin (eds), *Leisure in Britain 1780-1939* (Manchester, 1983), pp. 3-4.

10 R. Storch (ed.), *Popular Culture and Custom in Nineteenth-Century England* (1982).

11 D. Reid, 'The decline of Saint Monday 1766-1876', *Past and Present*, no. 71 (1976), p. 91.

12 P. Thompson, *The Edwardians: The Remaking of British Society* (1976), p. 40.

13 H. Cunningham, *Leisure in the Industrial Revolution, 1780-1880* (1980), p. 71.

14 See E. Yeo, 'Culture and constraint in working-class movements, 1830-1850', in E. and S. Yeo, *Popular Culture*.

15 J. Taylor, *From Self-Help to Glamour: the Working Men's Club, 1860-1972* (1972), pp. 44–56. S. Shipley, *Club Life and Socialism in Mid-Victorian London* (1983).

16 See Donajgradzki, *Social Control*. G. Stedman Jones, 'Class expression versus social control? A critique of recent trends in the social history of "leisure"', *History Workshop Journal*, no. 4 (1977). F. M. L. Thompson, 'Social control in Victorian Britain', *Economic History Review*, vol. 34 (1981). E. and S. Yeo, 'Ways of seeing: control and leisure versus class and struggle', in E. and S. Yeo, *Popular Culture*.

17 W. Vamplew, 'The economics of a sports industry: Scottish gate-money, 1890-1914', *Economic History Review*, vol. 35 (1982), pp. 549-50.

18 For further discussion, see Bailey, *Leisure and Class*, ch. 4. J. Walvin, *Leisure and Society, 1830-1950* (1978), ch. 5. H. Cunningham, 'Leisure', in J. Benson (ed.), *The Working Class in England 1875-1914* (1985).

19 J. Walvin, *Football and the Decline of Britain* (1986), p. 5. See also T. Mason, *Association Football and English Society 1863-1915* (Brighton, 1980). S. Tischler, *Footballers and Businessmen: The Origins of Professional Soccer in England* (New York, 1981).

20 See W. Vamplew, *Pay Up and Play the Game: Professional Sport in Britain 1875-1914* (forthcoming).

21 D. Rubinstein, 'Cycling in the 1880s', *Victorian Studies*, vol. 21 (1977); K. A. P. Sandiford, 'Victorian cricket technique and industrial technology', *British Journal of Sports History*, vol. 1 (1984).

22 Mason, *Association Football*, pp. 44-9. However, Tischler, following Marxists like Jean-Marie Brohm, has suggested that the commercial relationships among clubs were similar to the relationships among ordinary competitive firms, and that football became a microcosm of the wider business environment. Tischler, *Footballers*, ch. 4.

23 Tischler, *Footballers*, chs 5-6. See also W. Vamplew, 'Not playing the game: unionism in British professional sport, 1870-1914', *British Journal of Sports History*, vol. 2 (1985).

24 M. Arnold, *Culture and Anarchy* (1869). T. Veblen, *The Theory of the Leisure Class* (1925).

25 E. Hobsbawm, 'Mass-producing traditions: Europe, 1870-1914', in E. Hobsbawm and T. Ranger (eds). *The Invention of Tradition* (Cambridge, 1983), pp. 298-303.

26 R. D. Mandell, *A Cultural History of Sport* (Irvington, 1984), pp. 132–57.

27 Q. Hoare and G. Nowell Smith (eds), *Selections from the Prison Notebooks of Antonio Gramsci* (1971), p. 10.

28 F. L. Marquis and S. E. F. Ogden, 'The recreation of the poorest', *Town Planning Review*, vol. 3 (1913).

29 J. A. Mangan, *Athleticism in the Victorian and Edwardian Public School: The Emergence*

and Consolidation of an Educational Ideology (Cambridge, 1981), p. 86.
30 *Ibid.*, p. 9.
31 *Ibid.*, chs. 6–7.
32 *Spare Rib*, June 1984.
33 E. Hobsbawm, 'The formation of British working-class culture', in *Worlds of Labour: further studies in the history of labour* (1984), p. 191. Cf. A. Reid, 'Class and organisation', *Historical Journal*, vol. 30 (1987).
34 K. Burgess, *The Challenge of Labour* (1980), p. 55.
35 T. Nairn, 'The English working class', in R. Blackburn (ed.), *Ideology in Social Science: Readings in critical social theory* (1979), p. 198.
36 G. Stedman Jones, 'Working-class culture and working-class politics in London, 1870-1900; notes on the remaking of a working class', *Journal of Social History*, vol. 7 (1974).
37 Cunningham, *Leisure in the Industrial Revolution*, p. 128.
38 Hargreaves, *Sport, Power and Culture*. p. 67.
39 E. Dunning and K. Sheard, *Barbarians, Gentlemen and Players: A Sociological Study of the Development of Rugby Football* (Oxford, 1979), pp. 223-4.
40 E. Dunning, P. Murphy, J. Williams and J. Maguire, 'Football hooliganism in Britain before the first world war', *International Review of Sport Sociology*, vol. 19 (1984).
41 W. Vamplew, 'Ungentlemanly conduct: the control of soccer crowd behaviour in England, 1888-1914', in T. C. Smout (ed.), *The Search for Wealth and Stability* (1979). See also W. Vamplew, 'Sports crowd disorder in Britain, 1870-1914: causes and controls', *Journal of Sport History*, vol. 7 (1980).
42 *Nineteenth Century*, Oct. 1892.
43 *Contemporary Review*, Nov. 1898.
44 A. Ingham and S. Hardy, 'Sport: structuration, subjugation and hegemony', *Theory, Culture and Society*, vol. 2 (1984), p. 91.
45 A. Redfern, 'Crewe: leisure in a railway town', in Walton and Walvin, *Leisure*.
46 R. Holt, 'Working-class football and the city: the problem of continuity', *British Journal of Sports History*, vol. 3 (1986).
47 S. Shipley, 'Tom Causer of Bermondsey: a boxer hero of the 1890s' *History Workshop Journal*, no. 15 (1983). J. Lowerson, 'Brothers of the angle: match fishing, 1850-1914', *Bulletin of the Society for the Study of Labour History*, no. 50 (1985). G. Williams, 'How amateur was my valley: professional sport and national identity in Wales 1890-1914', *British Journal of Sports History*, vol. 2 (1985).
48 S. Yeo, 'A new life: the religion of socialism in Britain, 1883-1896', *History Workshop Journal*, no. 3 (1977). Hargreaves, however, stresses 'the British working-class movement's celebrated propensity to settle for "economism" and "labourism"'. Hargreaves, *Sport, Power and Culture*, p. 82.
49 *Nineteenth Century*, July and Sept. 1889, April 1890. T. Mann, *What a compulsory 8 Hour Working Day Means to the Workers* (1886). T. Mann, *The eight hours movement* (1889). T. Mann, *The Regulation of Working Hours: as submitted to the Royal Commission on Labour* (1891). C. Waters, 'Socialism and the Politics of Popular Culture in Britain, 1884-1914', PhD, University of Harvard (1985), pp. 12-20.
50 J. T. Brownlie, *The Engineers' Case for an Eight-Hour Day* (n.d. 1914?), p. 16.
51 Interestingly though, Brownlie was to serve as chair of the union committee

which negotiated a forty-seven-hour week in the engineering and shipbuilding trades in 1918.

52 L. Marlow, 'The Working Men's Club Movement, 1862-1912: A Study of the Evolution of a Working-Class Institution', PhD, University of Warwick (1980), p. 122. A. Salter, *What Socialism Means* (Manchester, n.d.), p. 18.
53 *Justice*, 24 June 1893.
54 Quoted in Mason, *Association Football*, p. 236.
55 S. Pierson, *British Socialists: The Journey from Fantasy to Politics* (Cambridge, Mass., 1979), p. 168.
56 Waters, 'Politics of popular culture', pp. 95-6; C. Waters, 'Social reformers, socialists, and the opposition to the commercialisation of leisure in late Victorian England', in W. Vamplew (ed.), *The Economic History of Leisure* (1982), pp. 114-15.
57 I. Britain, *Fabianism and Culture: A Study in British Socialism and the Arts c. 1884-1918* (Cambridge, 1982), p. 242.
58 For details of the Fabian Nursery, see Harvester Microform, Part 1: Fabian Society Minutes Books and Records, 1884-1918, cards 84-8.
59 *Fabian News*, July 1913.
60 H. Stratton, 'Socialism and sport, *Justice*, 26 Dec. 1891.
61 *Ibid.*
62 E. and S. Yeo, 'Perceived patterns: competition and licence versus class and struggle', in E. and S. Yeo, *Popular Culture*, p. 278.
63 Stratton, 'Socialism'.
64 R. Blatchford, *Merrie England* (1895), pp. 17-18.
65 Marlow, 'Working Men's Club Movement', pp. 356, 445-6.
66 J. I. Rushton, 'Charles Rowley and the Ancoats Recreation Movement', MEd, University of Manchester (1959), pp. 45-6, 65, 84, 94-6. Cf. Waters, 'Politics of popular culture', pp. 220-5.
67 Taylor, *Self-Help to Glamour*, pp. 57-70; Marlow, 'Working Men's Club Movement', pp. 591-659.
68 S. Rowbotham and J. Weeks, *Socialism and the New Life: The Personal and Sexual Politics of Edward Carpenter and Havelock Ellis* (1977), p. 75.
69 D. Clark, *Colne Valley. Radicalism to Socialism: The Portrait of a Northern constituency in the formative years of the Labour Party 1890-1910* (1981), pp. 32-5, 47-50, 117-25, 163-4, 181-96.
70 *Justice*, 1 July 1893.
71 P. Salveson, 'Working-class culture and leisure in Lancashire in the late nineteenth century', paper presented to the North-West Group for the Study of Labour History (1982).
72 ILP, *Annual Conference Report*, 1912, pp. 103-4.
73 Waters, 'Politics of popular culture', p. 253. Yeo, 'A new life', p. 38. D. L. Prynn, 'The Socialist Sunday Schools, The Woodcraft Folk and Allied Movements: Their Moral Influence on the British Labour Movement since the 1890s', MA, University of Sheffield (1971), p. 64. D. Cox, 'The Labour Party in Leicester: a study of branch development', *International Review of Social History*, vol. 6 (1961), p. 203.
74 Harvester Microform, ILP National Administrative Council Minutes and Related Records, 1894-1950, Memorandum for Social Secretaries, card 62.

75 Prynn, 'Socialist Sunday Schools', pp. 60-177. F. Reid, 'Socialist Sunday Schools in Britain, 1892-1939', *International Review of Social History*, vol. 11 (1966).

76 Prynn, 'Socialist Sunday Schools', pp. 30-42. See also D. Prynn, 'The Clarion Clubs, rambling and the holiday associations in Britain since the 1890s', *Journal of Contemporary History*, vol. 11 (1976).

77 K. S. Inglis, 'The Labour Church Movement', *International Review of Social History*, vol. 3 (1958), p. 449. Manchester Central Library Archives Department (hereafter MAD), 016/i/1, Birmingham CCC Minutes (Mins), 26 Feb. and 7 March 1894.

78 T. Groom, *National Clarion Cycling Club 1894-1944: The Fifty-Year Story of the Club* (Halifax, 1944). MAD, 016/i/1, Birmingham CCC Mins, 18 Dec. 1897.

79 Rubinstein, 'Cycling', pp. 68-9.

80 MAD, 016/i/1, Birmingham CCC Mins, 7 Feb. 1895. As Tony Mason has put it: 'They were inclined to lack seriousness of purpose at the Clarion.' Mason, *Association Football*, p. 236.

81 MAD, 016/i/1, Birmingham CCC Mins, 17 Oct. 1895, 13 July 1898.

82 MAD, 016/i/10, CCC Annual Meet Programmes and Year Books.

83 J. A. Fincher, 'The Clarion Movement: A Study of a Socialist Attempt to Implement the Co-operative Commonwealth in England 1891-1914', MA, University of Manchester (1971), pp. 181-93. Cf. Waters, 'Politics of popular culture', pp. 448-54, 459.

84 After the subscription was raised to 3s 6d in 1896 it was 'Resolved that ladies be admitted to the club without payment', MAD, 016/i/1, Birmingham CCC Mins, 12 Sept. 1895, 6 Feb. 1896. See also Clark, *Colne Valley*, pp. 34, 48-9. Waters, 'Politics of popular culture', pp. 460-71. K. Hunt, 'Women and the social democratic federation: some notes on Lancashire', *North West Labour History Society Bulletin*, no. 7 (1980-81).

85 MAD, 016/i/1, Birmingham CCC Mins, 1 May 1895.

86 MAD, 016/i/6, Minutes of a conference between the National Cyclists' Union and CCC, 10 Oct. 1908; National CCC Mins, 2 June 1912.

87 Fincher, 'Clarion Movement', p. 5.

88 *Ibid.*, p. 164.

89 MAD, 016/i/6, National CCC Mins, 27 Aug. 1911.

90 *Ibid.*, 9/10 Feb. 1912.

91 D. Pye, 'Fellowship is life: Bolton Clarion Cycling Club and the Clarion Movement 1894-1914', in North-West Labour History Society, *Labour's Turning Point in the North West 1880-1914* (1984).

92 MAD, 016/i/3, List of National CCC sections for 1913.

93 D. Rubinstein, 'An interview with Tom Stephenson', *Bulletin of the Society for the Study of Labour History*, no. 25 (1972), p. 29.

94 Pelling, quoted in Inglis, 'Labour Church Movement', p. 448. G. Pearson, *Hooligan: A History of Respectable Fears* (1983), p. 68.

95 Waters, 'Politics of popular culture', pp. 482-505, 516-36.

96 Fincher, 'Clarion Movement', pp. 7, 344, 349.

97 Pierson, *British Socialists*.

98 Yeo, 'New life', pp. 30-2.

99 S. Yeo, 'Towards "making form of more moment than spirit": further thoughts on labour, socialism and the new life from the late 1890s to the

present', in J. A. Jowitt and R. K. S. Taylor (eds), *Bradford 1890-1914: The Cradle of the Independent Labour Party* (Bradford, 1980), p.82.
100 Clark, *Colne Valley*, p. 52.

Chapter 3

Working-class sport in the years of peace, 1918–39

Introduction

The circumstances and pressures of the Great War (1914–18) produced important socio-economic and political changes in Britain. The precise nature of these changes, whether long-term or transient, beneficial or harmful, have been examined by a number of historians.[1] Although sports historians have yet to focus in any detail on the complex processes at play during this first 'total' mobilisation of the nation's cultural, as well as economic, resources, the legacy of war for sport was of some importance.[2] Not only had sports such as association football and horse-racing been severely curtailed by war, but the pattern of modern sports was reshaped in the post-war world. Crucially, the British economic environment on which sport ultimately rests underwent a process of structural adaptation and change.

It is therefore the purpose of this chapter to provide a general overview of the inter-war political economy of sport, stressing the major trends in the organisation and provision of working-class sport, and its continued limitations and possibilities. The opening section of the chapter will examine the most important trend in inter-war sport, namely its commercial orientation. This will be followed by a discussion of the wider cultural implications of the commercialisation process, in which neo-Marxist perspectives of the commodification of leisure will be applied critically. Finally, the chapter will end with a brief look at the place of voluntary sport in working-class society. But first an introductory discussion of inter-war economy and society.

The inter-war period witnessed a number of fluctuations in the trade or business cycle. After a short-lived boom in the immediate post-war demobilisation, there followed in 1920-22 the severest contraction in economic activity this century. The rest of the 1920s were marked by a mild recovery – some would say mild boom – to be stopped short by the world economic depression of 1929-33. From the mid-1930s the economy revived, though there were significant interruptions in 1937, and even in the spring of 1940 over one million people were without jobs.[3] Not only did the economy fluctuate over time, it also developed unevenly between different regions and sectors. Throughout the period there were regional disparities in growth. With the contraction of the major staple industries of coal, iron and steel, shipbuilding and textiles, whole regions in Wales, Lancashire, the North-East and central Scotland were blighted by mass unemployment, social decay and poverty. For most of the period there was never less than ten per cent of the insured labour force unemployed, and in 1933 the jobless figure approached three million; not to mention those in casual or short-time employment, or those out of work but not on the unemployment insurance register. On the other hand, the rise of new industries such as vehicle manufacture, electrical engineering, chemicals and services, located mainly in the Midlands and south of England, are viewed as revitalising the British economy, ushering in technical and organisational change, and bringing with them employment opportunities, higher real wages and the hope of a new start. Accepting the need for periodisation and regional differentiation in any account of the inter-war record, historians have attempted to assess economic and social performance as a whole.[4] In some ways the most far-reaching claims have been made by Chris Cook and John Stevenson, who point to the 1930s as a decade of economic growth, rising real wages, increased consumer spending, and better housing and health care – the 'dawn of affluence'.[5] In truth, however, as various historians have countered, material gains had their class boundaries. Rises in real income and, in turn, consumption, say little about inequality, the life chances of women, access to housing and health schemes, political rights, social alienation, attitudes, way of life, and perhaps most of all the character of manual labour in the workplace and the home. Quantitative evidence may suggest an improvement in average standards of living, yet this has to be supplemented by a qualitative assessment of the whole human condition as shaped by a far from neutral economic and social system.[6] It is important to appreciate this point as we proceed to discuss the commercial provision and organisation of sport.

Commercialisation and working-class sport between the wars

The sports of the inter-war working class cannot be understood without reference to the impact of total war, economic transformation, the ever-widening role of the State, and the configuration of class forces before, during and after the General Strike of 1926. But perhaps the most immediately direct socio-economic factor impinging on the development of sport was the further incursion of market relations into the sports domain. In the first place, it may well have been that sport was perceived as a lucrative market, a sector which would act as an outlet for surplus investment funds generated in the older declining areas of the British economy. Arguably, the demand for commercial sports was increasing in the period.[7] Real wages were rising – due to a drop in the cost of living – which when coupled with a fall in average family size, a change in the distribution of the National Income in favour of wages, and a shift in consumer spending away from food and beer, potentially freed scarce resources into the developing sports market. In addition, at a time when the bulk of the working population had comparatively insignificant holdings of money savings, hire-purchase and credit facilities were important in extending the market for sports.[8] Credit is especially pressing during periods of economic depression, for it allows consumer spending to rise and, most significantly, profits to be realised.

The demand for sport was also stimulated by the hours reductions of 1919–20, when the average working week came down from fifty-four to forty-eight hours. In 1919, approximately 6.3 million workers enjoyed reductions totalling over 40.5 million hours. It is true that the 1920s were rather barren in terms of hours reductions: in 1926 almost one million workers, mainly coal-miners (whose daily shift rose from seven hours to between seven and a half and eight), had to accept an increase of hours of about four million in total. Even so, marginal falls were recorded in the 1930s, so that by 1938 the average working week was in the region of forty-seven hours, though, of course, overtime, short-time working, occupational category, age and gender could make a mockery of such figures. Finally here, the growth of urban transport networks (trams, then buses) may have facilitated greater access to sport. All in all, the demand for sport was quite buoyant. However, this is not to argue that all sections of British society, particularly the unemployed, the low-paid, and working-class wives, had equal opportunities in exploiting commercial sports. As in the nineteenth century, people's relation to sport was very much dependent on social class. Those low in economic and cultural capital tended to have different tastes than their wealthy equivalents.[9] In overall terms, available data points to an increase in consumer spending on sport:

> Spectator sports expanded, taking their place alongisde radio, the cinema, and the dance-hall as a main component of a more commercialized, popular mass-entertainment industry. This was the golden age of football and cricket

attendances: professional football had ceased to be so strongly associated with the North and spread southwards in popularity; County Cricket became a truly more popular game; the Amateur Athletic Association Championships enjoyed a boom in attendances. New highly commercialised sports appeared in the 1920s, for example greyhound-racing, speedway, and Tourist Trophy (TT) motor-cycle racing, which gained in popularity with working-class people.[10]

Additionally, horse-racing, boxing and swimming continued to thrive, whilst other relatively new sports like ice-hockey began to make an impact – by the end of the 1930s there was perhaps £1 million invested in ice rinks, of which the multi-purpose Wembley Empire arena was the most well known.[11] Certainly, the price of admission was well within the range of many working-class spectators: newspaper advertisements testify that by the 1930s admission to football, greyhound racing, rugby league, skating, speedway and even boxing was as little as 1s.

To take football as an example, by the 1937–38 season the four divisions of the English league attracted a total of 31.43 million fans (plus many more in Scottish games and cup competitions), paying £1.57 million. In 1938, by way of comparison, 987 million people entered British cinemas, generating £41.5 million in gross receipts! More specifically, though, the average English first division gate rose from 23,115 in the 1913–14 season to 30,659 in 1938–39. On Merseyside, the attendances of Liverpool had grown from 25,300 in 1913–14 to 31,000 in 1927–28 to 35,250 in 1938–39, and those of Everton from 25,700 to 33,000 and finally 40,800 in the same seasons.[12] Note also the interesting findings of the early 1930s' social survey of Merseyside:

> There are probably a vast number of football and cricket enthusiasts, especially those of middle-age, who have never kicked a ball or handled a bat, but for whom the excitement of the sport consists solely of the thrills to be obtained by the spectator. Horse-racing, which only takes place once a year in Liverpool, greyhounds, motor races, and football are watched by multitudes. Liverpool, indeed, is said to provide better 'gates' at big football matches than anywhere except Glasgow and London. Thirty thousand is the average attendance when Everton or Liverpool is playing.[13]

High attendances were also enjoyed by such Midlands clubs as Aston Villa and West Bromwich Albion, and indeed clubs in London and Glasgow – the record attendance for a British league match is still 118,567 for the Rangers and Celtic fixture of January 1939. By the same token, figures for the English FA Cup show that more people watched the game at the end of the 1930s than ever before.[14] Although football, like horse-racing and rugby union, was linked to the health of the local economy and cyclical fluctuations in business activity,[15] as James Walvin has commented, 'Even in times of great economic distress, and often *especially* in those communities most severely damaged by the slump (the North-East for instance), the passionate commitment to local teams continued unabated.'[16]

Given the increased demand for football, it is hardly surprising that one popular newspaper should suggest that it was 'a matter of high finance'.[17] Football clubs were not profit-maximisers – the Football Association (FA) limited club dividends to 7.5 per cent and clubs were run not so much for financial gain as for influence in the community – yet there can be few doubts that they spawned a considerable economic enterprise. The conclusion of the Chester Committee in the late 1960s is applicable to the state of the game thirty years earlier: 'League football is not a 'commercial' operation in the same sense that a manufacturing or service industry is commercial; but it is subject to financial pressures like any other entertainment business. If its income does not meet its expenditure then, in the short run it will either have to reduce its level of operations or go out of business altogether.'[18] Because football clubs were (and are) limited liability companies, the relevant decision-making body was the Board of Directors, whose role was one of administration and financial control. They had to take stock of the fiscal aspects of the club, including such matters as the costs of operation, employment and marketing. During a period of poor results, perhaps relegation, directors had to consider the financial implications of their plight – they were not a charity, but a business dependent upon a certain level of turnover. When Bolton Wanderers were relegated from the First Division in 1933, the Board was forced to reduce levels of expenditure and to economise by cutting back on scouting, transfers and overheads.[19] Similarly, relegation from the Second Division in 1927 led the directors of Bradford City to introduce a series of special measures: a consultant was appointed to the Board, share capital was increased, and season and life members' tickets were issued immediately.[20] A period of good results, on the other hand, gave the Board the opportunity to think about expansion. On the eve of the 1934 FA Cup semi-final between Manchester City and Aston Villa, the City chairman, Albert Hughes, thus promised a 'progressive policy' of ground improvements and the addition of the best players on the market.[21] In a more general context, the fact that 'crowd attendances soared skywards' underpinned the increased commercialisation of the game: a more efficient business approach, including a concern for the financial integrity of clubs and an emerging relationship with the State; greater capital investment in stadia such as Wembley, Highbury, Maine Road and Upton Park; escalating transfer fees; the application of 'scientific' techniques, namely tactics, coaching, training and even deliberate foul play.[22] To be sure, by the end of the 1930s British football was in a healthy position. However, it must be added that many clubs had rather primitive facilities, whilst the FA remained conservative – reluctant to cement international contacts, introduce floodlighting or countenance Sunday play.

Much the same can be said about a number of other sports.[23] Rugby league established itself as a major preoccupation of the Northern working class. During the early post-war boom, which produced huge crowds, new ground records were set at Halifax, Hull, Rochdale, Swinton, Warrington and Widnes. From then on crowds rose steadily, no doubt stimulated by Wembley finals and Australian tourists: whereas the record attendance stood at 35,500 in 1922, it was just under 70,000 by the end of the 1930s.[24] And even the amateur sport of rugby union, which lost numerous players to the professional league, made considerable outlay on such stadia as the Cardiff Arms Park and Murrayfield.[25]

There was much investment in new sports like greyhound racing, which from its rather humble origins at Belle Vue, Manchester, in 1926, became immensely popular. In 1927 the *Daily Herald*, in welcoming the sport as a splendid alternative to the cruelty of coursing, believed 'that the new pastime will achieve a great democratic success'.[26] Time certainly justified such a prediction. In the following year, 154 companies had been registered to exploit the sport, and by 1932 there were 187 tracks with annual attendances of twenty million plus.[27] In a medium-sized city such as Hull, with its 300,000 inhabitants in the early 1930s, the two dog tracks attracted between 300 and 500 spectators each week-night, whilst in 1932 just over nine million attendances were recorded at the seventeen tracks in the metropolis.[28] According to Robert Sinclair, 'Uncounted numbers attend the score of London dog tracks which provide 2,000 nights' greyhound racing a year.'[29] Significantly, the trade union leader and Labour MP, J. H. Thomas, insisted in 1928 that dog racing disrupted family life, yet only six years later tracks were attempting to entice the whole family: nurseries were established at the Carntyne track (Glasgow) and Dens Park (Dundee) and even a child's playground at the Harringay track in north London.[30] Unsurprisingly, therefore, the Greyhound Racing Association Limited, formed by Alfred Critchley in the 1920s as a private company to manage a number of racecourses (later owned by the Greyhound Racing Association Trust Limited, set up in December 1927 with £1 million share capital), raised its trading profits from £36,000 in

1928 to £250,000 in 1939.[31] Even so, 'the dogs' was not a particularly secure form of long-term investment. Writing in the *Investors' Chronicle*, Austin Friars noted on 3 October 1931 that 'The popularity of the greyhound racing pastime in this country appears to have been stabilised.' Thus, although by the end of the decade some £6 million was invested in greyhound racing tracks – half of which represented the paid-up capital of public companies – and attendances were twenty-five million, the rate of expansion had slowed down. As *The Economist* put it: 'Greyhound racing leapt ahead from 1929 to 1932, the number of attendances rising fourfold. Between 1932 and 1938, however, they rose by more than a fifth but less than a quarter; the novelty had worn off, and the windfall profits of the first promoters had gone.'[32]

In fact, as *The Economist* went on to suggest, greyhound racing attempted to secure its operations through contact with other sports, Hence dog racing often shared its facilities with that other relatively new sport of speedway, first introduced in the 1920s from Australia by John Hoskins. In this way dirt-track riders helped to maintain the crowds and advertise the stadia. Though the sport failed to keep up its initial momentum, by 1933 there were five tracks in the London area attracting some 1,288,000 spectators.[33] On the other hand, many soccer clubs failed to exploit the commercial potential of their assets – grounds were used for football and little else.

The evidence also suggests that recruitment in the sports industry expanded. For example, the number of workers in England and Wales engaged in horse and dog racing rose from 4,485 in 1921 to 7,798 in 1931, and in golf from 8,116 to 13,007 in the same years. Interestingly enough, by 1931 there were 1,954 females employed in the golf business, forty of whom were employers, directors or managers.[34] Despite the glamour of professional sport, the industry which served it thrived on the back of an exploited and largely forgotten labour force, often employed on a casual basis with long hours of work, poor wages and low union density rates. The great Arsenal side of the 1930s thus benefited from cheap labour drawn from the poor district of Islington – casual workers were engaged on ground improvements, laying a running track, minding cars and motorbikes at home matches, making club mascots, and no doubt as gatemen, checkers and programme sellers.[35] Poor conditions of employment were also experienced by more permanent ground staff, cleaners of all descriptions, clerks, factory operatives in the sports requisites trade (the average weekly wage was little over £2 in 1935), stable lads, bar stewards, green keepers, and caddies who could be engaged for as little as half a crown a round in the 1920s.

Even athletes themselves, as in the case of professional footballers and boxers, were often denied rudimentary rights, conditions and contracts of employment. In association football, the notorious maximum wage and retain-and-transfer system effectively restricted the mobility of players. In boxing, where middle-of-the-bill fighters earned less than £1 a fight, promoters were exploiters of the labour market *par excellence*. Moreover, the main ruling bodies, first the National Sporting Club (1891) and then the British Boxing Board of Control (1929), practised a colour bar which meant that truly great black performers like Manchester's Len Johnson were excluded from top title fights, namely the British Championship with its Lonsdale Belts. For certain, racism was institutionalised in some sports.

The growing importance of a sports labour market is also evidenced by increased professionalisation, as in league cricket,[36] and notwithstanding certain difficulties, the existence of trade unions. It is true that the most notable of these, the Association Football Players' and Trainers' Union, slumped in the 1920s, but by the following decade, in a reorganised and healthier financial state, it continued to protect and promote the interests of professional footballers. Under the guidance of its secretary, Jimmy Fay, membership doubled to almost 2,000 on the eve of the Second World War, by which time the union had moved on the offensive, seeking changes to the contract system and, more specifically, immunity from income tax on benefits.[37] Equally, the National Union of Boxers, launched and supported by sports journalists and trade unionists like Harry Flower, Ben Tillett and George Sinfield, sought to get a fair deal for all those in the ring – decent conditions of employment, controls to stamp out abuses, and medical inspection.[38] The Transport and General Workers' Union also began to organise stable lads and the rest, albeit under great difficulties.

Sport had close links with other industries, notably the press, and the relatively new media of broadcasting and cinema. Indeed, according to Howard Marshall, the newspapers were 'mainly responsible for the grotesque development of the spectacular side of sport':

> This development has taken place largely since the War: before the War sport was covered, but it was covered modestly. It was not written up: it did not blossom into the news columns. Journalism is more powerful than some people care to admit: it creates atmosphere and fosters sensationalism. It created the Wimbledon tennis meeting, and the Cup Final at Wembley: it created greyhound racing and dirt track racing: it invested Test Matches with the importance of national events ... we are only now beginning to realise the

dangers of sensationalism run riot. The dangers are considerable: they affect not only our personal enjoyment, but our national well-being.[39]

Palpably, there is more than a degree of hyperbole in such comments. Yet, together with the BBC – radio, and then from 1936 television – and the newsreels whose most frequent item was sport, the papers contributed to and fed off popular sport: papers sold sport and sport sold papers.[40] From the *Advertiser's Annual* we know that by the end of the 1930s sports were advertised in such daily newspapers as the *Sporting Chronicle, Sporting Life* and *Greyhound Express*, as well as in the weekly specialist press: *Angler's News, Bicycling News, Football Pictorial, Golf Illustrated, Greyhound Outlook and Sports Pictures, Hockey World, Ice Hockey World, Lawn Tennis and Badminton, Racing, Racing Pigeon* and so on. Additionally, of course, there was the Saturday *Pink 'Un*, and the main daily and evening papers, purchased by many for their sports coverage.

Most of all, though, sport stimulated quite a thriving manufacturing industry. According to the Census of Production, by 1935 there were 146 establishments (each employing more than ten operatives) in the British sports requisites trade; forty-six per cent of them were located in the Greater London area, thirty-nine per cent in the rest of England and fifteen per cent in Scotland – which, as we might expect, specialised in the production of golf accessories and, to a lesser extent, fishing tackle. The eight largest firms produced thirty-four per cent of the gross output valued at nearly £3 million. In all that year, 588,000 golf clubs, 504,000 tennis and badminton rackets, 180,000 cricket bats, 108,000 hockey sticks, 108,000 skates, 23,000 pairs of boxing and other sports gloves, 12,924,000 tennis balls, 10,992,000 golf balls, 3,312,000 shuttlecocks, 360,000 footballs, 264,000 cricket balls, 72,000 sports bags, and other types of equipment were manufactured. This meant that between 1924 and 1925 the production index for sports requisites had shown an increase of twelve points, from eighty-eight to one hundred. Furthermore, notwithstanding the problems posed by changes in census classification and relative prices, the gross output of the industry had almost doubled, from £1,520,000 in 1912 to £2,919,000 in 1935.[41] Firms such as Dunlop, Slazenger and Spalding emerged as significant producers and employers – the average numbers employed in the trade as a whole rose from 6,775 in 1924 to 8,253 in 1935 – whilst department stores and variety chain stores were engaged in the retailing of sports goods.[42] Detailed analysis of the *Annual Statements of Trade* also reveals that by 1938 the total exports of sports and ancillary goods stood at £1,016,680 and imports at £683,928. No doubt this represented the origins of an international market in sport.

Seemingly then, sports manufacture was a small but expanding sector of the inter-war economy.

In fact, the sports division of the Dunlop Company is worthy of some attention. The Dunlop Rubber Company Limited was one of Britain's first multinationals. It began to manufacture golf balls as early as 1910, using scientific methods in weights, sizes and markings of balls. Further improvements followed in 1922 with the launch of the Dunlop 'Maxfli' which was so successful that demand quickly outstripped supply. By the end of the 1930s new lines had been introduced, including the 'Dunlop Warwick', 'Blue Flash', 'Goblin' and 'Sixty-Five' – so named after Henry Cotton's historic round of sixty-five at the 1934 British Open. Moreover, in 1924 the company extended its range with the production of tennis balls, soon to be improved by a new type of durable cover. And four years later, with the acquisition of F. A. Davis Limited, Dunlop diversified into the manufacture and sale of tennis rackets. At the now relatively autonomous sports division at Waltham Abbey much effort went into the development of machine-stringing and the ply-frame racket. Thus on the eve of the Second World War Dunlop had captured a large part of the growing market: the annual production of tennis rackets of 115,000 represented perhaps upwards of twenty per cent of the UK total, whilst judging from the *Annual Statements of Trade* increased production of golf and tennis balls helped to reduce import penetration from a peak of £126,075 in 1922 to £1,694 in 1936. This had much to do with a marketing strategy which associated the company name with national events like the Open and Wimbledon, together with cost-reducing innovations, the introduction of new lines such as racket presses, and the consolidation of distribution outlets. Also, of course, the Dunlop enterprise was heavily involved in the production and marketing side of cycling, motor-cycling, and motor-racing.[43]

Cycling as both a recreation and a mode of transport also created a major industry in its own right. Though H. R. Watling of the British Cycle and Motor Cycle Manufacturers' and Traders' Union (formed in 1910) could protest in the mid-twenties that the industry found it difficult to compete internationally due to protectionism, relatively poor labour efficiency, problems affecting design and reliability, high taxation, a lack of credit facilities and, especially, price factors, British bicycles were certainly sold overseas.[44] In the ten years to December 1931 the industry exported 2,355,189 bikes valued at £10,193,360, meaning that Britain controlled about half the world market. Moreover, it was estimated that during the summer months there were ten million bikes in use in the UK alone.[45] In 1933, after taking over Humber Cycles in the previous year, the Raleigh company made some 200,000 bikes; after all, it had gone 'all out to make customers of factory workers, clerks and shop assistants'.[46]

Of course, gambling had a systematic relationship with popular sports. Not only did horse and greyhound racing give rise to gambling on quite a phenomenal scale – stakes at dog tracks increased from £10 million in 1927 to over £75 million in 1938 – but also football, in the guise of the pools. In the mid-1930s, when gambling was a major industry with an annual turnover reaching perhaps £400 million, five to seven million people spent approximately £30 million on the pools. As a result, in 1934 the Football Pool Promoters' Association came into existence, 'comprising the principal firms in the business in general and protecting the interests alike of the Football Pool Promoters and of their clients'. Consisting of such firms as Littlewoods, Vernons, W. S. Murphy, Copes Pools and Western Pools, the business mushroomed, so that towards the end of the decade some 30,000 people were employed, the advertising budget reached £500,000 and profits were computed at no less than thirty per cent of amounts staked. And aside from this, additional economic activity was generated through diversification into the mail order business. John Moores, who had made his first million pounds out of the pools by 1932, founded Littlewoods Mail Order Stores in that year with an initial capital of £20,000, and this was followed three years later by Vernons' Mail Order Stores, which became a huge organisation extending the length and breadth of the country.[47]

As we shall see, participant sports continued to have an appeal, and amateur ideals were still prevalent, but the most important inter-war trend was that of commercialisation. Contemporary opinion thus pointed to the fact that sport was becoming big business. The *Daily Herald* lamented in 1924 that 'League football to-day is purely a commercial business and the spirit of sportsmanship is conspicuous by its absence', whilst a decade later W. F. Smith, the paper's sports editor, wrote that 'More than ever this year will Sport and Money go hand in hand.'[48] And in 1936, the *Spectator* complained about the professionalisation of sport, and once again the *Daily Herald* pointed to the high level of capital funding: 'Sports promoters have grasped the modern trend. All over the country they are building new palaces of sport. They know that by offering the right kind of attraction they can make money every night of the week.'[49] Or as one foreign visitor humorously put it: 'The real religion of Englishmen is balls.'[50]

Commercialised sport: towards a sociological and historical critique

Accepting that commercial influences were very much evident in inter-war sport, what implications did this have for the wider society and for the position of the working class within that society? Was commercial sport, for instance, an effective means of social control, consolidating bourgeois domination over the popular classes? One important approach to the commercialisation of sport has been derived from Marxist social theory. Such a theory views sport within a framework of accumulation, reproduction and legitimation systems. In particular, sport is tied to advanced capitalist society in terms of its organisation around the commodity form and wage labour. It is this which will serve as the theoretical background to the remaining sections of the chapter. According to a broadly conceived Marxian perspective, the commodification of sport can be viewed as an aspect of capitalist development and class domination, reproducing the *status quo* in the form of established economic, social and gender relationships. Rob Beamish, admittedly writing about the North American situation, has argued that sport is inextricably linked to what is happening at the level of the capitalist mode of production. Put simply, commodified sport is said to develop out of capital's search for new fields of profitable investment at a time when older market opportunities have diminished; especially when coupled with increased leisure time for the consumer, and the need to absorb the economy's greater production capacity. This leads to the formation of limited liability sports businesses, which both produce and market saleable commodities for profit, and in turn to the concentration of those businesses into fewer hands. It is of course capital, through its overall political and cultural domination, which owns, controls and manages the sports industry. Furthermore, the workers in the industry, be they stable lads or professional athletes, are compelled to sell their labour power to existing capitalist enterprises below their 'true' market value, whilst away from work people lose control over sport, as they are transformed into passive consumers dependent on capitalist industry for their pleasure.[51]

As noted, it is doubtful whether commercial enterprise in spectator sport was simply about the maximisation of profits, at least in inter-war Britain, where financial return was by no means the only reason for investing in team sports. Certainly in the British case it does seem a grave over-simplification, if not downright foolish, to assume that the commercialisation of spectator sport has developed in line with the logistics of capital accumulation. Entrepreneurs or 'committed amateurs' often failed to recognise the opportunities for profit. Nonetheless, the thesis that changes in leisure which involve the production and purchase of commodities to secure new markets in the face of late capitalism's crisis of profit realisation may have greater force in the context of inter-war Britain when referring to the ancillary sports industry, rather than simply the growth of spectator sport.[52] After all, the old staples were in decline whilst the production of sports goods and services rose in the period. There is also evidence that sport in Britain at this time was the victim of market relations, increasingly touched by commerce – manufacturers of stadia, amenities and equipment, the media, advertisers, and gambling concerns – and so *similar* to those commodities produced and sold on the mass consumer market for profits. But before we can be more definitive, work on the dynamics of inter-war commodity production and consumer capitalism has to be placed on the research agenda.

Recent empirical studies of football have in fact provided arguments in this direction, as well as a starting point for debate. First of all, it is true that many football clubs were limited liability entities and recipients of large investment funds. In claiming that football was perceived by social elites as good for national unity – as reflected in, for example, the way royalty became commonplace at the big occasion – N. B. F. Fishwick goes on to speculate that market considerations were a significant aspect of the game's ideological and social equipment. Fishwick proposes that not only was football's administrative hierarchy virtually closed to the working class, but even players and managers became removed from their proletarian origins, enjoying a higher status than most other workers.

Additionally, other important aspects of the game's commercialised sub-culture, such as the media and the pools, were owned or controlled by the wealthier, rather than the working, classes. Though the game may have depended on and belonged to working-class men, 'Most football followers had no more control over the game than any other consumers had over the product controlled.'[53] Likewise, Christopher Nottingham has criticised the notion that football clubs were organically linked to the local community, protesting rather that team selection, records and financial affairs were under the authority of an oligarchy of directors and managers from which working-class fans were largely excluded.[54]

The hierarchies of other commercialised sports were similarly dominated by the ruling elite – ownership of horses and stables in racing, limited access to such boxing venues as Earls Court in London, St James's Hall in Newcastle or Manchester's King's Hall – divorcing the 'people' from the centres of cultural production and the crucial decision-making processes. At a time when workers were benefiting from the hours reductions of the early post-war period, they were increasingly attracted to consumer markets in which they had little active involvement. Indeed, commercialised sport appears to have shared in the rise of the corporate economy; gate-money sport itself was a thinly-disguised form of cartelisation regulated by national governing bodies like the FA, MCC, British Boxing Board of Control and National Greyhound Racing Society, whilst there were fairly high levels of concentration in the ancillary media, pools and sports requisites trades. And at the same time, most professional sportsmen and women, though in no way comparable to a factory proletariat, often failed to receive from their employers earnings equal to the economic value of their endeavours. For certain, by the 1930s the sports industry, as with other capitalist industries, had a highly developed division of labour with proprietors at the top, followed by managers, professional athletes, and casual, part-time labour at the bottom. At least on the surface, there is some justification in the Marxian-inspired thesis that inter-war sport was related to wider developments in British capitalism; namely, declining staple industries on the one hand and new markets (as in sport) on the other, increased leisure time, passive consumption and a hierarchical sports industry with growing concentration levels and labour markets. But what did this mean for workers' control in sport?

To enter into a critical discussion, it is appropriate to recall that modern sports are contradictory cultural forms. Firstly, there is the question of control. At the outset, it should be recognised, as Roy Hay has done in a characteristically nuanced piece on Scottish football, that sports are not as effective a means of control as the wage system, the family or the State, if only in terms of the numbers of people directly involved or influenced by these respective institutions.[55] No one can doubt the widespread interest in sport, but this does not mean that it has ever been as socially potent or pervasive as work, family and the government of the day.

More specifically, accepting that inter-war sports were controlled ostensibly by the bourgeoisie, this should not disguise the fact that there were divisions within this class over commercial values and motivations. Capitalist penetration of sport often clashed with some of the conventions and traditional sporting ethos of the dominant order. The commercialisation and professionalisation of sport, and in turn the competitive urge to win, thus underpinned test cricket's imperial crisis of 1932–33 when the body-line bowling of Harold Larwood against Australia challenged the civilising traditions of British imperialist values.[56]

In a similar way, as Brian Stoddart has demonstrated, what lay behind the controversial England versus Germany football clash of December 1935 was the inability of the administrative elite, socialised in the amateur and sportsmanlike world of public school and university games, to come to terms with professional, bureaucratic and indeed political realities.[57]

There were also divisions based on regional and national differences between, say the ruling authorities of the English Football League in St Anne's, the English FA at Lancaster Gate (London) and the Scottish FA. The controversy over the transfer of top Scottish players to English clubs immediately springs to mind here. Even rugby union was a different kind of social force in South Wales than it was (and is) in the border towns of Scotland. And note also the contrasting values surounding rugby union and league. The northern game of rugby league had its own distinctive culture, based on particular regional lifestyles and interpretations of community concerns which differentiated it from the outlook and preoccupation of metropolitan elites. At any rate, there was no monolithic national cultural and intellectual leadership; rather, to borrow from Mike Featherstone, 'a structured social space in which various groups, classes and class fractions struggle and compete to impose their own particular tastes as *the* legitimate tastes, and to thereby, where necessary, name and rename, classify and reclassify, order and reorder the field'.[58]

Needless to say, middle-class moralists were also against the betting habit, believing that it was evil and corrupted every sport it touched. In 1925, the National Liberal Federation demanded legislative action to curb its growth, and thereafter Parliament debated a range of measures designed to regulate the football pools and the like. Though Sir Frank Meyer, the Conservative MP for Great Yarmouth, claimed during the debate on the 1928 Dog Racing Bill that the Liberal Party 'have been associated always throughout their history as a party with legislation of a kill-joy nature', the Liberals were in fact supported by other dominant interests drawn from sport, church and industry.[59] Even the great social historian, G. M. Trevelyan, could write in 1942: 'Gambling perhaps now does more harm than drink.'[60] Capitalist bookmakers and aristocratic followers of the turf may have had a vested interest in the spread of gambling, yet there were sections of the dominant class who articulated a different position. As in the Victorian period, disunity within the ruling class meant that it was difficult for the class as a whole to manipulate the forms and uses of popular sports. Generally speaking, on the gambling issue liberals, nonconformists and 'respectable' workers stood against Tory aristocrats, the new leisure entrepreneurs and the 'rougher' elements within the working class. Sports such as horse-racing, boxing and even greyhound and whippet coursing (if these cruel activities can be referred to as sports) were patronised by crowds drawn from high and low society, though breached by dress, manners and accent.[61]

Moreover, the working class was not without some form of control. There were penny capitalists or proletarian entrepreneurs in the entertainment industry.[62] It was not unusual in working-class districts for men to eke out their living from bookmaking, pedestrianism or sponsoring boxing booths. Johnny Boyd, a miner from Gallatown in Scotland, became a bookie after the General Strike even though he supported the Communist Party.[63] Also, professional athletes themselves, as highly-skilled workers, were able to exercise a limited degree of control and autonomy over their own particular 'productive' task. Their work could not be regimented or routinised like that of a factory worker, despite the evolution of 'scientific' approaches to sport. Indeed, professional sports presented (restricted) opportunities to escape from mean streets and factory labour.

In the case of association football, from the late nineteenth century the working class had fixed the game as their own: grounds were built in proletarian areas, and, notwithstanding the view of Fishwick and others, players, managers, shareholders and occasionally even directors were drawn from the working class with similar backgrounds and perceptions of the world. Revealingly, the majority of players and managers were born in the industrial heartlands of the North and Scotland.[64] Though first division players could expect to earn more than the average wage of a skilled artisan, they were by no means among the highest paid. Billy Liddell, the skilful Liverpool and Scotland forward of the 1950s – known as the 'Flying Scotsman' – may have claimed that the weekly wage of £5 he was offered for first team appearances when he signed professional forms in 1939 'represented wealth', but in fact the £5 received for 'A' team games was below the average industrial wage.[65] Stanley Matthews, arguably one of the greatest forwards, was truly representative of his class with a 'workers's face, like a miner's ... brought up among thrift and the ever-looming threat of dole and debt ... He came from that England which had no reason to know that the twenties were Naughty and the thirties had style.'[66] Much the same can be said about those other 'greats' of the period, Frank Barson, Charlie Buchan, Dixie Dean, Alex James (despite his penchant for night clubs), Tommy Lawton and the irrepressible Bill Shankly. Note in particular the retrospective views of Shankly, born into a large family in the poor Scottish mining village of

Glenbuck, and inspired by the writings of Robert Burns:

> I'm a socialist, though I do not have any great faith in any of the political parties. The socialism I believe in is not really politics. It is a way of living. It is humanity. I believe the only way to live and to be truly successful is by collective effort, with everyone working for each other, everyone helping each other, and everyone having a share of the rewards at the end of the day. That might be asking a lot, but it's the way I see football and the way I see life.[67]

By the time Shankly achieved his managerial successes with Liverpool in the 1960s and 1970s top players may well have become alienated from their working-class constituents, but this was far from the case in the 1930s. Then 'Football was not so much an opiate of the people as a flag run up against the gaffer bolting his gates and the landlord armed with his bailiffs.'[68] And for Hibernians and Glasgow Celtic, of course, football had radical overtones given their link with the Irish republican movement.[69]

Interestingly enough, league cricket as 'essentially a game controlled by working men' has also been viewed as having 'features which represented a latent challenge to the cricket establishment'.[70] It is fascinating to know that during the miners' lock-out of 1926 such leading cricketers as Jack Hobbs, Harold Larwood, Herbert Sutcliffe and Frank Woolley, together with other sportsmen, supported 'the wives and children of the miners, who are the real victims of the great industrial stoppage now going on'.[71] Likewise, in 1929, the Sports Fellowship was urging the collection of money at sports meetings for the Coalfields Distress Fund.[72] By way of speculation, professional boxing, greyhound racing, speedway and rugby league may also have thrown up implicit challenges to the establishment.

In a slightly different context, capital was invested in the manufacture of sportswear and sports equipment for profit and thereby exploited factory operatives in the production process, yet this tells us very little about consumption. Once working-class consumers made their purchases from the retail outlets they could impose controls on usage, as in the case of hobbies in the home or football equipment in the myriad of neighbourhood teams. Crucially, the new, emergent consumer lifestyles of the 1930s, as initially defined by advertisers, films, the popular press, pulp fiction, records and even sports stars, must not be reduced to the level of a conformist mass culture, for the signs, images, meanings and uses of consumerism can be decoded by individuals and classes in creative and indeed nonconformist ways.

A further speculative, even controversial, point to make is that spectatorship was potentially disruptive of the capitalist mode of production insofar as it led to absenteeism, ill-discipline and insobriety, factors which could undermine certain prerequisites of the accumulation process. On occasions, sport could interfere with production schedules, as on Saturday afternoons when available labour time was reduced. Moreover, it was not unknown in the Lancashire cotton industry for operatives to absent themselves from work to enjoy sport.[73] Cotton masters began to question the repercussions of sport, especially in relation to the hours reductions of the early post-war period: 'I sometimes wonder if we haven't all got pleasure on the brain, from bosses of mills and works down to the lads straight from school. Pleasure never built a business up, but it can easily knock one down.'[74] Another contributor to the local press believed that 'we are getting a little bit too much' sport, whilst yet another protested 'that to-day work is neglected for sport'.[75] Or as that enlightened despot, William Morris, put it: 'I think there is too much sport in England. I have seen factories in the Midlands brought to a complete standstill owing to a mid-week football match. I shall not allow that to happen at my works. I work my full weight. I expect my men to.'[76] Gambling and an elaborate system of bookmakers' agents was also commonplace in many factories, whilst sport continued to be a topic of conversation at work, one of many forms of resistance to the labour process proper.[77] In such ways was production disrupted and labour time lost. Now, undoubtedly, there were managerial experts who asserted that sport could actually improve labour productivity and hence business performance. And, of course, absenteeism may have diminished due to the spread of evening greyhound and speedway meetings. Even so, any theory which locates sport as an agent of the status quo must recognise that as far as certain sections of the inter-war business community were concerned it could also have negative consequences.

Spectator sport, especially when accompanied by drink, posed a threat to the social order in the guise of violence. Games and play reflected aspects of working-class culture and community such as toughness, harshness, parochialism and chauvinism which had evolved as a response to the rigours of wage labour, poor housing, poverty and hostile state interference. Though some sociologists and historians claim that football hooliganism is a post-Second World War phenomenon,[78] there is evidence to suggest that crowd disorder amongst sections of the working class was not unknown before then. As already noted, spectator violence existed in the late nineteenth century, and this continued into the twentieth. By the 1920s Birmingham City's Spion Kop had a reputation for its bottle fights, and in the mid-1930s Leicester fans were known for train-smashing.

Grounds were even closed down temporarily for bad behaviour, for instance at Queen's Park Rangers in 1930, Millwall in 1934 and Carlisle in 1935, whilst complaints were even made to the Metropolitan Police that when grounds were full officers found themselves 'helplessly jammed' by the crowd.[79] In January 1923 also, a Durham coroner commented on the conduct of crowds after one supporter had died from injuries caused by being pushed under a bus:

> It is only a typical instance ... of what happens at the close of football matches in this part of the country. You get two or three men, more or less ruffians, and they set all at defiance. They are a disgrace to the North of England. I have had to stand an ugly rush of 15 or 20 ruffians before the train stopped and have had to call for protection. Unless soon stopped it will be unsafe for people to travel who are not properly protected.[80]

Four months later, of course, the most notorious crowd disorder of the inter-war years occurred at the first Wembley cup final between Bolton and West Ham. According to official sources, there were 200,000 to 250,000 spectators in the ground, 10,000 to 15,000 of whom actually gained access to the pitch. Though allegations had it that casualties amounted to 1,000, apparently only twenty-four cases were treated. Certainly the authorities – some 700 police (though estimates vary), thirty-eight official Wembley staff, 281 paid employees and even 120 boy scouts – failed to control the situation. In the end, order was restored by mounted police, the good sense of the fans and seemingly the appearance of King George V: 'His Majesty's arrival undoubtedly contributed very largely in calming the excitement of the crowd, thus making the task of the Police easier than perhaps it otherwise would have been.'[81] After the final, one Scottish Labour MP commented humorously that the authorities should consider transferring the event 'to Glasgow in order that it may be properly conducted'.[82] However, little did he know that two years later the *Sporting Chronicle* would protest that 'Disorderliness has been the big problem of Scottish football since the war.'[83] Indeed, as H. F. Moorhouse and Bill Murray have cogently argued, the coupling of ethnic antagonism with football in inter-war Glasgow led to violence between the supporters of Protestant Rangers and Catholic Celtic, so that each match became a 'potential flashpoint'.[84]

By the same token, there appears to have been some trouble at racecourses in the early 1920s due to the exploits of racetrack gangs, and even in rugby union, leading the *Western Mail* to blame crowd indiscipline on 'Reds on the terraces'.[85] And in a different environment, that of the informal street community, games and gambling could lead to all kinds of disagreements and disputes between (and within) opposing social classes. Now, even if it can be postulated that such violence acted as a kind of safety valve for the status quo, ensuring that grievances did not spill over into oppositional political forms,[86] there can be few doubts that it disrupted social order and, possibly, the accumulation process. Needless to say, sport disorderliness was far from constructive or socially progressive, yet it is salutary for those theorists who regard sport as a cultural support of the capitalist system to appreciate that it could lead to confrontation with administrators, police and judiciary, and make it harder for industrial capital to secure a disciplined labour force. At the very least, sports disorder as it becomes threatening to the established system may reflect other types of conflict in the wider society and demonstrate that the forces of law and order are under stress.[87] In the final analysis, Ingham and Hardy are right to note that 'we should not overlook the possibility that sport can meaningfully dramatise the reality which subordinate groups actually experience or the possibility that sport can be a vehicle for the expression of subordinate group aspirations'.[88]

Non-commercial outlets

Given the need for further research – most of the discussion has been concerned with football – the claims about commercialisation can only hope to be tentative and partial. Moreover, though commercialisation rose in importance during the period under discussion, voluntary or amateur sports continued to play a substantial role. This is a salient point, for ruling groups had the opportunity to exercise control through voluntary bodies. Did the 'play' of the Boy Scouts and Girl Guides help to reproduce militarist and imperialist values? Did works sports clubs encourage a more harmonious relationship between capital and labour? Or did female organisations like the Women's Institutes and Women's League of Health and Beauty perpetuate established patterns of femininity and domesticity? Clearly such questions can only be answered through a detailed empirical and theoretical research programme. At this stage one can suppose that the working classes were resonant enough to influence voluntary organisations in accordance with their own world-view.

The uniformed youth movement was particularly strong between the wars, the membership of the Boy Scouts rising from 232,000 in 1920 to 422,000 in 1930.[89] Bearing in mind the membership fall of the 1930s and the fact that the various lads' brigades were in decline, the uniform movement was popular with sections of working-class youth. By the 1920s the Scouts were firmly behind 'middle opinion', emphasising social harmony, national unity and peaceful reconstruction. Yet, at the very least, their ideology implied patriotism and service to the Crown and Empire. There is no reason to believe, however, that working-class boys were taken in by the ritualised style of Scout life, the pledges to King and country, the jamboree or saluting the Union Jack. As Gary Whannel has speculated: 'Many may well have joined to use the organisations' facilities without subscribing to the ideas they peddled.'[90] In short, camping, games and comradeship were what mattered, not ideology. In fact, John Springhall claims that the working classes were antagonistic to militarism, and this may well have been behind the reorientation of scouting away from patriotic fervour to world brotherhood. If not, the inter-war years witnessed the growth of alternative non-uniform groupings like the boys' and girls' club movement, which catered for working-class sports.

For working-class adults, possibly ruling groups attempted to influence their outlook through the industrial recreation movement. True, 'backward' employers were suspicious of the efficacy of sport. Even so, by the 1930s many large corporate firms had the resources to afford recreational facilities, among them some of the largest enterprises in the country, who came together in business federations in such major industrial centres as Birmingham, Coventry, Hull, Liverpool, London and Sheffield.[91] Detailed research on the Lancashire cotton industry has found that sports provision was connected to the size, structure and technological base of firms, and the nature of market conditions. In brief, it was the larger mills and those companies engaged in the more buoyant sectors which tended to have outlets for sport: the Fine Cotton Spinners' and Doublers' Association (FCSDA), the English Sewing Cotton Company, Tootal Broadhurst Lee, the Calico Printers' Association, Ashton Brothers, the Amalgamated Cotton Mills Trust.[92]

To be sure, captains of industry moved in a highly complex ethical and cultural world where religion and humanistic ideas played such a complicated role, and where morality and capitalism could be conflated. Hence, employers were interested in sport for numerous reasons, though arguably the main motivation was to improve the health and physical fitness of the workforce, and so increase labour productivity. The opinion thus expressed by the welfare expert, J. G. Patterson, could well have been applied to a number of firms: 'in as much as the employer is interested in industrial efficiency, he cannot afford to ignore the potential vitalizing effect of ordered and intelligently planned leisure occupation'.[93]

Indeed, some firms in the Glasgow area made company sport a condition of employment, apparently because there was 'a disinclination among young people to take healthy exercise'.[94] Equally, industrial sports often aimed to foster smooth industrial relations, improve morale and make the workforce feel as though they were an integral part of the firm. At least the sources are replete with references to the spirit of *esprit de corps*.

Having said this, it does not appear that employers analysed data rigorously to demonstrate the effectiveness of sports facilities in raising efficiency or promoting good industrial relations. Fundamentally, sports could not mask the structural divisions between labour and capital or absolve employers from wage cutting or 'speed-up' of the production process. In the case of enlightened bosses such as Cadburys there were tensions between economic interests and social ideals, business performance and worker welfare.[95] Furthermore, though some workers were deferential, sports schemes could not operate by employer fiat alone. Many had been set up and managed by the workforce: the sports clubs of the Lyons' catering chain were thus 'run by the members for the members; the company does not interfere or dictate', whilst the recreation sections of the FCSDA were 'controlled and maintained by the Workers themselves'.[96] Even if workers were without direct control, factory sports could have been appropriated by the working class for their own ends. Employees attended social functions on their own terms, even using them for drinking and other boisterous activities. And finally, it must be added that not only were there rich alternatives such as fishing and bowls clubs in proletarian communities and the commercial sector, but also opposition from the labour movement, as the next chapter will discuss.

As for other forms of voluntary provision, it is true that lawn tennis, which had spawned 2,874 clubs with over 75,000 members by the mid-1930s, golf with some 1,200 clubs by the late thirties, and athletics with 720 bodies affiliated to the Amateur Athletic Association (AAA) in 1939, catered mainly for the middle classes.[97] Nonetheless, outdoor participations attracted considerable sections of the working class. There was even limited working-class penetration of golf, reflected in the formation of the Artisan Golfers' Association in 1921, and the gradual spread of public courses, reaching some thirty on the eve of the Second World War. Additionally, however, continued discrimination against the so-called lower orders was even more surreptitious when directed at the Jewish community, who responded by setting up their own clubs.[98]

Of course, an array of amateur sports teams were found in working-class neighbourhoods. In 1937, when there were 35,000 clubs affiliated to the FA and perhaps 40,000 Sunday footballers in London alone, the President, W. Pickford, could state with some justification:

> Owing to the intense interest aroused by the doings of the big clubs and the space given to them in the Press, there is an idea that ours is a professional game. It is only partly so. I should be surprised if there are more than 500 clubs that engage the services of more than one paid player. Compared with the vast army of players, ours is really an amateur association with a mere platoon of professionals. Every Saturday afternoon now more than a million amateurs are enjoying the sport.[99]

Similarly, in the 1930s, workers' interests in the countryside had been fully awakened, and as chapter 5 demonstrates, many joined organised clubs. Though a good proportion of these catered for the middle classes, workers were certainly found in their ranks: a rough estimate of the occupational composition of the Youth Hostels Association put one-third as manual workers.[100] By 1938 the membership of those bodies covering angling, camping, cycling, holidays, rambling and other outdoor pursuits was at least half a million, and a good number must have been drawn from the proletariat.

It is also a moot point that the First World War smashed old ideals of female gentility and passivity, especially amongst middle-class women, who experienced the harsh realities of munitions work or nursing in military hospitals. Active female participation in the war economy, together with the demographic transformation wrought by the loss of male soldiers and of course the pre-war campaign for female suffrage, meant that women emerged in the 1920s more independent and sure of themselves.[101] This is not to deny that the female sphere was still subordinate – for working-class wives in particular everyday life was one continuous struggle against poverty, unremitting domestic labour, and control over economic and biological reproduction – but rather that women were able to express themselves in new ways through work, the vote, fashion and sport. The period witnessed a growth of female participation in athletics (the Women's AAA was founded in 1922), cycling, physical fitness, swimming, tennis and the like. A Women's Keep Fit Movement in the North-East, for instance, launched in 1929 with one class and 127 women, had increased to nine weekly classes with 500 people within the year. At national level, the membership of the middle-class Women's League of Health and Beauty, started in the late twenties, rose from 30,000 in 1933 to 120,000 in 1937 and 166,000 by 1939. Interestingly, there is also evidence of rising attendance by working-class women at football matches.[102] Even though women have been able to find spaces for sporting endeavours, on the whole it should still be concluded that patriarchal relations in the home and the wider society severely limited women's access to sport. The major spectator and participant sports, namely football, rugby, boxing, cricket and racing remained male preserves.

One final point here, there was no question of the working class closing down its institutions and associations in response to the attractions of commercial sports. Even in the 1930s there were still approximately 50,000 members of pigeon-racing unions, drawn from such occupations as mining and weaving, and perhaps one million in the Working Men's Club and Institute Union with its wide array of games facilities.[103] Numerous miners' institutes also organised sport, the most spectacular schemes having 'football, hockey and cricket grounds, several tennis courts and bowling greens, a children's playground, a park space with bandstand and perhaps a dancing area, a putting course, one or more pavilions, shelters, seats, lavatory accommodation, a refeshment kiosk, trees, shrubberies and flower beds, a groundsman's corner and possibly a green house and a residence for the groundsman'.[104] True, Viscount Chelmsford, chair of the Miners' Welfare Committee, denied 'the gibe ... that it spends all its money on play and recreation'.[105] Yet the fact is that from the outset, when the Committee first considered recreation and reported 'that the great majority of the recommendations so far received from the district Welfare Committees are for recreational schemes', play remained more material than such pressing concerns as health, convalescent homes, ambulance associations, education and research.[106] Likewise, as this study will discuss, the labour movement continued to generate quite a thriving cultural and recreational nexus.

Conclusion

This chapter has not considered all aspects of inter-war sport. Subsequent chapters will raise the interesting issues of municipal sport and informal street activities. Most importantly, sports evolved against the general background of economic restructuring. This meant that for those sections of the working class displaced due to unemployment and short-time working, obstacles were placed in the way of freely-chosen sports participation. Much the same point can be said about certain other 'marginal' groups, such as casual and female domestic labour. However, it has to be recognised that for those workers in permanent full-time employment and the so-called socially upwardly mobile, the economic growth of the time meant that there were greater opportunities to exploit sport. Indeed, sport shared in the growth process, evidenced by spiralling attendances and high consumer spending. In some ways the expansion of the mass market in sport may have incorporated working-class consumers into a system of passive, administered pleasures increasingly permeated by profit. Accordingly sports have been analysed by some commentators as a form of class domination, an integral part of those forces said to produce a submissive and docile proletariat. To be sure, the further consolidation of consumer culture modified the range of working-class sports. However, the working classes' relationship with commercialised sports was inherently ambiguous, at the same time subordinate and independent. Sport could reproduce male chauvinism, nationalism and the competitive ethic, yet it could also re-cast proletarian collective identity and suspicion of authority.

Various bourgeois groupings were extremely sensitive to the spread of commerce in the field of culture. On occasions, the exploitation of sports markets clashed with some of the mores and conventions of the dominant social order. The internal fragmentation of the ruling class presented some difficulty in the use of sports as a vehicle of straightforward class domination.

Moreover, the working classes were not passive recipients of the sports product. Commercialised sports and their ancillary products were part of a proletarian milieu, precisely because the workers stamped their own meanings and culture on them. Although the demand for sport was determined ultimately in the context of bourgeois political economy, such demand was not simply imposed from above, for it reflected the realities and experiences of working-class life. The popular classes were able to bring to commercialised sports their own distinctive culture, whether as producers or consumers. Economic and cultural subordination in terms of the wage form, unemployment and the sexual division of labour should be acknowledged, but this did not prevent the wider proletarian culture from remaining under proletarian control and linked to the community experience. Thus commercial forms had to fit in with a pre-existing culture based on communal activity, mutuality and shared ideas and attitudes. The commodification of sport was differentiated along class lines, as shown in the social composition and segregation of football, dog-racing, speedway and other crowds.[107] The sports ground, billiards room, and even the weekly ritual of filling in the football pools were part of a collective culture, bringing people together to share their leisure, producing common identities and reference points. This is not to romanticise the richness of the working-class spirit; sports could often be violent as in foul play, crowd disorder or squabbles over bets. Despite the imposition of rules and regulations, working-class sports continued to be rough and ready: in contrast to the bourgeois amateur ethic, professional sportsmen played to win and in so doing were prepared to 'bend' the rules, whilst on the terraces supporters adapted the game to express and exemplify aspects of an essentially dynamic and active working-class culture. At times the sharpness and potentially explosive character of lower-class sport could even disrupt the capitalist accumulation and legitimation process. In sum, there were established structures of constraint in industrial capitalism, but commercial sports as received by human agents had their creative and transformative elements. In the context of inter-war Britain, the tensions and frictions inherent in commercial sports meant that it was not impossible for workers to adapt games to satisfy group needs and fit in with their own sub-culture, ideas and institutions.

Good use was also made of sport in the non-commercial sector. Workers had the capacity to turn company sports clubs, street teams and the vast array of voluntary organisations to their own advantage. Importantly, voluntary sports were not isolated from commercial influences: local league cricket and football teams often had contacts with professional sportsmen and made outlays on stadia and expensive equipment, whilst street teams or homing societies encountered the sportswear industry, sports requisites, gambling concerns and even a growing trade in pet-keeping. By the end of the 1930s the 'residual' experiences, meanings and values of earlier associational forms were adapted to fuse with an 'emergent' consumer culture.[108] Even so, as the following chapters will demonstrate, the labour movement posed alternatives to the hierarchies and principles of capitalist sport and the 'new' consumer culture.

Notes

1 See, for example, A. Marwick, *The Deluge: British Society and the First World War* (1965).
2 But see A. Marwick, 'British life and leisure and the First World War', *History Today*, vol. 15 (1965). C. Veitch, 'Play up! Play up! and win the war: football, the nation and the first World War', *Journal of Contemporary History*, vol. 20 (1985). D. Birley, 'Sportsmen and the deadly game', *British Journal of Sports History*, vol. 3 (1986).

3 For further details, see D. Aldcroft, *The Inter-War Economy: Britain 1919–1939* (1970).

4 For an overview of the different interpretations, see R. Middleton, *Towards the Managed Economy: Keynes, the Treasury and the fiscal policy debate of the 1930s* (1985). P. K. O'Brien, 'Britain's economy between the wars: a survey of counter-revolution in economic history', *Past and Present*, no. 115 (1987).

5 J. Stevenson and C. Cook, *The Slump: Society and Politics During the Depression* (1977). But see the more balanced perspective in J. Stevenson, *British Society 1914-45* (Harmondsworth, 1984).

6 See, for example, A. Howkins and J. Saville, 'The 1930s: a revisionist history', *Socialist Register* (1979).

7 S. G. Jones, *Workers at Play: A Social and Economic History of Leisure, 1918–1939* (1986), ch. 1.

8 See P. Johnson, *Saving and Spending: The Working-Class Economy 1870–1939* (Oxford, 1985), pp. 155-65.

9 M. Featherstone, 'Lifestyle and consumer culture', *Theory, Culture and Society*, vol. 4 (1987), pp. 61-2.

10 J. Hargreaves, *Sport, Power and Culture: A Social and Historical Analysis of Popular Sports in Britain* (Cambridge, 1986), p. 86.

11 *Economist*, 8 April 1939.

12 See N. B. F. Fishwick, 'Association Football and English Social Life 1910––1950', DPhil, University of Oxford (1984), esp. pp. 139-41.

13 D. Caradog Jones (ed.), *The Social Survey of Merseyside*, vol. 3 (Liverpool, 1934), p. 293. See also T. Mason, 'The Blues and the Reds', *Transactions of the Historic Society of Lancashire and Cheshire*, vol. 134 (1984).

14 S. G. Jones, 'The economic aspects of association football in England, 1918-1939', *British Journal of Sports History*, vol. 1 (1984), pp. 288-90.

15 *Economist*, 17 April 1937. W. Vamplew, *The Turf: A Social and Economic History of Horse Racing* (1976), pp. 68-9. G. Williams, 'From grand slam to great slump: economy, society and rugby football in Wales during the Depression', *Welsh History Review*, vol. 11 (1983).

16 J. Walvin, *Football and the Decline of Britain* (1986), p. 49.

17 *Daily Herald*, 28 Aug. 1936.

18 *Report of the Committee on Football* (1968), p. 33.

19 P. M. Young, *Bolton Wandereres* (1961), pp. 126-7. J. Power, 'Aspects of Working-Class Leisure During the Depression Years: Bolton in the 1930s', MA, University of Warwick (1980), pp. 64-7.

20 *Sporting Chronicle*, 5 May 1927.

21 (Manchester) *Evening Chronicle Special Cup-Tie Supplement*, 15 March 1934.

22 See G. Green, *The History of the Football Association* (1953), pp. 285-355. J. Walvin, *The People's Game. A Social History of British Football* (1975), pp. 115-35. S. Wagg, *The Football World: A Contemporary Social History* (Brighton, 1984), pp. 21-65. S. Studd, *Herbert Chapman, Football Emperor: A Study in the Origins of Modern Soccer* (1981), pp. 96-138. C. Korr, *West Ham United: the Making of a Football Club* (1986), *passim*.

23 For the financial aspects of modern sport, see the summary article of the growing literature by J. Cairns, N. Jennett and P. J. Sloane, 'The economics of professional team sports: a survey of theory and evidence', *Journal of Economic*

Studies, vol. 13 (1986).

24 K. Macklin, *The History of Rugby League Football* (1974), chs. 7–12.

25 D. Smith and G. Williams, *Fields of Praise: The Official History of the Welsh Rugby Union 1881–1981* (Cardiff, 1980), pp. 218–20, 225, 284.

26 *Daily Herald*, 26th April 1927. For the labour journalist, R. B. Suthers, however, the sport was 'mechanical' and lacking in thrills. *Railway Review*, 14 Oct. 1927.

27 *House of Commons Debates*, 14 March 1928, col. 1927. Public Record Office (hereafter PRO) HO 45/15853.

28 R. Evans and A. Boyd, *The Use of Leisure in Hull* (Hull, 1933), p. 10. H. Llewellyn Smith (ed.), *The New Survey of London Life and Labour, vol. 9 Life and Leisure* (1935), p. 55.

29 R. Sinclair, *Metropolitan Man: The future of the English* (1937), p. 120.

30 *House of Commons Debates*, 14 March 1928, col. 571; 27 June 1934, col. 1159.

31 D. J. Jeremy, 'Critchley, Alfred Cecil (1890–1963): greyhound racing promoter and industrialist', in D. J. Jeremy (ed.), *Dictionary of Business Biography*, vol. 1 (1984).

32 *The Economist*, 8 April 1939.

33 Llewellyn Smith, *Life and Leisure*, p. 56.

34 *Census of England and Wales 1931. Industry Tables* (1934), pp. 10, 719.

35 J. White, *The Worst Street in North London: Campbell Bunk, Islington, Between the Wars* (1986), pp. 40, 54, 109, 165. At West Ham United, however, the essential services were provided by volunteers, and even Arsenal suffered from unofficial programme sellers. Korr, *West Ham*, p. 133. S. Inglis, *Soccer in the Dock: A History of British Football Scandals 1900 to 1965* (1985), p. 4.

36 J. Hill, 'The development of professionalism in English league cricket, *c.* 1900 to 1940', in J. A. Mangan and R. B. Small (eds), *Sport, Culture and Society: International historical and sociological perspectives* (1986).

37 B. Dabscheck, '"Defensive Manchester": a history of the Professional Footballers' Association', in R. Cashman and M. McKernan (eds), *Sport in History: The Making of Modern Sporting History* (Queensland, 1979), pp. 244–6. *Sporting Chronicle and Athletic News*, 6 April 1938.

38 See M. Hill, *George Sinfield – his pen a sword* (n.d., 1986?), pp. 18–22.

39 *Listener*, 1 July 1931, supplement no. 14.

40 See Fishwick, 'Association football', pp. 266–320.

41 *Fifth Census of Production*, 1935, Part III (1940), pp. 583–98.

42 *Ibid.*, p. 593. J. B. Jeffreys, *Retail Trading in Britain 1850–1950* (Cambridge, 1954), pp. 414–19.

43 See Dunlop Rubber Company, *50 Years of Growth* (1938).

44 *Minutes of Evidence taken before the Committee on Industry and Trade* (1925), pp. 448–65.

45 H. R. Watling, 'The cycle and motor-cycle industry', in H. J. Schofield (ed.), *The Book of British Industries* (1933), pp. 126–7.

46 J. Woodforde, *The Story of the Bicycle* (1970), p. 168.

47 Jones, 'Economic aspects', p. 295. See also Fishwick, 'Association football', pp. 321–74. B. West, 'Moores, Sir John (1896–): football pool promoter and retailer', in Jeremy, *Dictionary*, vol. 4.

48 *Daily Herald*, 1 April 1924, 19 March 1934.

49 *Spectator*, 28 Feb. 1936. *Daily Herald*, 6 March 1937.

50 *Nation and Athenaeum*, 26 Jan. 1929.
51 R. Beamish, 'Sport and the logic of capitalism', in H. Cantelon and R. Gruneau (eds), *Sport, Culture and the Modern State* (Toronto, 1982). See also R. Goldman, '"We make weekends": leisure and the commodity form', *Social Text*, vol. 8 (1984), in which he states that 'The most visible aspect of the commodification of leisure has been the emergence of the sports spectacle' (p. 86).
52 See E. Mandel, *Late Capitalism* (1978), p. 394. R. Butsch, 'The commodification of leisure: the case of the model airplane hobby and industry', *Qualitative Sociology*, vol. 7 (1984).
53 Fishwick, 'Association football', p. 407.
54 C. J. Nottingham, 'More important than life or death: football, the British working class and the social order', paper presented to the fifth Anglo-Dutch Labour History Conference, 1986, p. 17.
55 R. Hay, 'Soccer and social control in Scotland 1873–1978', in R. Cashman and M. McKernan (eds), *Sport: Money, Morality and the Media* (New South Wales, n.d., 1982?).
56 See R. Sissons and B. Stoddart, *Cricket and Empire: the 1932–33 Bodyline Tour of Australia* (1984).
57 B. Stoddart, 'Sport, cultural politics and international relations: England versus Germany, 1935', in N. Müller and J. K. Rühl (eds), *Sport History* (Niedernhausen, 1985).
58 Featherstone, 'Lifestyle', p. 60.
59 *Liberal Magazine*, June 1925. *House of Commons Debates*, 14 March 1928, col. 562. This was most forcefully demonstrated in early 1936 when the Football League twice rescheduled the fixture list to disrupt pool betting. See Inglis, *Soccer in the Dock*, ch. 7.
60 G. M. Trevelyan, *Illustrated English Social History: 4* (Harmondsworth, 1964 edition), p. 208.
61 See R. Graves and A. Hodge, *The Long Week-End: A Social History of Great Britain 1918–1939* (1940), pp. 234–5, 391.
62 J. Benson, *The Penny Capitalists: a study of nineteenth-century working-class entrepreneurs* (Dublin, 1983) pp. 65–72.
63 I. MacDougall (ed.), *Militant Miners* (Edinburgh, 1981), p. 82.
64 Based on data derived from F. Johnston (ed.), *The Football Who's Who* (1935). Alternatively, as Charles Korr has argued in his case study of West Ham United: 'footballers remained part of the class and neighbourhood in which they were born [, they] lived near the ground, took local buses and trams or walked to training sessions'. Korr, *West Ham*, pp. 92, 93.
65 B. Liddell, *My Soccer Story* (1960), p. 34.
66 A. Hopcraft, *The Football Man: People and Passions in Soccer* (1968), p. 30.
67 B. Shankly, *Shankly* (St Albans, 1977), p. 41. Cf. Wagg, *Football World*, p. 140.
68 Hopcraft, *Football Man*, p. 23. Thus for Charles Korr, West Ham United was 'a collection of shared traditions and beliefs ... a captive of the community'. Korr, *West Ham*, pp. 23, 27.
69 Hay, 'Soccer and Social Control', pp. 239–40. B. Murray, *The Old Firm: Sectarianism, Sport and Society in Scotland* (Edinburgh, 1984), esp. pp. 60–75.
70 Hill, 'English league cricket', p. 116.

71 *Lansbury's Labour Weekly*, 24 July 1926.

72 *The Times*, 4 March 1929.

73 *Cotton Factory Times*, 11 March 1927. It must be added that there were fewer cases of sport-related absenteeism by the 1920s. *Cotton Factory Times*, 4 Feb. 1927.

74 *Textile Weeky*, 10 Aug. 1928.

75 *Textile Weekly*, 29 June 1928; *Manchester Evening News*, 16 Aug. 1930.

76 Quoted in R. Whiting, 'The Working Class in the "New Industry" Towns between the Wars: the case of Oxford', DPhil, University of Oxford (1978), p.161.

77 *Minutes of Evidence taken before the Royal Commission on Lotteries and Betting* (1932), *passim*. G. Brown, *Sabotage: A Study in Industrial Conflict* (Nottingham, 1977), pp. 91, 311-12. R. McKibbin, 'Work and hobbies in Britain 1880-1950', in J. Winter (ed.), *The Working Class in Modern British History* (Cambridge, 1983), pp. 135-40.

78 I. Taylor, 'Class, violence and sport: the case of soccer hooliganism in Britain', in Cantelon and Gruneau, *Sport*, pp. 41-2, 60-1. Walvin, *Football and the Decline*, p. 66.

79 See, for example, G Pearson, *Hooligan: A History of Respectable Fears* (1983), pp. 29-31. C. M. Downham, 'The problem of Millwall Football Club: an historical and sociological approach', in D. Benning (ed.), *Sport and Imperialism* (1986). *Sporting Chronicle and Athletic News*, 2 Dec. 1935. PRO MEPO 2/2219.

80 *Daily Mail*, 5 Jan. 1923.

81 PRO HO 45/11627.

82 *House of Commons Debates*, 30 April 1923, col. 971.

83 *Sporting Cronicle*, 28 Jan. 1925.

84 H. F. Moorhouse, 'Professional football and working-class culture: English theories and Scottish evidence', *Sociological Review*, vol 32 (1984); Murray, *Old Firm*, pp. 169-78.

85 Vamplew, *The Turf*, pp. 141-2. Smith and Williams, *Fields of Praise*, pp. 228-9.

86 Walvin, *Football and the Decline*, p. 109. Wagg, *Football World*, pp. 210, 214; Murray, *Old Firm*, pp. 3, 136. Goldman, '"Weekends"', p. 90. J-M. Brohm, *Sport – A Prison of Measured Time* (1978), pp. 15, 51. See also the interesting discussion in A. Guttmann, *Sports Spectators* (New York, 1986), pp. 147-58.

87 Hay, 'Soccer and social control', p. 240. Cf. N. Elias, 'Introduction', in N. Elias and E. Dunning, *Quest for Excitement: Sport and Leisure in the Civilizing Process* (Oxford, 1986), pp. 54-7.

88 A. Ingham, and S. Hardy, 'Sport: structuration, subjugation and hegemony',*Theory, Culture and Society*, vol. 2 (1984), p. 87.

88 This paragraph is based on J. Springhall, *Youth, Empire and Society: British Youth Movements, 1883-1940* (1977).

90 G. Whannel, *Blowing the Whistle: The politics of sport* (1983), p. 83. Cf. J. MacKenzie, *Propaganda and Empire: The manipulation of British public opinion 1880-1960* (Manchester, 1984), pp. 110, 243-8.

91 See Jones, *Workers at Play*, pp. 69-71. Fishwick, 'Association football', pp. 36-46. J. Crump, 'Recreation in Coventry between the wars', in B. Lancaster and T. Mason (eds), *Life and Labour in a 20th-Century City: The Experience of Coventry* (Coventry, n.d., 1986?), pp. 268-77, 284.

92 See S. G. Jones, 'Work, leisure and the political economy of the cotton districts between the wars', *Textile History*, vol. 18 (1987). S. G. Jones, 'The survival of industrial paternalism in the cotton districts: a view from the 1920s', *Journal of Regional and Local Studies*, vol. 7 (1987).
93 *Industrial Welfare*, May 1934.
94 (Glasgow) *Daily Record and Mail*, 30 Nov. and 1 Dec. 1928.
95 C. Dellheim, 'The creation of a company culture: *Cadburys*, 1861–1931', *American Historical Review*, vol. 92 (1987).
96 *Economist*, 19 June 1920, 28 June 1930. Jones, 'Survival of industrial paternalism'.
97 A. Howkins and J. Lowerson, *Trends in Leisure 1919–1939* (1979), pp. 42, 53.
98 G. Cousins, *Golf in Britain: A social history from the beginnings to the present* (1975), chs. 13, 18, 26.
99 *Listener*, 29 Sept. 1937.
100 Jones, *Workers at Play*, pp. 65–6. M. Rooff, *Youth and Leisure: A Survey of Girls' Organisations in England and Wales* (Edinburgh, 1935), p. 21; A. Holt, 'Hikers and ramblers: surviving a thirties fashion', *International Journal of the History of Sport*, vol. 4 (1987), pp. 59–60.
101 J. Walvin, 'Sport, social history and the historian', *British Journal of Sports History*, vol. 1 (1984), pp. 11–12.
102 Guttmann, *Sports Spectators*, pp. 108–9.
103 J. Mott, 'Miners, weavers, and pigeon racing', in M. A. Smith, S. Parker and C. S. Smith (eds), *Leisure and Society in Britain* (1973), p. 92. *Minutes of Evidence taken before the Royal Commission on Licensing (England and Wales)* (1930), pp. 1217–52.
104 *Report of the Departmental Committee of Inquiry into the Miners' Welfare Fund* (1931), cmd. 4236, p. 32.
105 PRO POWE 1/46, Minutes of Proceedings at Ninth Annual Conference of District Welfare Committees, 18 Nov. 1930.
106 PRO POWE 1/1, Miners' Welfare Committee, Minutes of first meeting, 3 Feb. 1921. PRO POWE 1/46, Minutes of Conference of Miners' Welfare Committee, 28 Nov. 1922.
107 Power, 'Aspects of working-class leisure', pp. iii, 18, 67, 92–3. White, *Worst Street*, pp. 83, 165. J. Lowerson, 'Studying inter-war leisure: the context and some problems', in A. Tomlinson (ed.), *Leisure and Social Control* (Brighton, 1981), p. 72. J. E. Cronin, *Labour and Society in Britain 1918–1979* (1984), p. 92. J. Clarke and C. Critcher, *The Devil Makes Work: Leisure in Capitalist Britain* (1985), p. 75.
108 For further discussion of this point, see R. Williams, *Marxism and Literature* (Oxford, 1977), ch. 8.

Chapter 4

'Up the Reds': workers, socialists and sport

Introduction

The British Labour movement made important organisational gains during the First World War. Trade union membership doubled to 8,348,000 in the six years to 1920, bringing increased negotiating strength. The unions were able to gain a number of significant concessions in the radical industrial and political atmosphere of the early post-war period, the most notable of which was the shorter working week. As already mentioned, shorter hours contributed to the growth of inter-war sport.[1] As in the nineteenth century, organised labour was instrumental in the social reform movement, and as such helped shape the place of sport in the broader structures of industrial capitalism. It is true that union membership declined with the slump in economic activity, though still by 1926 it was above the pre-war level at 5,219,000. No doubt the union amalgamation movement of the post-war years helped to prevent a collapse in membership, whilst advances on the political front, especially the formation of the first Labour Government in 1924, represented the working classes' coming of age. Indeed, such commentators as Martin Jacques and James Cronin have claimed that the period between 1918 and 1926 was one of 'aggressive labour insurgency' and 'unprecedented militancy', when organised workers believed that capitalism was under the threat of imminent collapse, and so were prepared 'to use industrial action in order to influence political decisions'.[2] The class politics of the early 1920s culminated in the 1926 General Strike, seen by some as a kind of watershed in inter-war labour history. Though this is not the place to rehearse the various interpretations and nuances of these salient political developments, any discussion of organised labour's relationship with sport must at least recognise the subtle interactions of capitalist structures, socialist opposition and resistance, and the overall balance of class forces. Big assumptions to make, but, in the context of this chapter's discussion of socialism and sport, important ones nonetheless. The chapter will trace the origins of the British Workers' Sports Federation in the early 1920s, the subsequent takeover by communist activists and the Marxist approach to sport in the first half of the 1930s.

Workers' sport in the early 1920s

During the inter-war years, sport was undoubtedly a major working-class leisure activity; games like football and cricket were often grouped together as the 'Englishman's religion'. Given these circumstances, the broad labour movement could hardly ignore the importance of sport and the influence it exerted in everyday life. As noted, socialists of the late Victorian and Edwardian era were quick to realise this, so that by the 1920s there was already a specifically socialist sporting tradition. In fact, this tradition as linked to the religion of socialism was recast in the inter-war years. Far from socialist forms of recreation being generated spontaneously with little emphasis on efficient organisation, as was the case with the religion of socialism, the labour movement sought to respond to the further commodification of sport in a more systematic fashion through a national workers' sports movement. With some certainty, this reflected the wider institutionalisation of labour and socialist politics, notably the Labour Party's new constitutional arrangements of 1918, the formation of the Communist Party in 1920 (as closely defined by the new Soviet Republic), the election of the first Labour Government, and the union amalgamation movement.

After the Great War, the workers' movement was consolidated by both the political and industrial wings of organised labour. There is evidence to suggest that from the beginnings of the 1920s, local trade unions and labour organisations were taking an interest in sport. The sports meetings held in the immediate pre-war period by, for example, the Amalgamated Society of Carpenters, Cabinet-makers and Joiners were heralded as models for future adaptation.[3] And at a time when commercial sport was booming and organised labour was articulating the demand for leisure, reports on sport began to appear in union journals and party publications: the *AEU Journal* had a regular section on social events, the *Workers' Union Record* frequently covered football and motor-cycling, and the *Railway Review* hosted a 'Sporting Column'. There were many contributions, including one from G. D. H. Cole, urging the need for trade union sport – seemingly, the dullness of the branch room or political platform was to be variegated and made pleasant by expansion into sport.[4] In the *London Citizen*, for example, 'Sporticus' advocated the formation of labour and co-operative sports clubs, envisaging the day when the British co-operative commonwealth would play a test match against the Australian co-operative commonwealth, and a labour sports club would win the FA Cup.[5] In fact, a number of clubs were formed like the Guildford Co-operative Society's ladies' football team, the King's Lynn Labour Sports Club, the North London Workers' Union Team and the Southampton Transport Workers' Social and Athletic Club, many of them having sections for boxing, cricket, football, socials and entertainment, children's treats, drama and music.[6] If a club was fortunate enough it might also possess a sports ground – the Leicester Co-operative Society thus had cricket squares, tennis courts, bowling greens and football pitches, together with the necessary changing rooms.[7] Aside from this, the Clarion Cycling Club (CCC) still provided opportunities, if in a less dynamic form, for cycling and general sporting activities. Despite the fact that membership had declined to about 2,500 in 1921, there were still strong local unions, and the annual Easter meet continued to play its traditional festive role, comprising a whilst drive, an international football match with the French, a walk around the walls of Chester, political discussion, a drama and smoking concert, a grand dance, swimming and, of course, a cycle ride.[8] There were numerous cycling and even motor-cycling clubs – 'Ladies are especially invited' – as well as camps and clubhouses, fellowships and vocal unions. It is therefore clear that the official labour movement was sponsoring sport in the early 1920s.

Indeed, a British Workers' Federation of Sport was established in April 1923 under the auspices of Clarion cyclists, Labour Party sympathisers and trade union officials, with the object of promoting labour sport on an international basis 'to further the cause of peace between nations'.[9] The main driving force behind the Federation, soon to take on its formal name, the British Workers' Sports Federation (BWSF), was thus a desire for international unity. This is hardly surprising as the leading figure was none other than Tom Groom, a convinced internationalist. As chairman of the CCC, he attended the first international workers' sports conference in 1913, and the founding conference of the social democratic Socialist Workers' Sports International (SWSI) in 1920 – to which the BWSF was affiliated – disseminated the related ideas on internationalism and sport among his socialist comrades, and was even asked to stand as a Clarion Parliamentary candidate.[10] With mottoes and phrases like 'Footballs instead of Cannon Balls' and 'Peace through Sport', the BWSF immediately established contacts with the SWSI in the 'hope that the future peace of the world may be secured in the democratic arenas of international sporting Olympiads'.[11] Even though the belief that global athletic gatherings would promote international fraternity and substitute the spirit of sport for the spirit of militarism was somewhat idealistic, even utopian, it gave the Federation a source of political legitimacy. And no doubt this commitment mirrored wider socialist, even trade union, sentiment, one Sheffield branch of the Amalgamated Engineering Union thus hoping to see 'International sport as a means to promote peace'.[12] This is not to deny that there were no other concerns: socialists of all descriptions not only had a passion for sport – the Parliamentary Labour Party had its own cricket team – but also were critical of the social system that denied adequate sporting facilities, playing grounds and open spaces, and encouraged an aristocratic outlook to games like cricket.[13] Yet it was the pacifist and internationalist ideas engendered by the non-chauvinistic left before, during and after the First World War which gave the BWSF ideological commitment, a theme which will be returned to in later sections of this study.

In spite of the Federation's precarious organisational structure, there were some initial successes. The Scottish group had a number of sections embracing football, cycling, swimming, athletics, gymnastics and boxing, with a membership of about 1,000.[14] In London, contacts were also made with some trade unions – engineers, railwaymen, builders, clerks, transport workers – as well as trades councils, Independent Labour Party (ILP) and Labour Party branches; at least sixty-three associations contributing towards the organisation of a sports day.[15] As far as sport was concerned, the BWSF participated in gala days which, judging from one programme, were colourful occasions: tug-of-war, one-mile walk, sprints, children's events, three-legged races, egg and spoon races, and a ladies' thread-the-needle race.[16] At the same time, the London group sponsored a tour of Germany, and, most important of all, the national trade union movement began to offer greater levels of assistance.[17]

In the early part of 1925, representations were made with Fred Bramley the general secretary of the Trades Union Congress (TUC), and it was decided that workers' sport would best be served by a policy of formal co-operation with the unions, rather than by isolated growth through individual sports clubs.[18] At the annual conference of trades councils a favourable resolution was passed, stressing the need for labour-sponsored sport, following further developments at both the national and local levels.[19] As Jack Cohen commented: 'The agitation for the formation of a Workers' Sports Organisation has been growing more and more popular.'[20] All sections of the official labour movement were prepared to consider the question of workers' sport, and in 1927 the TUC officially recognised the Federation.[21] Moreover, sporting activities were extended: tours were made of various Continental countries, culminating in the participation of Clarion cyclists in the Workers' Olympiad at Prague in July 1927.[22] And locally, certain ethical socialists in, for instance, the North-West, were pleading for sport as 'a living, pulsating, satisfying fellowship', whilst others were busy organising annual rallies as in the Colne Valley and sports galas as in Oldham.[23] All of this was rather suggestive of the religion of socialism. Indeed, if the activities of the ILP Guild of Youth with its 171 branches by 1925, the Clarion and the numerous semi-independent and autonomous socialist bodies like the Gorton ILP Rambling Club, Willesden Socialist Cycling Club, and the Printing and Allied Trades Amateur Boxing Club were also brought into the account, it would appear that the BWSF and similar groups were providing a plentiful recreational supply.

However, at least in terms of efficient national organisation, outward appearances do not always reflect what lies beneath. The Federation was neither particularly dynamic nor a popular sporting organisation. At an early stage, leading members like George Bennett, an old member of the Social Democratic Federation, and Tom Groom complained that enthusiasm for labour sport was 'a trifle shop-worn and soiled', that pleasing initiatives had petered out, and that little help came from the Labour Party and its supportive newspaper, the *Daily Herald*.[24] It is true that improvements were being made, but in comparison with the Continental workers' sports movement – the German association had close to one million members by 1927 – the BWSF was a mere fledgling, growing, but very slowly indeed.[25] The description made as late as 1927 by the *People's Year Book*, though perhaps a little unkind, was not far off the mark: 'The British Workers' Sports Federation is a weak and puny body; hardly worthy of the name of a Federation.'[26] Equally, the Young Communist International supposed that until Marxist influence was brought to bear in 1927 the BWSF 'had existed more dead than alive'.[27] There was indeed some justification in this comment for only when a more militant, dynamic and communist-inspired group exerted pressure did the Federation begin to make some kind of sporting and political impact.

The British communist movement interpreted sport as a legitimate political issue in the early 1920s. It is likely that Marxists participated in some of the sports organised by the local socialist societies, ILP scouts, Clarion cyclists and Socialist Sunday Schools. As one young Marxist put it, in a way which seemed to imitate the creed of certain public school masters:

The benefits of athletic and other manly exercises, from an educational as well as a recreative point of view, are generally admitted. There is no better means of promoting healthy growth and development than sensible indulgence in sports and pastimes. Further, boys and girls are assisted in attaining self discipline through the game, by being induced to put the common welfare before personal interests, to act in concert with the various elements of the company, and in using initiative and directive ability during the course of play.[28]

Hence, it was quite widely believed that 'Communist organisations must turn the proletarian youth into a healthy people'.[29] Communist sport was to be pure, clean and uplifting, purging the revolutionary of any sympathy he or she might have for capitalist sport. Even so, it was only after the formation of the Communist Party (CP) in 1920 that a coherent ideological and political approach to sport can be observed. It is true that some communists thought sport to be 'the best antidote to Bolshevism', 'a dope for the working masses', but the Party leadership quickly realised that workers' interests could not be ignored.[30] In 1922, the Party Commission on Organisation, no doubt encouraged by trends in international communism, stressed the political significance of sport.[31] As this study will discuss, the Red Sports International (RSI) was formed in Moscow in 1921 as an ideological alternative to the SWSI. Based on the idea that 'Physical culture, gymnastics, games and sport are a means of proletarian class struggle', by 1924 it was seemingly 'accessible to all proletarian elements which recognise the class war'.[32] This, of course, included British communists. Similarly, the Young Communist International drafted policies on sport which espoused the message of struggle.[33] A synthesis of developments in Moscow and indigenous factors therefore signalled the beginning of a movement for the organisation of 'communist' sport in Britain.

At first it seemed as though the communists were going to establish their own organisation, the Young Communist League (YCL) initiating in 1923 a campaign for revolutionary sport. The aims of the workers' sports movement were publicised, calls were made for 'real' working-class sport to assist the workers in their fight against capitalism, and a number of 'Red' sports clubs were formed by local branches of the YCL at Barrow, Bethnal Green, Croydon, Edinburgh, Erith, Kentish Town, Kirkcaldy, Manchester, Sheffield, Shipley, Stepney and Tooting.[34] Interestingly enough, this aroused the interest of the national press – the *Daily Mail* wrote of a communist plot, whilst *The Times* drew attention to 'Communist Sports Propaganda'.[35] These developments were, however, checked by the establishment of the British Workers' Federation for

Sport. It soon became apparent that both the CP and YCL wished to shape the Federation's political and ideological personality. Although there was no formal policy of infiltration, it is clear that the criterion for success was the extent of influence achieved in the BWSF. After all, the Federation was considered to be 'an outcome of the class struggle' which had to be joined, assisted and supported in order to 'give an impetus towards acceptance of the basis of the Red International of Sports'.[36] The Walthamstow CP was admitted into the ranks, whilst the Federation co-operated with the YCL, and advertised in the *Young Communist* and *Sunday Worker*.[37] Yet, despite policy statements to the contrary, the Party leadership was lukewarm about the relevance of workers' sport, and at least initially the BWSF remained a small London-based organisation.

In 1926, however, the YCL began to examine the question of sport a little more systematically: recreational activities were organised during the General Strike and miners' lock-out, a number of positive contributions were made to the League's fortnightly journal, the *Weekly Young Worker* (said to have a circulation of 6,000) and out of this came a further drive to build up the sports movement.[38] The ubiquitous nature of capitalist sport was opposed; that is, the system by which the minds of young workers were apparently 'carefully doped with imperialist and anti-working class teachings', and the YCL canvassed for sport 'entirely controlled by the workers, without any capitalist influence'.[39] Most notably, the period witnessed the beginnings of a sustained campaign against the ideas and activities of the boy scouts who were lampooned as obedient wage-slaves, militarists and unthinking servants of the Empire.[40] The extent to which Marxists believed that working-class youth were simply taken in by scouting ideology is difficult to say. Yet the fact that the YCL itself was able to act as an oppositional force is just one indication of the transformative elements at play. Even if the scouts were ideological instruments of the status quo, they did not have it all their own way.

By 1927, it appears from the Marxist-influenced *Sunday Worker*, which had a circulation of about 100,000, that there was some success in this direction. Capitalist-controlled sports bodies were opposed, whilst socialist sport was actively promoted: a cricket league was instituted, two football leagues with teams like the 1917 Sports Club were set up in London, and contacts were established between the metropolis and provinces.[41] Moreover, the National Committee of the BWSF included two communists, Walter Tapsell and George Sinfield, and it was under their guidance that the Federation was won over to the communist cause. Tapsell had first come to the forefront in the mid-1920s when elected to the National Executive of the YCL. Though the Scottish Marxist, David Proudfoot, thought him a 'windbag', Tapsell devoted his life to the working-class movement.[42] He was a leading figure behind the communist *Daily Worker*, and was eventually 'killed by fascism' during the Spanish Civil War.[43] Similarly, Sinfield was active in the labour movement all his life, serving first from 1935 as sports editor and then from 1942 as industrial correspondent of the *Daily Worker*. Born in 1899 into a family of ten, he became the main inspiration behind the BWSF, and despite his turn to journalism, maintained an active interest in boxing and football. But above all, George Sinfield matured into an outstanding journalist who communicated the Left's position on industrial, political and sporting issues very powerfully and clearly.[44]

The political complexion of the London group was revealed with the organisation of a football tour to Russia in August and September of 1927. As the first British football team to tour Soviet Russia, six matches were arranged from Moscow to Leningrad, Kharkov to Kiev – all of them ending in defeat, one by eleven goals to nil.[45] Even so, the tour gave ordinary workers – railwaymen, woodworkers and furniture makers – the opportunity to see the so-called 'Workers State' for themselves. Although, in retrospect, the Soviet Union of 1927 was not exactly Utopia, one cannot doubt the sincere feelings of a small group of British workers as they expressed their commitment to the idea of international fraternity. Working-class solidarity was illustrated in one match, played against a Russian representative side in Moscow in front of 35,000 spectators, when the BWSF team gave their share of gate receipts to the Russian Air Fleet. On their arrival home, George Sinfield summed up the results of the trip: 'It was a most amazing experience. From all points of view, it was an experience of a lifetime.'[46] The London group, supported by certain CP functionaries, was now convinced of the need for a militant sports movement and resolved to end the social democratic leadership of the Federation.[47] Sinfield wrote a pamphlet which described the proceedings of the BWSF side in the Soviet Union, and also put forward the case for communist sport in its 'struggle against all types of capitalist sport organisations'.[48] Tom Groom and his colleagues repudiated such statements and, not surprisingly, opposed the action of Londoners regarding the Russian Air Fleet.[49] The communist position was vigorously defended in the Marxist press, which seemingly encouraged further growth – over 100 meetings were addressed by London members and a number of communist sport groups were formed in various parts of the country.[50]

The political differences between the social democrats and the communists came to a head at the First National Congress of the BWSF, held in Birmingham in April 1928. It was here that a new and Marxist-inspired leadership was elected. George Sinfield replaced Tom Groom as national secretary, and, even more importantly, the main task of working-class sportsmen and women as enshrined in a new constitution was 'an unrelenting struggle against the existing capitalist domination of sport and the introduction of a socialistic content into sport and physical recreation'.[51] Thus, after five years of slow and uneven progress, a communist-styled sports organisation had finally been created.

In many ways, the split in the workers' sports movement was inevitable. The division merely reflected opposing political ideologies, one Marxist, the other labour socialist or social democratic. It is certainly true that the Labour Party and TUC were intransigent to anything remotely communist, which made a compromise very difficult to achieve. But reading through the sources, one is struck even more by the sectarian stance of the Marxist left. The split was welcomed by revolutionaries, for they interpreted working-class sports as being sabotaged by conspiracy and reaction. Predictably official labour was characterised as an agent of capitalism and its approach to sport stigmatised as, to use the contemporary jargon, 'mondism in sport' – a form of class collaboration or 'sell-out' on the recreational front.[52] Even though it is difficult to accept such exaggerated polemics, it does seem that communist activists were pleased to be rid of TUC and Labour Party influence; groups in Brighton, Manchester and Newcastle felt that 'B.W.S.F. stood to lose nothing by the T.U.C. action'.[53]

The old, social democratic leadership soon found the militancy of the Federation incompatible with its own politics. The General Council of the TUC could not approve the new constitution and soon withdrew its recognition; the Labour Party Executive was unsympathetic to the fact that 'Communist influence dominated the British Workers' Sports Federation'; and the CCC, in complaining about the links with the RSI, also severed its connections.[54] Similarly, at local level, the newly formed sports section of the Sheffield Trades and Labour Council, previously sympathetic to the aims of the Federation and a delegate body at the first national congress, curtailed its association, ultimately having to dissolve because of financial troubles.[55] Eventually, the social democratic forces re-grouped and in 1930 formed an opposition body, the National Workers' Sports Association (NWSA). The process of disunity was complete by the end of the 1920s, when the CP initiated its 'Class Against Class' programme of policies. Put briefly, 'Class Against Class' was developed by the Communist International in line with the general backdrop of world economic crisis. In the mistaken belief that the capitalist system was about to collapse, the British Labour Party and TUC were labelled staunch supporters of the status quo – 'social fascist' – and as such had to be replaced by some other form of left-wing alignment, generated and sustained principally at local level.[56] Indeed, the fight against the labour sports movement and Clarion cyclists was to be intensified.[57]

Marxists and the British Workers' Sports Federation

The discussion up to now has shown how a communist sports movement was formed in the political conjuncture of the late 1920s. However, to fully understand the communist approach to sport something must be known about the ideology of the BWSF; that is, its values, sympathies, policies and general ethos. Already, the narrative has acknowledged that the novelty of the Federation, at least from 1928, was its Marxist personality – a personality only rarely evinced in the late nineteenth century by the recreational forms of the religion of socialism. Yet this Marxism still needs to be dissected and examined in a little more detail. At this time, Marxism in Britain was theoretically immature, gripped by a powerful strain of economic reductionism. It is true that after the 1917 Revolution Marxism began to enjoy an extended relationship with the British working class, but given the industrial slump and the rise of unemployment, this was more often than not couched in crude economistic terms. In a rather mechanical way, the owners of production were said to control wider political and cultural life, enabling them to spread anti-socialist values and divert the proletariat from their proper place in struggle.[58] Trotsky's notion that discontent had been 'diverted along artificial channels with the aid of boxing, football, racing and other forms of sport' was frequently recast in the British Marxist press.[59] In brief, sport under capitalism was viewed simply as a kind of superstructural tool to aid the exploitation of the workers. Hence, the most important principle of the BWSF, as revealed in so many policy statements, was a rigorous critique of capitalist sport in all its forms. Whenever the opportunity arose, leading members sought to expose and oppose the capitalist control of sports, and to this end the propaganda of the Federation focused on commercial, amateur and factory-sponsored sports.

The early issues of the *Daily Worker* (the organ of the CP launched in 1930 with an initial circulation of 10,000) are full of derogatory articles and reports on the character of commercial sports. Given that the period witnessed the commercialisation and capitalisation of sport (as discussed in the previous chapter), it is perhaps unsurprising that Marxists attempted to illustrate the profit-making objectives of all types of sporting endeavour. 'Boss' sport or 'bankers'' sport was exposed constantly during 1930 and there were many references to profiteering in football, class hatred in cricket and corruption in boxing. A diary of 'boss-controlled sport' in 1930 thus had 'the object of showing the decline of British capitalist sport from the point of view of playing success, financial support and morale':

> Any writer can see the decadence of capitalism and of its sport goes side by side.
> Is boss sport played to improve the physique? No! The welfare of the individual player is considered from the point of view of his transfer value.
> Is boss sport played for any reasons but for dope and finance? Definitely, no!
> Results, in kind and cash, are all the financiers aim for. Dope, fighting, wangling, and sham pretences of boss-administered law achieve the desired results.
> The puppets give their health, their lives; the spectators give their money.
> Boss sport exposes itself more clearly every day. Forward to the time when 'Red Sport' in Britain shall be workers' sport in fact as well as in name.[60]

Association football in particular was given a great deal of attention. When West Ham United decided to increase their minimum admission price to 2s and refuse the BBC broadcasting facilities for the sixth round cup tie with Arsenal, the BWSF advocated a boycott, 'an alternative to the swindling, profiteering exhibitions which pass for sport under capitalism'.[61] Needless to say, despite the fact that the boycott campaign led to some new recruits, workers attended the match in droves to see Arsenal win 3–0.[62] Equally, activists believed that the professional aspects of the game implicated players in such questionable activities as transfers, coaching and illegal play, 'adopted to ensure, not merely victory, but financial supremacy as well': 'Fouling at Charlton, Arsenal, West Ham, Huddersfield and most other grounds where the final matches were being played with almost reserve sides: Gallacher, Lambourne, Barson ordered off; disorder at Cardiff, Stamford Bridge and on other grounds.'[63] In the face of this barrage of criticism the positive aspects of professional sports in terms of, say, the opportunities they presented to disadvantaged groups were never seriously posed. There was little detailed evaluation of professionalism and its relation to working-class culture; analysis, at least in the first year of the *Daily Worker*, tended to be no more than rhetoric.

Voluntary sport also came under fire. Amateur games were seen as intrinsically linked to professionalism. It was alleged in the first week of the *Daily Worker* that amateurs took part in professional sport for which they received illegal payments, and that this was all part of a scheme 'for doping the workers into submission to worsening conditions'.[64] Moreover at those levels where commercial transactions were frowned upon, sport was still said to be tainted by its organisation on a capitalist basis: 'What of the exhibitions of chauvinism, colour and class hatred expressed many times at the Olympic games, and which have now become a regular feature of these events?'[65] In the opinion of the leadership, the class character of amateur sport was just one further indication of an inegalitarian social system, though somewhat hypocritically, subscriptions were still paid to the AAA.[66]

The antipathy shown towards those youth movements viewed as militarist and fascist, of course, continued. The Manchester branch of the Federation was following established policy when it informed a well-attended camp that groups as diverse in membership and outlook as the Boy Scouts, cadets, Rambling Federation and Cyclists' Touring Club were preparing working lads and girls for a war against the USSR.[67] Though such a warning was so obviously exaggerated, the hostility shown towards competing youth organisations was clear for all to see. Even the personal intervention of the Prince of Wales could not persuade Rebecca Goldman and other members of the Federation to support his youth scheme.[68] Confrontation continued on an ideological and practical level, with references to Baden-Powell's activities as a military spy, strike-breaker and capitalist 'puppet', attendance at anti-Scout rallies, distribution of anti-Scout leaflets, and continued opposition to those activities and events, like the Meridan War Memorial service, considered to be part of 'the imperialist drive to war'.[69]

The assault of the Federation on the third category of capitalist provision, namely factory-controlled sport, was waged even more intensely. Industrial welfare clubs, which, as discussed, were proliferating at this time, were perceived as an integral part of managerial strategy – 'a soothing syrup to mitigate the growing discontent that the continual worsening of conditions is producing', is the way one contribution expressed it.[70] Propaganda sought to amplify how 'boss'-subsidised sports clubs 'doped' the workers and created an environment in which it was easier to impose rationalisation, 'speed-ups' and wage cuts, and so reproduce an energetic labour force vital for the extraction of surplus value. The BWSF tried to show how employers used sport to manipulate the workforce and provide them with a ready-made vested interest in the running of the firm. Not only this, factory sports clubs were regarded as undermining militancy, and further stimulating the development of a labour aristocracy to act as scabs and spies for the employer.[71] The welfare policies of firms like the glass-makers, Pilkington Brothers (with its dozen rugby teams, including St Helens Recs who finished Rugby League runners-up in 1927), were thus disclosed in such a way as to emphasise their inherent capitalist bias: 'The recreation side of rationalisation keeps the workers up to scratch and also keeps them under the influence of the boss at play as well as at work.'[72] However, without entering into detail, there was a failure to appreciate that company sports could be taken over by workers and used in ways very different from their original purposes.

Lastly here, the important relationship between sport and gambling was also placed in the overall context of capitalist political economy, both as a commercial activity in its own right and a means of ideological conditioning. Gambling had been received with a great deal of hostility from the beginnings of the socialist movement in the late nineteenth century. Labour leaders judged that gambling was interfering with politics and education, and encouraging instead a new faith in 'get-rich-quick consumptionism'.[73] In particular, Ramsay MacDonald, who had been an arch-enemy of betting in his early political career, expressed contempt for 'the most distressing evils that are arising out of Greyhound Racing': 'Unfortunately, so many of our people regard (betting) as a luxury of the rich which ought to be shared by the poor. This indiscriminate imitation of opportunities which are only destructive is doing a great deal of harm to the moral life of our country at the present moment.'[74] Addressing a meeting at Rochester in 1927, MacDonald thus reaffirmed that the problem of betting would be discussed by a future Labour Government, for socialism was not just concerned with economics but also morality: 'The State that took no interest in moral issues was not fulfilling its duty. The Labour movement was one that united to produce not merely economic qualities, but human qualities.'[75] For many socialists, gambling was not just morally wrong, it was also against the basic materialist interests of the workers; they regarded it as an irrational activity which reinforced the cycle of poverty and deprivation. According to one critic, it was wasteful and led 'to the ruination of the homes of thousands of people'.[76] Likewise, a number of correspondents to the *Railway Review* made the point that gambling damaged individuals, and perhaps more significantly, the labour movement itself.[77] If workers could be shown the light, all well and good; if they could not, it was the responsibility of the labour leadership to protect their best interests. Betting had to be regulated or, if regulation proved ineffective, ultimately prohibited. However, notwithstanding this opposition, as the various Parliamentary debates over the Racecourse Betting, Dog Racing, and Betting and Lotteries Bills demonstrate, there were many socialists who countered by arguing that workers should be allowed to gamble without undue interference.[78] In fact there was no official Labour Party line, evidenced by the National Executive Committee's decision not to participate in a public conference on greyhound racing arranged by the National Emergency Committee of Christian Citizens.[79]

It is therefore interesting that when the *Daily Worker* first came into circulation there was a wide-ranging debate about whether the paper should cover horse-racing and include gambling form; a debate in some respects reminiscent of the battle over the proposed contents of labour's first daily newspaper, the *Daily Citizen*, launched in October 1912 with space for sport but not gambling tips. A range of contributions came from the provinces, some of them taking the line that there should be no attempt to compete with the sports journalism of the so-called capitalist press. In the end, the CP decided to ban racing results and tips from the columns, 'on the grounds that the *Daily Worker* cannot possibly assist the capitalists in the carrying on of a gigantic swindle and money-making concern, which at the same time is used to dope and divert the workers from the real bread-and-butter questions which concern them'.[80] Though some activists claimed that the inclusion of racing would be an attractive selling device on the shop floor, this decision received backing from important sections of the Party. The BWSF recorded its support for 'the eradication of the bad tendencies from our movement', whilst the Marxist literary intellectual, Ralph Fox, writing from Moscow, called on the paper not to 'give way to the racing fiends'.[81] Moreover, Rajani Palme Dutt, one of the Party's leading theoreticians whose column in the *Labour Monthly* was very influential, also offered his support. According to him, gambling was a dangerous pursuit as it provided an 'alternative to the class struggle'. Racing coverage may have been a way to boost sales of the paper, but Palme Dutt asserted that this was no reason to betray 'Communist ideology'. In acknowledging that 'Sport is a gigantic organising instrument', he concluded: 'Our task is to head the workers, not hang at their tails; to express the outlook of the best, most conscious workers, not the reactionary tendencies, survivals and moods which are artificially fostered by capitalism, and which we must fight, not hide behind.'[82] For someone who listed his leisure interests as 'anything except sports', such a position is perhaps not entirely surprising.[83] More seriously, the important point is that in the early 1930s the communist leadership decided that gambling was basically an anti-proletarian activity. This perspective continued to form the basis of communist policy on sport for the rest of the decade, though a more moderate approach evolved during the late thirties when George Sinfield protested that it was not the business of outside agencies 'to force workers not to bet on football'.[84]

It is obvious that the ideological position of the BWSF was incorporated within a materialist conception of society. Indeed, since the Federation was a cultural adjunct of the CP, it was intimately involved in the life of the British communist movement. One clear instance of this is that the revolutionary tenets of the Federation were disseminated almost exclusively in the communist press. Activists applied Marxism, if only crudely, as a means to explain the political foundations of sport: Michael Condon, who had once played football for Leyton Orient, can be found quoting Lenin in order to illustrate the revolutionary potential of physical culture.[85] Additionally, the Party leadership used the sports question as another way to challenge capitalist supremacy; not only through the writings of Palme Dutt, but also via the practical intervention of Harry Pollitt, who attended sports events and claimed that the lack of playing fields, recreation grounds and gymnasia was directly attributable to capitalism.[86] Though Jack Cohen talked about 'the disgusting passivity on the part of the Party with regard to the British Workers' Sports Federation', endless contributions point to the symbiotic relationship between Party and Federation.[87] In political, industrial and cultural terms, there were many instances of co-operation.

There is some evidence to suggest that the CP and YCL manipulated the Federation, in Martin Bobker's words, as a 'transmission belt' to transmit ideas and policy to the apolitical masses, and so involve them in both sport and politics.[88] No doubt the sports movement laid on opportunities for recruitment, as well as entertainment and sociability – even the revolutionary Marxist needed to relax.[89] On a more serious level, since it was thought that the aims of workers' sport could only be attained 'under the revolutionary leadership of the Communist Party', the Federation helped Party candidates during elections.[90] Hence, the Stepney Workers' Sports Club gave financial assistance to Harry Pollitt in a local by-election in 1930 and, four years later, continued to support the communist candidate, this time John Gollan, in the London County

Council elections.[91] Given this mutuality of interests, it was hardly unexpected when the Party sought to intervene more directly in the affairs of the Federation.[92]

The industrial wing of organised communism was another possible avenue for Federation involvement. Leading members considered that there was a role to be played in the factory and mine in counteracting the employers' sports clubs, and in fostering an attitude conducive to the growth of trade unionism. Working through rank and file organisations, an alliance was made with the National Minority Movement (NMM) – the communist satellite concerned with industrial relations. The NMM, though obviously having more important considerations than sport, received instructions from the Agitprop Department of the Red International of Labour Unions to consider this question, and at least one thriving football team was set up in Fife by the United Mineworkers of Scotland.[93] It was also envisaged that groups catering for sport would be useful in publicising the 'Workers' Charter' of industrial demands, in addition to granting 'assistance for workers on strike, or lock-out, by the organisation of sports, competitions, galas etc'.[94] Indeed, though the conceived alliance was not as strong as it was made out to be, there were some successes: The Minority Movement approached the Federation for advice, eventually requesting that a representative sit on their national bureau, and help was given to workers on strike – Yorkshire textile operatives, West Fife miners and London lightermen.[95]

Furthermore, under the initiative of Clem Beckett (a future vice-president of the BWSF) marginal influence was even achieved in the sports industry. Beckett began his speedway career at the Audenshaw track in 1928, and by the end of the year had set twenty-eight track records and established a reputation for broadsliding. By the 1930s he was one of the top performers, once being engaged to ride at Coventry, Manchester and Rochdale in the same day, and as such was responsible for the inauguration of the so-called 'Wall of Death' in Sheffield. Yet he was very much against certain aspects of commercialised sport, believing that speedway entrepreneurs exploited riders – 'bleeding the men who risk their lives on the dirt track'. Though suspended from competition for exposing the employer-backed Auto-Cycle Union in a bad light, he formed the Dirt Track Riders' Association to improve conditions of work and prevent unfair treatment at the hands of 'shady' promoters. True, Beckett' suspension proved more permanent than at first thought – in any case speedway was in decline by 1932 – yet this could not conceal the need for union organisation in sport.[96]

The BWSF also promoted joint activities with the workers' theatre and cinema organisations. Both Tom Thomas and Vic Farrant argued that there were financial and intellectual reasons to relate sport to cultural pastimes and, indeed, there were many collaborative ventures at socials, dances, political meetings and sports events.[97] For certain, the Federation also worked with the National Unemployed Workers' Movement (NUWM) – assistance being given to hunger marchers – and the Workers' Defence Force, which had Michael Condon on its National Executive.[98] And though the evidence is a little thin on the ground, contacts were made with the Society for Cultural Relations with the USSR, Friends of Soviet Russia, the League Against Imperialism, International Class War Prisoners' Aid, the Teachers' Labour League, and the Young Pioneers.

Having outlined the ideological and political stance of the BWSF it is now possible to make some kind of considered appraisal. Certainly the critique of capitalist society was strengthened by a quasi-scientific evaluation of sport which, though problematic, provided a partial answer to multifarious working-class recreational grievances, an answer so obviously denied by other contemporary accounts. Into the bargain, Marxist interpretations of sport in the 1930s went beyond the moral homilies of nineteenth-century utopian and ethical socialists. Even so, in addition to the fact that considerable sections of an otherwise sympathetic potential membership were alienated by the obvious signs of communist tutelage, the Marxist approach to sport led to various theoretical misconceptions and practical difficulties. There was a tendency to dogmatism in argument and sectarianism in position.

The consequences of a doctrinaire, inflexible analysis of sport un-doubtedly led to a degree of isolation. George Brown, then a member of the Manchester YCL, was alarmed at 'the puritanical act of dismembering the sports page [of the *Daily Worker*] by eliminating the racing articles'. He claimed that those who had taken such a step did not understand the workers and likened the decision to the act of 'a Bible thumper trying to stop a gang of navvies from swearing and drinking'.[99] This was a valid point, yet may communists failed to accept that workers' commitment to sport often transcended political sentiment. The leadership did not realise, at least in public discussion, that the working class was organically linked with various commercial sports, especially football; although the Federation was right to reveal the unsavoury aspects of capitalist patronage and control, the 'people's game' had evolved from the real experiences of the workers themselves, their ranks supplied the overwhelming majority of players and the bulk of spectators, and it was they who had the knowledge and ability to make their participation count. It was manifestly wrong to regard football and other sports as simply subsumed under bourgeois dominance, a kind of superstructural image of the overall capitalist arrangement. Comment on sport of this order is perhaps a reflection of the fact that the inter-war labour movement in Britain applied Marxism from the Continent in a fairly mechanical and reductive way. Not only did this empty sport of human capabilities and creativities, but it also failed to even pose the complex, and often ambiguous, relationship between popular sports and radical politics. Indeed, there is no reason why a supporter of a premier football team could not also be a militant trade unionist or, for that matter, a member of the CP.[100] If a Marxist sports organisation was to have credibility in the eyes of the workers, it had to understand the subtlety and complexity of working-class culture and, in a critical sense, the BWSF did not always possess such an understanding. Initially, it neglected pragmatic considerations and relied on 'phrase-mongering', political 'wordspinning' and an abstract philosophy which must have perplexed many workers. A Marxist version of sport was digested by Party members, but for a worker who relied on the racing results or the Saturday afternoon on the football terraces for recreational stimulus, such a challenge to working-class passions was less easy to digest. The idea that professional sport would go bankrupt in the face of advanced opinion and that the role of spectator was a mug's game probably did not go down too well in working-class circles. It is more likely that even those workers influenced by BWSF pronouncements, admittedly not that numerous anyway, found the view that 'boss' sport was in the process of disintegration a little puzzling when in reality it seemed to be getting stronger by the day. It is not that a socialist analysis of sport can be rejected out of hand, but rather the way in which Marxism was theorised and applied. The 'pure' ideology of the BWSF, which also stressed the need for discipline, did not take into account the prejudices, sympathies and motivations of those workers interested in sport.

Clearly, the political atmosphere of 'Class Against Class' and the feeling that the revolution was just around the corner did not encourage a 'balanced' perspective.[101] In fact, it merely engendered a suspicion of reformism and a reluctance to consider non-Marxist developments, however advanced. The NWSA, though including many socialists and trade unionists, was depicted as a comic outfit of 'social fascists' and 'renegades', 'a hot-house plant pruned and cultivated by job-hunters of the T.U.C.'.[102] Thus, on one occasion when addressing a conference of

Clarion cyclists, Ernest Bevin was heckled, cajoled and eventually driven from the platform by a group of communist supporters.[103] It was this very form of action which widened the gulf in the workers' sports movement and reduced even further the Federation's sphere of influence.

The general picture of sectarianism, however, needs to be qualified. Oral history has shown that the ideas of 'Class Against Class' did not impinge on everyone in the BWSF. The North Manchester group is said to have been very broad-minded, stressing sport rather than politics, while George Sinfield himself had a very rounded character, with a keen interest on unity in sport.[104] Moreover, the dogmatism of those in the higher echelons of the organisation was eventually recognised and the need for compromise accepted. This did not mean a negation of Marxist principles, rather a modification of tactics and policy. The reality of the political and sporting wilderness meant that the application of revolutionary purity was impossible from the start. The rank and file of the BWSF were, on the whole, lacking in political education and were not the extraordinary purveyors of class-conscious thought which the leadership had envisaged. As one member put it: 'Your chaps swear and play for medals, and are just ordinary fellows.'[105] Like other organisations, the Federation was not free from the 'petty' realities of everyday life, whether they were squabbles over financial debts, personality clashes or instances of incompetence.[106] If the BWSF was revolutionary, this should not detract from the fact that the majority of members were ordinary people who wanted sport as much as, if not more than, politics.

From the early part of 1931, the militancy of the Federation was moderated, though never subjugated altogether. Members realised that 'to generalise on the relationship between politics and sport is fatal when approaching your young chum, who can probably tell you, by heart, the names of the last 20 winners of the F.A. Cup, the holders of the world's boxing titles and Hendren's average for last cricket season'.[107] The secretary of the south-east London BWSF further suggested that sport and not 'unintelligible politics' should be provided, whilst other contributions in the *Daily Worker* began to play down the political significance of the Federation and criticise the role played by the Party and the YCL.[108] Depending on circumstances, co-operation began to replace confrontation as the major organising principle. The groups in Scotland and Derby, for example, recognised the need to work with bourgeois youth groupings, and this found expression in the move towards unity.[109] Eventually, in 1933, as a response to the rise of fascism, 'Class Against Class' was dropped and the 'United Front on the field of Sport' became official Federation policy – activities were to be widened out to include participation with all progressive forces of the anti-fascist front.[110]

There were obvious tensions in the Marxism of the BWSF and challenges to the prevailing orthodoxy of revolutionary class politics, but this did not preclude growth. When the communists first seized control, the Federation was only small, 'not developing quickly'.[111] By 1930, though, it had grown into something approaching a national organisation, with branches in some of the major industrial centres of Britain.[112] There is little evidence relating to membership levels, but, appreciating the difficulty of confirming internally produced information, some estimates can be made. Even during the period of political isolation in 1930 the Federation could claim 3,000 members, more than that enjoyed by its mother organisation, the CP itself; when activities broadened out membership increased, so that by 1931 there were 5,000 footballers associated with the BWSF and club affiliations were 'coming in at the rate of two a week'.[113] Later in the year, one particular minute noted that there were ninety clubs in the Federation – though only nineteen had made financial contributions – with a membership of 6,000.[114] As influence widened into the united front, it is more than likely that membership again rose. Thus when the Federation helped to organise the campaign for Sunday League football in 1933, 585 teams were represented.[115] The BWSF was effective enough to attract large numbers of young workers into its ranks and it was this working-class composition which made it so different from the predominantly middle-class character of other national organisations. Even if the negative repercussions of 'Class Against Class' militated against the organisational objective of creating a mass-based workers' sports movement, the attempts made to recruit youth from the mines, factories and railway depots were not without their rewards.

Undoubtedly the BWSF was a proletarian body, but to what extent did it cater for women as well as for men? This is a topical point to raise, for, as feminist scholars have theorised, women's access to sport and leisure is said to be structured by patriarchal society; that is, a situation of dominance by men over women due to the sexual division of labour and strong ideological forces like femininity, gentility and domesticity.[116] Now it is true that the BWSF was not free from chauvinistic mentality, tending to be male-dominated. Indeed, the Federation was entrapped in a society where working-class women continued to be unfairly treated at work and in the home, with unequal pay, hard domestic drudgery and large families. It was therefore very difficult for women to 'escape' into sport.

An analysis of the credential forms for the 1930 national conference shows that for the nineteen clubs for which information is available only 288 (or eighteen per cent) of the 1,614 membership were women. Even so, the Federation must take credit for developing women's sections, particularly in London. where Clara Deaner organised a specialist department affiliated to the women's AAA. Apparently netball was the most popular interest – fifty teams competing in the cup competition in 1931 – though hockey, gymnastics, rambling and swimming also featured.[117] However, in sum, the BWSF may have placed 'women and men on an equal footing', but as Gladys Keable of the Red Star Netball section explained, 'there are too many in our movement who regard women as a bit of a nuisance, pushing themselves forward when the men want to get their important revolutionary changes'.[118]

There is little information about the extent of local sporting activities, though it appears from the reports in the communist press and the records in the CP archives that a number of sports were provided, ranging from football and cricket to wrestling and ju-jitsu. In Newcastle and parts of Scotland, boxing seems to have been the major interest, highlighted by some well-organised exhibition matches; in Manchester, outdoor pursuits like camping and rambling were favoured; and in London, football was the major concern. In fact, there were labour Football Leagues in London, South Wales, Derby and Glasgow in which players were 'instructed to play the ball and not the man'.[119] Most branches had cycling and rambling sections, a number of which were relatively autonomous – the Spartacus, Equity, Whitehall and Red Wheeler cycling clubs – and many had gymnasia and premises of their own, the Essex group even having a permanent camp by the sea. The Collyhurst gym was the centre of the north Manchester activities, where boxing, running, skipping and weightlifting were performed; for many youngsters it was the focal point of their leisure time, as they 'were there every night and Saturdays and Sundays'.[120] Originally set up at the beginning of 1929, the branch also arranged socials, had a wall newspaper and international correspondence section, links with boxers and weightlifters from Oldham, and eventually an active and militant rambling group.[121] It is evident from the sources that the Federation performed a useful role in adding to what, at times, was limited recreational and social provision. A diary of events produced by the Hackney club illustrates the rich diversity: something to do on every night of the week, including education and cultural development on Tuesday, boxing and road-running on Thursday, and rambles on Sunday.[122]

Additionally, special sports meetings took place at High Beech and Victoria Park in London. In April 1930 two major football games went ahead between representative sides from England and Wales – one of them attracting a crowd of 3,000, seemingly more than attended the Merthyr Town versus Fulham Third Division game in the Football League – and a Red Sports Day was organised, with about 1,000 spectators and competitors from ten clubs.[123] Sports meets of this kind were designed to attract workers to a combination of counter-cultural events, which also included plays, music and a host of amusements. There were, however, complaints about Federation sport: one correspondent pointed out that the BWSF or, as he called them, the 'Bolshies With Sporting Feelings', were totally against individualism on the football field, preferring mass action, even mass shooting for goal; another correspondent, described as a 'Near Communist – Now Fascist', referred to a Manchester BWSF camp as 'bedlam', characterised by sexual immorality, 'filthy' jokes, drinking and Marxist 'depravity'; and on a further occasion, a ramble arranged by the Stockport group was a 'wash-out' since only two persons appeared at the meeting place.[124] Furthermore, the activities of the Federation were principally for the young and the healthy, rather than for those older or perhaps unfit. Yet, notwithstanding these comments, provision was made for the enjoyment of many leisure pursuits, bringing greater variety and colour into young workers' everyday lives.

Despite the effort and enthusiasm which went into sport, it should be recalled at this stage that political and ideological questions remained the main preoccupation. Put simply, sport was not regarded 'as an end in itself, but as a means of fitting the workers with the necessary energy and stamina to face up to the class struggle of to-day, and the greater ones of the future'.[125] In the first place, the Federation's politics were underpinned by wide-ranging proposals for improvements in sports provision. Ideally it was believed that communism would lay the foundations for truly emancipated sport, but for gains to be made under capitalism the working-class movement had to articulate the necessary demands and embark on the appropriate course of action. Throughout its short history the Federation therefore pursued all kinds of short-term objectives, especially access to the countryside, organised Sunday sport and better playing facilities. Secondly, the Federation's politics were clearly reflected by its international perspective and commitment. In brief, the political colour of the Federation's internationalism is vividly shown by the way in which it courted the Soviet Union: from the first football tour of 1927, BWSF delegations were apt to praise the sporting and economic achievements of the 'Workers' Fatherland'. Subsequent chapters of this study will focus on both the domestic political campaigns and global position of the Federation. But all in all, it was the conspicuous political behaviour of the BWSF, ranging from support of Russia to the use of the hammer and sickle as a club motif and the presentation of red banners to successful teams, which distinguished it from traditional sporting structures.

Conclusion

In the first half of the 1930s sports of all descriptions were organised by the BWSF, whilst certain political advances were made. However, a question posed by a Bethnal Green supporter in November 1933 clarified what was definitely a position of weakness: 'What has become of the British Workers' Sports Federation and all the old comrades who used to take part in this workers' movement?'[126] Even a statement of repudiation from George Sinfield could not hide the apprehension felt about the future.[127] There were fairly regular features in the *Daily Worker* during 1934, but by the following year reports were very few and far between, so that by the end of 1935 it appears that the Federation had been dissolved. This did not mean that Marxists suddenly lost interest and vacated the sporting sphere. Activists continued to organise sports festivals, exhibitions, gala days and the rest, whilst, on a more theoretical level, the importance of sport in the social formation was still alluded to. In some areas local branches were replaced by YCL sports sections, in others they simply disappeared, took on a non-political form, or were supplanted by the NWSA. As a distinctive Marxist cultural organisation the BWSF fell victim to the popular front; that is , it was at odds with the aim 'to establish close and friendly relations with ... non-fascist sport organisations'.[128] Even so, the demise of the Federation was more deep-rooted and can be traced to a range of organisational and political constraints.

Organisation had always been a formidable problem in the sense that it was difficult to co-ordinate sporting and politcal activities on a national scale. Since the leadership was drawn from the working class, organisation was hindered by a dearth of spare time and finance. The arrangement of forthcoming events usually took place after working hours and it was commonplace for the committee to adjourn their meetings late in the evening. It was no coincidence that those who gave most time were invariably out of work. Then there was the problem of money. The Federation was self-financing through dances, socials and so on, though the funds raised tended to be insufficient for the purchase of equipment, for the hiring of premises or for the publication of a sports paper – the journals of the Federation all collapsed after a short period, first the London group's *Worker Sportsman* at the end of the 1920s, then *Sport and Games* in 1932, and finally the *Worker Sportsman* also in 1932 (despite a circulation said to be 3,000 strong, a £60 debt had been run up). Early on, Michael Condon was led to confess that the facilities of many BWSF clubs were 'contemptible', and the situation improved only marginally.[129] Organisation on a national scale was nearly impossible under such circumstances, so activity tended to be local in character. Indeed, the leaders of the Manchester group have recalled that the Federation was not really a national body at all, as it was so loosely constituted.[130] Judging by one contemporary comment that the 'B.W.S.F. stills acts in a disjointed and uncoordinated fashion', such recollections seem to contain more than a grain of truth.[131] Even though there were affiliations, this does not mean that the Federation acted as a national organism – there was confusion over policy statements and the arrangements for sports events, a certain degree of disunity, and little sense of democratic centralism. Once the initial enthusiasm of the leadership began to wane, then these organisational obstacles became increasingly more difficult to overcome, and all hopes of building a mass Federation less and less likely.

A genuine explanation of decline must also take into account the political identity of the Federation. Aside from the various theoretical misconceptions and distortions of 'Class Against Class', the relationship with the CP did not exactly encourage growth. The political position of the Federation may have been moderated, yet it remained a sympathetic adjunct of the Party. Due to the fairly open dialogue with the CP, it lay open to criticism from both left and right – from the left because it wished the Federation to be more of a forum for revolutionary politics, and from the right because it did not like to see a sporting body have dominating political aspirations. Even within the ranks, so to speak, on the one hand Johnny Douglas was critical of sport as 'an unpolitical thing' which leads to 'growth of abstractions, of opportunism (a "non-political" sports movement)', whilst, on the other, John Morris was critical of sport being used as a vehicle for communist propaganda.[132] Such ideological in-fighting did not create favourable conditions for mass growth. The Federation never really had the will to pronounce a clear, coherent position of its own, free from political expediency and the policy dictates of a party, often unfairly vilified by the ruling bourgeois order. In short, it failed to be autonomous, to gain an autonomy which would have made it possible to propagate a more sophisticated approach to working-class culture.

The amalgam of organisational and political constraints reduced the potential for national growth, especially since the Federation faced a capitalist culture which was the very antithesis of what it stood for. It could not hope to compete with commercialised sport or the many establishment clubs if it could not even put its own structures and politics on a sound basis. There was the absurd contradiction of some branches co-operating with church groups, whilst others were reluctant to approach local trade unions. Moreover, the Federation may have perpetuated gender divisions in sport, if only by giving more attention to such male-centred endeavours as football and boxing. Under such conditions, it was difficult to create and sustain a viable Marxist sporting alternative.

Without doubt, the BWSF made various mistakes, but to portray it in this way alone is unfair. In fact, what is more surprising is not the BWSF's ultimate demise, but rather that it appeared in the first place and survived for more than a decade. Some of the constraints faced, particularly those relating to finance, were unavoidable and difficult to overcome with all the organisational and political will in the world. Moreover, as Alun Howkins has concluded, the Federation was a significant part of a lively and productive oppositional culture in which sport, literature and the arts were used as counters to the orthodoxies of capitalism and social democracy: 'It was certainly a successful organisation both in political and sporting terms.'[133] This, at least, is the opinion of some of the men and women who were first-hand observers. Mick Jenkins, writing about the Manchester branch, has concluded that it 'did a very find job'; Joe Jacobs, on the Stepney branch, regarded the Federation as a 'good organisation'; and Marion Henery has applauded the way that the Glasgow group made 'headway among the youth'.[134] The oral recollections of Manchester activists, though not without reservations, also point to the positive contribution of the BWSF.[135] Even if these opinions are somewhat partisan, they seem to be reliable enough. The Federation organised an array of sports, providing many workers with an active recreational outlet they might not otherwise have had. It is true that the working class provided sport for themselves before the CP arrived on the scene, and that there was also a proliferation of proletarian sports clubs during the inter-war period, many of them the unrecorded street-corner variety. And furthermore, outside the auspices of the BWSF, sport and recreation were an important part of those counter-communities in Mardy, Lumphinnans and the Vale of Leven – the so-called 'Little Moscows'.[136] Yet the BWSF did show explicitly that this was all possible without middle-class patronage. In a sense, they offered a clear political alternative to capitalist modes of spare-time activity. It is creditable that a politically-motivated leadership shaped a movement, not perfect by any means, which challenged British sporting traditions and questioned the dominant structures of sport. The BWSF was indeed a novel departure in both the history of sport and the history of the labour movement.

Notes

1 For the hours issue, see G. Cross, 'The political economy of leisure in retrospect: Britain, France, and the origins of the eight-hour day', *Leisure Studies*, vol. 5 (1986).

2 M. Jacques, 'The Emergence of "Responsible" Trade Unionism, A Study of the "New Direction" in T.U.C. Policy 1926-1935', PhD, University of Cambridge (1976), pp. 89, 103-8. J. E. Cronin, 'Coping with labour, 1918-1926', in J. E. Cronin and J. Schneer (eds), *Social Conflict and the Political Order in Modern Britain* (1982).

3 *Daily Herald*, 27 May 1919.

4 See, for example, *Railway Review*, 12 March 1920, 11 March and 13 May 1921. *Workers' Union Record*, Sept. 1920. *Post*, 12 Nov. 1921, 2 Sept. 1922. *Locomotive Journal*, Dec. 1922. *Record*, June 1924.

5 *London Citizen* (Tottenham edition), June, July and Oct. 1921, Jan. and Feb. 1922.

6 *Daily Herald*, 27 March 1922. *New Leader*, 1 Dec. 1922. *Workers' Weekly*, 17 Feb. 1923. *Workers' Union Record*, April 1923. *Record*, Dec. 1924, Sept. 1925.

7 *New Dawn*, 8 Dec. 1923.

8 Manchester Central Library Archives Department (hereafter MAD), 016/i/10, Programme of the 21st Annual Meet, Chester, 1921. *Clarion*, 1 April 1921.

9 British Workers' Sports Federation Minutes (hereafter BWSF Mins), 5 April 1923. (All minutes and related records of the BWSF are located in the Communist Party Archives, London.) *Daily Herald*, 5 and 13 April and 1 May 1923.

10 T. Groom, *The Fifty Year Story of the Club: National Clarion Cycling Club 1894-1944* (Halifax, 1944). *Forward*, 3 Feb. 1923. *Clarion*, 13 June 1924; *New Leader*, 26 Sept. 1924. MAD, 016/ii/19, Minutes of the Annual General Meeting of the CCC, 12 April 1925.

11 *Labour Magazine*, May 1923.

12 EP Microform, Sheffield Trades and Labour Council Minutes, 18 Aug. and 1 Sept. 1925.

13 However, there was no compunction in affiliating to the bourgeois Amateur Athletic Association or making contacts with the National Cyclists' Union and the London Football Association. BWSF Mins, 16 Aug. 1923. *Clarion*, 31 Aug. 1923.

14 *Forward*, 10 March 1923. *New Leader*, 13 April 1923. *Daily Herald*, 1 May 1923. *Clarion*, 29 June 1923.

15 BWSF Mins, 1923-24, *passim*.

16 MAD, 016/i/31, Programme, BWSF First Annual Sports and Gala, 3 May 1924.

17 *Clarion*, 29 Aug., 5 Dec. and 12 Dec. 1924. BWSF Mins, 26 Nov. 1924; MAD, 016/ii/19, Minutes of the National Committee of the CCC (hereafter CCC Mins), 5 Oct. 1924, 8 Feb. 1925.

18 BWSF Mins, 12 Jan. 1925.

19 National Trades Councils, *Annual Conference Report*, 1925, pp. 16-17. See also TUC, *Annual Report*, 1926, p. 66. *Trade Unionist*, Jan. to March 1926, *passim*.

20 *Worker*, 3 April 1926. *Young Worker*, 1 May 1926. *Sunday Worker*, 2 May 1926.

21 *Industrial Review*, April 1927. BWSF Mins, 21 July 1927. TUC, *Annual Report*, 1927, pp. 150-1.

22 See chapter 7.

23 *Rochdale Labour News*, May 1925. Colne Valley Divisional Labour Party, *Annual Report*, 1924. *Oldham Labour Gazette*, June and July 1926.

24 *Clarion*, 8 June 1923, 11 Jan. 1924; BWSF Mins, 12 April 1923, 28 Feb. and 22 May 1924.

25 *Labour Year Book*, 1927, p. 422.

26 *People's Year Book*, 1927, p. 272. See also *Clarion*, 29 April 1927.

27 CP, *The Young Communist International: Between the Fourth and Fifth Congresses 1924-1928* (1928), p. 100.

28 National Council of British Socialist Sunday Schools Union, *The Young Socialist Crusaders: Aims, Objects and Method of Organisation* (Glasgow, 1920), p. 14.

29 *Workers' Dreadnought*, 18 June 1921.

30 *Communist*, 21 Jan. 1922.

31 CP, *Report on Organisation presented by the Party Commission to the Annual Conference of C.P.G.B.*, 7 Oct. 1922, p. 62.

32 J. Riordan, *Sport in Soviet Society: Development of Sport and Physical Education in Russia and the U.S.S.R.* (Cambridge, 1977), p. 354. *International Press Correspondence*, 18 Dec. 1924.

33 See *International of Youth*, Sept. 1922, March 1923. *Resolutions adopted at the 4th Congress of the Young Communist International* (1924), pp. 92-6.

34 *Workers' Weekly*, 9 June 1923. *Young Worker*, Aug. 1923. The membership of the YCL was rather unstable: 500 in 1924, perhaps 5,000 in 1926 and 1,000 in 1928. K. Newton, *The Sociology of British Communism* (1969), p. 161. Cf. *International Of Youth*, May 1928.

35 See *Times*, 12 Jan. and 10 Feb. 1923. *Workers' Weekly*, 10, 17 and 24 Feb. 1923.

36 *Workers' Weekly*, 28 April, 5 May and 12 May 1923. *Young Worker*, Sept. and Nov.-Dec. 1923, Jan. 1924.

37 BWSF Mins, 17 May 1923, 1 Feb. 1924, 15 July 1925.

38 *Sunday Worker*, 2 May 1926. *Workers' Weekly*, 9 July 1926. *Fight Like Hell*, 23 July 1926. *A Congress of Young Fighters: A Report of the 4th Congress of the Y.C.L. of G.B.*,

Dec. 1926, pp. 26-7. *Report of the Executive Committee to the 4th National Congress of the Y.C.L. of G.B.*, 1926, pp. 18-19. *Weekly Young Worker*, 5 June, 7 Aug., 21 Aug., 4 Sept., 18 Sept., 9 Oct. and 18 Dec. 1926. CP, *The Young Communist International*, pp. 99-100, 147, 182-7, 240.

39 *Workers' Life*, 22 July 1927. W. Rust, *The Case For the Y.C.L.* (n.d.), pp. 18-19.

40 See Anon., *Baden-Powell Exposed* (n.d.) *Young Worker*, Oct. to Dec. 1927, *passim*.

41 *Sunday Worker*, 17, 24 and 31 July, 7 and 14 Aug., and 6 and 27 Nov. 1927.

42 I. MacDougall (ed.), *Militant Miners* (Edinburgh, 1981), pp. 289-90. Rebecca Casket stresses that he was an extreme left-wing communist, very 'bright' and lively – 'he was such a happy boy'. Rebecca Casket (née Goldman), interview with the author, 17 Aug. 1981.

43 *Challenge*, 28 July 1938.

44 *Morning Star*, 27 Nov. 1973. M. Hill, *George Sinfield – his pen a Sword* (n.d., 1986?).

45 See *Sunday Worker*, 28 Aug. and 4, 11 and 18 Sept. 1927. *Young Worker*, 27 Aug. and 10 and 17 Sept. 1927.

46 *Sunday Worker*, 25 Sept. 1927. See also *Young Worker*, 24 Sept. 1927; G Sinfield, 'Chelsea? No!: Soviet football', *Russia To-day*, Sept. 1939; *id.*, 'Soviet football', *Labour Monthly*, Feb. 1958.

47 CP, *Reports, Theses, and Resolutions of the 9th Congress*, 1927, p. 104.

48 G. Sinfield, *The Workers' Sports Movement* (n.d., 1927?), p. 11.

49 BWSF Mins, 8 Jan. 1928. *Daily Herald*, 9 Feb. 1928.

50 See *Sunday Worker*, 5 and 12 Feb., and 4 March 1928. *Young Worker* 18 and 25 Feb., and 3 and 10 March 1928. *Workers' Life*, 17 Feb. 1928.

51 Minutes of the first National Conference of the BWSF, 28 April 1928. *Young Worker*, 5 May 1928. *Worker Sportsman*, June 1928.

52 *Report of the 5th National Congress of the Y.C.L.*, 1928, pp. 11-14. *Workers' Life*, 24 Feb. 1928. *Sunday Worker*, 17 June 1928. *Young Worker*, 23 June 1928. *Communist*, Aug. 1928.

53 BWSF Mins, 12 Oct. 1928.

54 TUC General Council Minutes (hereafter TUC GC Mins), 23 May 1928. (All TUC Minutes are located in the TUC Archives, London.) Labour Party Executive Committee Minutes (hereafter Labour Executive Mins), 23 May 1928. (All Labour Party Minutes are located in the Labour Party Archives, London.) MAD, 016/ii/19, CCC Mins, 6 May and 14 Oct. 1928.

55 EP Microform, Sheffield Trades and Labour Council Minutes, 3 and 17 Jan., 6 March, 12 and 19 June, 3 July and 8 Oct. 1928.

56 See J. Jupp, *The Radical Left in Britain 1931-1941* (1982), ch. 4.

57 CP. *The New Line: Documents of the 10th Congress of the CPGB*, Jan. 1929, p. 127.

58 S. Macintyre, *A Proletarian Science: Marxism in Britain 1917-1933* (Cambridge, 1980).

59 L. Trotsky, 'Where is Britain going?', in R. Chappel and A. Clinton (eds), *Leon Trotsky, Collected writings and speeches on Britain*, vol. 2 (1974), p. 123.

60 *Daily Worker*, 2 Oct. 1930.

61 *Daily Worker*, 22 and 26 Feb. and 1 March 1930.

62 BWSF Mins, 28 Feb. 1930. *Daily Worker*, 3 March 1930. Ironically, a decade or so later, West Ham were enthusiastic contributers to the Aid to Russia Fund. C. Korr, *West Ham United: The Making of a Football Club* (1986), p. 199.

63 *Daily Worker*, 2 Jan. 1931.
64 *Daily Worker*. 3 and 4 Jan. 1930.
65 *Daily Worker*, 2 Jan. 1930.
66 BWSF Mins, 1 Nov. 1929, 14 Feb. and 11 April 1930. By 1932 the Federation even had a club in the National Amateur Rowing Association. BWSF Mins, 28 Oct. 1932.
67 *BWSF Camp Souvenir* (Manchester, n.d., 1932?), p. 1.
68 Casket, interview, in which she claimed that the Prince of Wales had a personal meeting with her and other leading members of the YCL. I have been unable to substantiate this claim any further.
69 J. L. Douglas, *"Be Prepared" For War!* (n.d.).
70 *Fan*, 22 Nov. 1930.
71 *Daily Worker*, 14 Feb., 28 March, 12 July and 2 Oct. 1930; *Hornsey Star*, 27 June 1931. A. Hutt, *The Condition of the Working Class in Britain*, (1933), pp. 241-2.
72 *Daily Worker*, 25 Jan. and 13 Feb. 1930. Cf. *St Helens Newspaper and Advertiser*, 7 Feb. 1930. J. Arnold, 'The Influence of Pilkington Brothers in the growth of sport and community recreation in St Helens', MEd, University of Liverpool (1977).
73 R. McKibbin, 'Working-class gambling in Britain 1880-1939', *Past and Present*, no. 82 (1979), p. 176.
74 PRO 30/69/1437/554, Ramsay MacDonald Papers, Ramsay MacDonald to Sir Walter Gibbons, 11 Oct. 1927.
75 *Rochester, Chatham and Gillingham Journal*, 1 Feb. 1928.
76 *Labour*, May 1934.
77 *Railway Review*, 22 April, 13 and 20 May and 10 and 17 June 1927.
78 See, for example, *House of Commons Debates*, 16 March 1928, cols 2275-364; 11 May 1928, cols 545-636; 27 June 1934, cols 1137-263.
79 Labour Executive Mins, 7 Feb. 1928. By February 1933, four socialist MPs – Aneurin Bevan, Thomas Groves, John McGovern and Neil Maclean – could attend the annual meeting of the National Greyhound Society of Great Britain. *Times*, 14 Feb. 1933. Even so, opposition to greyhound racing was still prevalent in the 1947 Labour cabinet. A. Robertson, *The bleak midwinter* (Manchester, 1987), p. 119.
80 *Daily Worker*, 22 Jan. 1930.
81 BWSF Mins, 23 Feb. 1930. *Daily Worker*, 28 Jan. 1930.
82 *Daily Worker*, 25 Jan. 1930. Dutt later invited Sinfield to write an article for the *Labour Monthly*. BWSF Mins, 14 Feb. 1930. *Labour Monthly*, March 1930.
83 J. M. Hoberman, *Sport and Political Ideology* (1984), p. 110.
84 *Daily Worker*, 4 March 1936. Racing results and tips returned to the papers in 1934.
85 *Daily Worker*, 11 Feb. 1930. See generally, J. Riordan, 'Marx, Lenin and physical culture', *Journal of Sport History*, vol. 3 (1976).
86 *Worker Sportsman*, May 1932.
87 *Communist Review*, Feb. 1930. Cf. BWSF Mins, 23 Feb. 1930.
88 Martin Bobker, interview with the author, 18 Aug. 1981.
89 See, for example, *Communist Review*, April 1930.
90 *Daily Worker*, 2 June 1930.
91 *Daily Worker*, 21 Nov. 1930, 5 March 1934.

92 BWSF Mins, 7 and 14 Oct. 1932.
93 *Trade Union Propaganda and Cultural Work*, Oct. 1928 to Nov. 1929, *passim*: MacDougall, *Militant Miners*, pp. 127-8. See the photograph of the UMS team in the *Daily Worker*, 22 April 1935.
94 H. Pollitt, *The Workers' Charter* (n.d., 1930?), p. 12. National Minority Movement, *On Strike!: A Word to all Workers in Dispute* (1929), p. 8. *Daily Worker*, 1 Nov. 1930, 16 Feb. 1931. *Worker*, 16 May 1931. *Sport and Games*, Jan. 1932. *Busman's Punch*, April and May 1933.
95 BWSF Mins, 4 Oct. 1929, 3 Jan., 19 Sept., and 3 and 24 Oct. 1930. *Daily Worker*, 21 Jan., 14 May and 3 June 1930, 30 July 1931, 29 Jan. 1932.
96 *Daily Worker*, 1 Oct. 1930, 14 Jan., 13, 17 and 20 Feb., and 20, 21 and 23 May 1931. *Worker Sportsman*, 1 May and 1 June 1932. W. Rust, *Clem Beckett: Hero and Sportsman* (Manchester, n.d., 1937?). E. and R. Frow, *Clem Beckett and the Oldham Men Who Fought in Spain: 1936-1938* (Manchester, n.d., 1980?).
97 *Daily Worker*, 27 Jan. 1930, 8 Jan. 1931. BWSF Mins, 14 Feb., 14 March, 31 Oct. and 28 Nov. 1930. *Red Stage*, Jan., Feb. and June–July 1932.
98 *Casket*, interview; *Daily Worker*, 18 March and 7 May 1930. BWSF Mins, 14 March and 11 April 1930. Cf. H. Francis and D. Smith, *The Fed: A History of the South Wales Miners in the Twentieth Century* (1980), pp. 143, 193-8.
99 *Daily Worker*, 3 Feb. 1930. In fact, Harry Pollitt also seemed to imply that horse-racing would continue in a communist society of the future. J. Mahon, *Harry Pollitt: A Biography* (1976), p. 165.
100 See R. Miliband, *Marxism and Politics* (Oxford, 1977), pp. 51-2. Accounts of industrial conflict in the USA in the 1930s are replete with stories of workers on strike listening to ball-games. M. Naison, 'Lefties and righties: the Communist Party and sports during the Great Depression', *Radical America*, vol. 13 (July–Aug. 1979), p. 51.
101 Mick Jenkins, interview with the author, 7 Sept. 1981. Confirmed in a conversation with Edmund Frow.
102 *Labour Monthly*, April 1930. See also *Daily Worker*, 20 and 26 Feb., 25 July and 6 Aug. 1930, 20 June 1931. It does seem, however, that BWSF representatives attended the initial meetings of the NWSA. BWSF Mins., 17 Jan. and 25 July 1930.
103 Bernard Rothman, interview with the author, 3 Aug. 1981.
104 *Casket*, Rothman, interviews.
105 *Daily Worker*, 14 Nov. 1930. Earlier, even Michael Condon had admitted that the BWSF was not free from 'bad elements'. He suggested a purge! *Sunday Worker*, 10 March 1929.
106 See BWSF Mins, 24 May, 7 June, 19 July, 6 Sept. and 13 Dec. 1929, 28 March 1930.
107 *Daily Worker*, 12 Feb. 1931.
108 *Daily Worker*, 25 June 1931.
109 BWSF Mins, 7 June 1931. *Daily Worker*, 8 Nov. 1932.
110 BWSF, 3rd National Conference Report, 1933. *International of Youth*, Aug. 1933.
111 *International of Youth*, Nov. 1929.
112 By 1932, the Federation had branches in Derby, Doncaster, Edinburgh, Fife, Gateshead, Glasgow, London, Manchester, Nottinghamshire and the Rhondda. *Sport and Games*, Jan. 1932.

113 *International of Youth*, April–May 1930. *Daily Worker*, 31 Oct. 1930, 27 Feb. 1931.
114 BWSF Mins, 7 June 1931.
115 T. M. Condon, *The Case for Organised Sunday Football* (1933), pp. 1-2.
116 See, for example, C. Griffen *et al.*, 'Women and leisure', in J. A. Hargreaves (ed.), *Sport, culture and ideology* (1982). Cf. N. Theberge, 'A critique of critiques: radical and feminist writings on sport', *Social Forces*, vol. 60 (1981).
117 BWSF Mins, 30 Nov. 1928, 14 March 1930. 7 Feb. 1932. *Sunday Worker*, 16 Dec. 1928. *Daily Worker*, 28 Jan. and 3 June 1930, 30 Jan. 1932. *Sport and Games*, Jan. 1932.
118 *Daily Worker*, 13 Jan., 29 Aug. and 21 Nov. 1930.
119 BWSF Mins, 14 March 1930.
120 Casket, interview.
121 *Daily Worker*, 1930, *passim*.
122 *Daily Worker*, 27 Jan. 1932.
123 *Workers Illustrated News*, 13 Dec. 1929. *Daily Worker*, 8 and 28 April and 2 May 1930. BWSF Mins, 2 May 1930.
124 *Red Stage*, Feb. 1932. *Blackshirt*, 7-13 Oct. 1933. Stockport Archive Centre, B/MM/3/23, Stockport Labour Fellowship, Executive Committee Minutes, 20 June 1933.
125 *Daily Worker*, 13 Nov. 1930.
126 *Daily Worker*, 30 Nov. 1933.
127 *Daily Worker*, 7 Dec. 1933.
128 *Report of Comrade M. Woolf, 'The Day is Ours!'. 6th World Congress Young Communist International* (1935), pp. 30-1. *The Tasks of the United Front of the Youth: Resolutions adopted at the Sixth Congress* (1935), p. 11. See also D. Steinberg, 'Workers' sport and the united front, 1934-1936', *Arena Reveiw*, Feb. 1980.
129 *Sunday Worker*, 9 Dec. 1928.
130 Bobker, Casket and Rothman, interviews.
131 *Daily Worker*, 20 Aug. 1931.
132 *Daily Worker*, 13 Jan. and 19 June 1933.
133 A. Howkins, 'Class against class: the political culture of the Communist Party of Great Britain, 1930-35', in F. Gloversmith (ed.), *Class, Culture and Social Change: A New View of the 1930s* (Brighton, 1980).
134 M. Jenkins, 'Early days in the Y.C.L.'., *Marxism Today*, vol. 16 (1972), p. 53; J. Jacobs, *Out of the Ghetto: My Youth in the East End, Communism and Fascism 1913-1939* (1978), p. 113. M. Henery, 'The Y.C.L. and the 1930s', *Scottish Marxist*, no. 21 (1981), p. 18.
135 Bobker, Casket and Rothman, interviews.
136 S. Macintyre, *Little Moscows: Communism and Working-Class Militancy in Inter-War Britain* (1980).

Chapter 5

The Labour Party, the unions and sport in the 1930s

Introduction

By the early 1930s the official labour movement had experienced a number of industrial and political reverses. The 'defeat' of the General Strike in 1926, and the resulting Trade Disputes and Trade Unions Act in the following year, effectively constrained the bargaining position of organised labour. Moreover, the fact that unemployment reached three million by 1933 undoubtedly undermined Labour's industrial strength. And politically, the 'betrayal' of MacDonald's Labour Government in 1931 arguably drained the movement of strong ideological notions of solidarity and co-operation. Yet, despite all this, there were signs of a new approach to economy and society, and the germ of a new confidence and assertiveness. Although political battles were still fought and industrial disputes still commonplace, especially in the mining sector, Labour responded to the period in opposition in the 1930s by modernising its policy position.

In the first place, the trade unions were not demoralised after the débâcle of 1926, and as Sidney Pollard has argued, their authority was little impaired due to a lack of blacklegging, the moderation of employers and the support of the National Unemployed Workers' Movement (NUWM).[1] Stephen Shaw, in his thoughtful study of the Trades Union Congress (TUC) and unemployment, has rightly concluded that 'in the 1930's the trade unions succeeded in preserving their membership in a manner which had not proved possible in the 1920's', and though 'severely handicapped by the depression, they emerged from it with a record of successful defence of their members' living standards'.[2] With the upswing in the economy, union membership recovered from a low of 4,392,000 in 1933 to reach 6,298,000 by the end of the decade. Significantly, those militants who had been unemployed for years started to trickle back into the workshops. The long period of unemployment had hardened the resolve of such men and women, and a new defiance began to take root in the embryonic shop stewards' movement. It is also fair to say that at another level by the 1930s the unions had gained access to the official policy-making machinery. As Middlemas, Martin and others have asserted, the TUC was drawn into the process of consultation which accompanied state intervention in the economy.[3] Writing from a different perspective, Rodney Lowe has also demonstrated that under the sway of industrial depression, the Ministry of Labour defended 'trade-unionism in order to safeguard industrial self-government and social peace'.[4] Far from declining in strength, by the end of the 1930s the unions may actually have consolidated their position in the British political system.

The unions also played a vital role in the affairs of the Labour Party. Not only did the 1930s witness a resuscitation of the Party's National Council of Labour on which the union representatives sat, but also the growing influence of trade union leaders such as Ernest Bevin, the powerful head of the Transport and General Workers' Union. Now, John Saville is quite right in assuming that 'for the mass of working people in the thirties what Labour had to do was to rehabilitate itself in terms of its collective capacity to govern'.[5] Arguably, such rehabilitation was achieved. Though Ben Pimlott and Alan Booth have cast doubts on Labour's ability to grasp new ideas and policies,[6] on the eve of the Second World War, the Party had advanced significantly from its inertia of the 1920s. In particular, Labour made substantive contributions in the field of economic and financial policy, and perhaps to a lesser extent in the drafting of blueprints for a new welfare settlement covering social security, health, housing and educational provision.[7]

It is of course this recovery of union strength and reorientation of policy in the 1930s which provides the essential backdrop for discussion of Labour's approach to sport. In much the same way as Labour's overall position in society was structured by new economic and political realities, then so, too, was the decision to take an interest in recreational and cultural questions. The growing importance of sport in everyday life meant that Labour could not afford to neglect it altogether. And the fact that the TUC and Labour Party were antagonistic to the communist-inspired BWSF necessarily led to the establishment of a sporting organisation under the guardianship of the official labour leadership. This chapter will focus on Labour's political and ideological interest in sport, and attempt to assess the role played by the National Workers' Sports Association from its inception in 1930 to the end of the decade.

The growth of the National Workers' Sports Association

After the British Workers' Sports Federation fell under communist control the official labour movement promoted sports organisations of its own. The origins of a national labour sporting body are to be found in the activities of the London Labour Party. During the 1920s the London Party, under the leadership of the future Cabinet Minister, Herbert Morrison, built a reputation for its cultural outlets. Morrison admired the sub-culture found in the German Social Democratic Party with its wide array of cultural and recreational services, and in this he saw a model for London socialism. In establishing speakers' classes, a legal advice bureau, a choral union, a dramatic federation and a Young People's Advisory Committee, he sought to shape a form of counter-culture: 'There will be an Art of the People, produced by the people, for we will not be content with the commercialized stuff of modern capitalist society.'[8] Though these experiments were not particularly successful, the Party also began to take an interest in sport.

London labour activists must have been aware of the pulling power of commercial sports and the associated attractions of gambling. Thousands of spectators ventured to the capital's sporting occasions: test cricket, the Wimbledon fortnight, professional boxing at the White City, and, on a more regular basis, football, greyhound racing and speedway. Thus as an alternative there were various relatively autonomous labour organisations catering for sport. The Tottenham Labour Sports Association, for example, was formed in 1927, and by the following year building work undertaken by its own members had resulted in a sports ground with facilities for cricket, football, netball and tennis, as well as a pavilion containing three dressing rooms.[9] It is therefore unsurprising that towards the end of 1928, the London Labour Party, supported by the London Trades Council, should form a Sports Association.

Set up in the wake of a successful Festival of Labour at the Crystal Palace, the London Labour Party Sports Association comprised twelve clubs, and was soon reported to be developing strongly.[10] Both the national Party Executive and the TUC General Council sanctioned the scheme in principle and a number of sporting initiatives were made: a football competition was inaugurated for which the winners received the Ramsay MacDonald Cup; an athletics meeting was organised at Herne Hill: and a football team toured Germany, winning one match, drawing two and losing two.[11] Furthermore, the chairman of the Association, Alec Macleod, initiated a 'Soccer for Sixpence' campaign, protesting that 'It is scandalous that football clubs should spend their large surpluses in securing "fashionable" players under the transfer system instead of improving their accommodation or reducing their prices.'[12] Though there certainly was a spiralling transfer regime at this time, like an earlier trades council campaign of 1922,[13] the protests of Macleod made little impact, aside from the counter-opinions voiced by such labour leaders as Herbert Dunnico, the Baptist minister and Deputy Speaker of the Commons, and Frederick Roberts, the Minister of Pensions.[14] Even so, as suggested at the time, organisational developments in London formed what was to be the 'nucleus' of a national movement.[15]

At the beginning of 1930 delegates to a conference at Transport House agreed to the formation of a sports organisation, later to be christened the National Workers' Sports Association (NWSA).[16] Once again, the Labour Party Executive and the TUC General Council approved the constitution, both finding it worthwhile enough to appoint a representative to the newly instituted National Council.[17] The major aim was to 'encourage, promote and control Amateur Sport and Recreation among Working Class Organisations' by federating sports bodies 'organised under the auspices of the Trade Union Congress and the Labour Party', and it was along these lines that the Association developed during the 1930s.[18]

By 1932, the NWSA consisted of eighteen sports bodies, with nine district committees and a total of 145 sections catering for approximately 5,000 members.[19] Unfortunately the Association was formed at a time of severe economic and political dislocation. Economic crisis and the concomitant problems of unemployment, social decay and poverty, especially in the industrial heartlands of South Wales, the North-East, and central Scotland, 'made workers' sports a distinctive luxury'.[20] On the political front, the fall of the Labour Government in 1931 and the disaffiliation of the left-wing Independent Labour Party (ILP) the following year constrained party organisation and recruitment, at least temporarily. Nevertheless, the position of the NWSA was consolidated so that by 1936, excluding union links, there were said to be over 380 clubs and sections with a membership some 13,000 strong.[21] There were particularly energetic organisations in Bath, Birmingham, Bristol, London, Reading and Swindon, and, as will be discussed, also a number of supporting trade unions and trades councils.

Without the affiliation of the Clarion Cycling Club (CCC), however, it is doubtful whether growth would have appeared impressive. As Judith Fincher has rightly claimed, the CCC was rejuvenated in the 1930s, based as it was on a wealth of outdoor recreations and a particularly dynamic way of communicating the socialist message.[22] In continuing to function as a means of organising 'Cyclists for Mutual Aid, Good Fellowship and the Propagation of the Principles of Socialism, along with the social pleasures of Cycling', it participated in all kinds of events, from cycle shows and exhibitions to conferences and competitions (including bicycle polo), published its own journal, the *Clarion Cyclist*, which had a circulation of 5,575 by November 1936, arranged educational classes, sponsored clubhouses, sleeping accommodation and cultural amenities, and entered into all kinds of practical campaigns.[23] In overall terms, there were 1,915 people on the rolls of the CCC in 1931, rising to 8,306 in 1936, and it is this which primarily explains the growth of the NWSA.[24]

In contrast to the BWSF, the major concern of the NWSA appears to have been sport, and not politics. From its inception in 1930, the Association provided a host of recreational activities, ranging from football and cricket through to table-tennis and chess – fourteen sports in all by 1935.[25] Most of the affiliated bodies seem to have made provision for a variety of sports, though there were specialist sections such as the Acton Labour Party Netball Club, London Labour Football Club, Reading Labour Rowing Club and of course the CCC. The ranks of the London football club, for example, were restricted to members of trade unions and the Labour Party; clad in labour colours and using a first-class enclosed ground as its home stadium, it entered a senior amateur league, as well as knock-out competitions, and played against and beat teams like Fulham 'A' which had five professional players.[26] Moreover, various leagues were established specifically for labour sport: football, netball and table-tennis leagues in London, shove-ha'penny and whist leagues in Reading, darts and skittles leagues in Bath.

Yet it was the annual galas, gatherings, championships and competitions which were the highlight of labour sport. There was the NWSA football cup, the traditional Easter meet of the CCC, and the annual athletics, cycling, swimming and tennis championships. In 1938, for instance, the athletic and cycling championship held at Herne Hill was the most successful of the decade. About 500 entries were received and participants came from Dover, Hexham, the Home Counties, Lancashire, the London area, Middlesborough, Portsmouth and Wales to compete in a range of track and field events, including cycle races, high jump, sprints, the ten-mile walk and tug-of-war competition.[27] Perhaps even more interesting was the tennis tournament, which assumed the name 'Workers' Wimbledon' when launched in 1932. Interestingly enough, Fred Perry, who won the official Wimbledon singles in three consecutive years in the mid-1930s, was the son of Samuel F. Perry, the secretary of the Co-operative Party. In referring to his son's success, Samuel Perry noted revealingly that 'our pleasure is shared by co-operators throughout Britain, by whom Fred is justly regarded as one of ourselves'.[28] In fact, there were autonomous labour lawn tennis clubs at Ealing, Oxford, Salford, Slough, Tottenham, Ware, Woolwich and elsewhere, so it certainly seems that the Workers' Wimbledon had numerous players upon which to draw.[29] The event was still popular in 1938, when it attracted 101 competitors to its venue of Southsea, and was described as 'a great success from every point of view'.[30] Additionally, as the final chapter will discuss, the NWSA was also involved in international competition, representative teams visiting the Continent for the Workers' Olympiads and other events, and international meetings being organised in England.

It is apparent that the Association organised a variety of sports for both domestic and international competition. Underpinning this was the encouragement of a plethora of auxiliary services. It has to be remembered that by the 1930s professional, and to a lesser extent amateur, sport was becoming more technically sophisticated. In association football, for instance, top club sides were beginning to take cognizance of wider developments in scientific management, through more efficient financial and administrative structures, the transfer market, and the application of coaching and tactics, including sports medicine.[31] In the mid-thirties, the Football Association introduced a coaching sheme, instructional classes for schoolboys and training films.[32] Sports enthusiasts in the labour movement must have been aware of these trends, and as a means of improvement sought to emulate them. The NWSA provided technical assistance to local labour sports events, galas and fêtes, though it was the introduction of supporting tertiary activities which was in fact the most significant step. Advice and tips were given on all aspects of sport, culminating in the publication of a pamphlet on sprinting and athletic training; the CCC had an insurance scheme whereby cash benefits were paid for personal accidents, and the Association even made arrangements for osteopath treatment.[33] Sports services were also part of a wider entertainment which included the use of lantern slides in lectures, a Clarion stand at the London lightweight cycle show, a workers' exhibition and a three-reel silent film of the Liège sports gathering of 1939.[34] Furthermore, there were attempts to maintain some level of control over sports grounds and premises. Thus, one useful adjunct to the movement was the National Workers' Football and Sports

Grounds Limited, formed to provide stadia for workers' clubs.[35] Needless to say, as with other initiatives, this appears to have been crippled by lack of cash.

But, focusing on the sporting preoccupations of the NWSA should not lead us to believe that politics were unimportant. The Association did not seek to follow the position of the BWSF and use sport as a means of revolutionary class struggle, yet political issues were constantly raised. As the next chapter will show, the labour sports movement had its own political programme of demands from which certain campaigns sprang. Most importantly, in contrast to 'establishment' clubs, the membership was clearly drawn from the working class. At the Crystal Palace sports meeting of July 1935, one commentator noted the occupational diversity of the competitors:

> In the tug-of-war, dockers from Southampton ... vied with drivers and stokers from Willesden ... whilst the men who handle our letters at the G.P.O. held on strenuously to the team of London bus drivers ... Tram men from Birmingham, and N.A.T.S.O.P.A. [National Society of Operative Printers and Assistants] members from Fleet-street also turned up to show their speed against South Wales miners and C.W.S. [Co-operative Wholesale Society] employees from Silvertown.[36]

In addition, there were boot repairers and teachers, and amongst the women, 'drapery assistants and clerks from Woolwich'. The proletarian character of the membership necessarily structured the ideological and policy position of the Association. In brief, the NWSA sought to represent the demands and needs of those workers interested in sport.

As with the BWSF, however, the labour sports movement tended to be male-dominated. Evidence suggests that the majority of NWSA members were men, whilst in the mid-1930s there was only one female representative on the fifteen-strong executive committee. True, women participated in tennis and netball, but sports like football, cricket and athletics were ostensibly for males. Arguably, the role of women in the social side of sports or in such rituals as thread-the-needle competitions tended to reinforce domesticity, femininity and the female sphere. Moreover, the subordinate position of women is reflected in the failure of policy statements to raise the particular problems and disadvantages faced by women in sport and, more generally, in the wider society.

To be sure, the aims, objectives and sympathies of the Association were shaped by its close relationship with the (male) leadership of the Labour Party and TUC. Though the Association did not depend on the labour leadership for finance, aside, that is, from small grants and contributions, it worked through formal labour policy-making channels. The central bureaucracy was located initially at Transport House, and all the principal officials were well-known members of the Party or TUC. Herbert Elvin (1879-1949), for example, who served as chairman of the Association for many years, was general secretary of the National Union of Clerks and, in 1938, president of the TUC. Partly due to his religious convictions – he was a lay preacher and sympathised with the broad tenets of Christian socialism – Elvin was a vigorous advocate of temperance, serving on the hierarchy of the Workers' Temperance League. No doubt Elvin's desire to wean workers away from the public-house, and his sincere belief in the 'Socialist Commonwealth' inspired a commitment to labour sport, a commitment which had much in common with earlier socialist ideals.[37] Significantly, by 1935 Elvin's son, George, was both general secretary of the Association of Cine-Technicians and the NWSA.

By the end of the 1930s there were a variety of trades councils and unions either affiliated directly or aligned to the Association. As previously noted, from an early stage the trades councils attempted to promote sport, and no doubt with this in mind the Association courted local groupings.[38] In fact, a Reading delegate to the annual conference of trades councils in 1933 'urged that the fullest support should be given to the NWSA'.[39] And in 1937, the University towns of Oxford and Cambridge decided to launch labour sports sections, though many failures were recorded as in the case of the Sheffield trades council.[40] The first union to affiliate was NATSOPA with a membership of 20,000, and this was soon followed by the National Union of Commercial Travellers with 700 members; by 1935, unions representing building employees, clerks, commercial travellers, iron and steel workers, printers and textile operatives were connected with the Association.[41] Additionally, a degree of financial and moral support came from engineering, clerical, post office and transport workers.[42] Further, union branches were often represented at national and local sports events. At the Workers' Wimbledon in 1937 many unions were present, including the Amalgamated Engineering Union, Amalgamated Union of Upholsterers, Association of Women Clerks and Secretaries, Chemical Workers' Union, National Union of Railwaymen, Transport and General Workers' Union, and United Patternmakers' Association.[43] Needless to say, the Labour Party was also concerned 'to make the work of the Association better known and more popular', and formal contacts were made with agencies of the Party.[44] It is appropriate at this point to make a digression about wider labour sports provision, and the organisation of socialist youth.

Outside the Association, numerous local labour recreational bodies continued to thrive in the 1930s. Most of all, it is apparent that the co-operative movement catered for a range of leisure occupations. Labour history has tended to focus on the nineteenth-century origins and development of co-operation, but it should be understood that the 1920s and 1930s were halcyon years for co-operation as a retailing, political and indeed social movement. The membership of co-operative societies rose from 4.1 million in 1919 to 8.5 million in 1939, whilst the highly popular Co-operative Women's Guild was a salutary attempt at voluntary self-help by committed working-class women. The total environment of co-operation spawned opportunities for critical debate, education, drama, film-making and other cultural interests. As for sport, by the 1930s many societies had their own sports clubs and teams, some with grand amenities. The Soap Works at Irlam had a recreation society, the Longsight Printing Works had cricket, swimming and tennis clubs, the Silvertown Productive Factory had a social and athletic committee, the Reading Works had a ladies Gymnasium Class, the Avonmouth Flour Mill had an athletic club, the Trafford Wharf had a football club, the Newcastle-upon-Tyne Boot and Shoe Department had cricket and football clubs, and the list goes on. All sports were catered for, and, most interestingly, the fact that young women had formed cricket and hockey clubs, netball teams and gymnastic classes was said to be 'outstanding'. Further, in 1929 the CWS granted £10,000 for the purchase of sports facilities, and grounds were established in Batley, Birmingham, Hebden Bridge, Leicester, Liverpool, Manchester, Reddish and elsewhere. By 1932, for example, the London Co-operative Society Employees Sports club had 6,900 members, a fine ground at Chingford, and accommodation for many sports. Similar developments occurred in the main provincial societies, and at a time when perhaps half of CWS works had sports sections there was a demand for a national organisation. Admittedly the British Co-operative Employees' Sports Association, established in 1932, had foundered by 1937 – 'although the idea had to some extent germinated and borne some fruit'. Nonetheless, at least at local level, co-operation was still active in the sports field, a clear instance of proletarian sociability and creativity.[45]

Many local Labour Parties and trade unions also had their own social and sports clubs. The executive of the Working Men's Club and Institute Union had a fairly close connection with the Labour Party, whilst in the North-West of England the National Union of Labour and Socialist Clubs was under the effective tutelage of the official labour movement, with seventy-two affiliated clubs by 1932.[46] Apparently, a number of games were catered for – bowling, darts and especially billiards – though 'the greatest privilege' was said to be 'good fellowship and comradeship'.[47] In its search for proletarian solidarity, there was even a motion submitted by the Victoria Labour Club that the Union should not 'entertain or play any games with any other political organisation'.[48] Similarly in London, a national Trade Union Club was formed in April 1930 with a membership of 3,000. In addition to a 'cosy lounge' with three May Day cartoons by Walter Crane on the walls, the Club had a billiards room, table-tennis equipment and a card playing room.[49] Evidence shows that members of the NWSA used the club's facilities.[50]

By the same token, the NWSA had contacts with the TUC-inspired Unemployed Associations, which had been set up in 1932 to meet the increasingly demanding problems of enforced leisure.[51] Though it is no mere coincidence that the Associations were established at the same time as the institutional base and ideas of the left-wing NUWM and 'bourgeois' National Council of Social Service were spreading, they were also a pragmatic attempt to keep the out of work in touch with the unions by means of the educational and recreational outlets.[52] Initially numbering sixty-four, they had grown to some 100 in 1938 with 400,000 unemployed members, concentrated in Lancashire, Yorkshire, the Midlands and South Wales.[53] In the summer of 1932 the NWSA offered to place their expertiese at the disposal of the unemployed,[54] though perhaps more interesting was the part played by the National Playing Fields Association (NPFA). The NPFA had been launched in 1925 to campaign for more recreation grounds and open spaces, and in this role was relatively successful. At the beginning, leading labour personalities such as George Lansbury and Ramsay MacDonald offered their support, whilst the indefatigable dockers' leader, Ben Tillett, represented the TUC on the NPFA's Governing Council.[55] By all appearances, the relationship was consolidated in the 1930s, Herbert Elvin of the NWSA taking over Tillett's representative position, and the Playing Fields Association supplying the unemployed with games equipment: cricket and football gear, golf clubs, hockey sticks, sets of boxing gloves, sportswear, and indoor games like darts, dominoes, draughts and ping-pong.[56] No wonder the NPFA reported in 1933 that 'Formal adhesion by the General Council of the Trades Union Congress was secured early in the year'.[57] With some justification, the communist-led National Minority Movement protested that the alliance between the TUC and NPFA was tantamount to collaboration with 'well-known class enemies', of whom the Duke of York and the Earl of Derby were the most prominent.[58] Despite the militant exhortations of the communist movement during its notorious 'Class Against Class' phase, it is difficult to escape the conclusion that at both national and local level certain labour activists were attempting to provide sporting possibilities for employed and unemployed alike.

With reference to socialist youth, one of the first pressures for a youth section within the Labour Party appears to have come in May 1919 from members in Leigh, who impelled the National Executive to follow their example and establish a League of Young Labour.[59] Though it is hardly appropriate here to trace the tortuous steps in the eventual founding of the League of Youth, it should be noted that by 1920 a National Young Labour League had in fact come into being, and it was this which provided a platform for the development of Young People's Sections by mid-decade.[60] Significantly, before these Sections had been re-organised into the League of Youth in 1926, the National Executive had stressed that aside from education and participation in election work, opportunities were to be found for sports and other recreational interests.[61] Indeed, at an early stage, William Jacob, the Parliamentary agent to the West Wolverhampton constituency and president of the BWSF, urged the new youth grouping 'to protect the young people from the great danger of commercialised sport and assist the Working-Class Sports Movement throughout the country'.[62] To some extent, the aim to provide an avenue for sports may have been motivated by the leadership's desire to marginalise the influence of young socialists on important policy issues. After all, as early as 1924 the National Executive had stressed that 'The work of the Young People's Sections should be taken not to over-emphasise their political side.'[63] Be that as it may, by 1930 there were 335 branches in the League of Youth, and sport was emerging as a premier activity; the League's National Advisory Committee was soon to make contacts with the NWSA.[64] In fact, political work could be combined with sport, as John Ferris has suggested:

> rambling and cycling groups could venture forth into the countryside or nearby towns to leaflet or swell the ranks of a neighbouring L.O.Y. branch or local Party's meeting, canvass or recruiting drive. This recreational side, the L.O.Y.'s social life, was seen as especially important. Members enjoying themselves together would provide a spirit of fellowship which was '... the true basis of socialism'. If there was a monthly political meeting then branch officers should ensure that a monthly social was also held in order to encourage the less politically minded. Public dances, tennis, football, rambling, cycling and swimming groups; visits to local places of interest, especially municipal

undertakings, were to overcome the reluctance of many young people to become involved or committed to political activity.[65]

It is also fascinating to discover that a feature of Hugh Gaitskell's candidature at Chatham in the mid-1930s 'was his lavish attention to the Labour League of Youth. On summer Saturdays he went with them on midnight rambles, talking politics, and often ending up with political chores into the small hours.'[66] To what extent were similar patterns found in other constituencies? – a question which would surely profit from further detailed research. More definitely, the League's relationship with the NWSA was solidified in 1932 when Herbert Elvin addressed the young socialists' annual conference, and from then on fraternal links were maintained.[67] The Leeds branch of the League, for instance, after setting up sections for sport, decided to join the Association as a 'sympathetic body'.[68]

Lastly here, it should be recalled that there were certain other non-Marxist recreational organisations which catered for socialist youth. Perhaps the most important was the Woodcraft Folk, which first got off the ground in 1925 as a kind of ideological counter to the Boy Scouts. The history of the Folk has been outlined admirably by David Prynn, who rightly claims that the Woodcraft idea 'shared a reverence for nature, the idealisation of the primitive and a recoil from industrialisation and city life'.[69] Interestingly, the Folk's veneration of nature and the 'natural' human condition meant that there were even pioneering attempts at sex education for young people, as under the auspices of the Sheffield Folk Supporters' Council.[70] Once again, there was a degreee of continuity here from the earlier religion of socialism tradition. It is evident that similarities existed between the utopian ideology, environmentalism and recreational nexus of the Folk and the late nineteenth-century Clarion movement, the New Life Fellowship and the endeavours of Edward Carpenter and friends. But more than this, the Woodcraft Folk was closely related to the labour and co-operative movement – Leslie Paul and Joseph Reeves of the Royal Arsenal Co-operative Society giving it a distinctive 'socialist orientation' – and as such even believed in the emancipation of the proletariat from 'wage slavery'.[71] In the words of Reeves:

The Woodcraft Folk represents the militant part of the co-operative youth movement. It aims at inspiring young people with the ideals of co-operation by bringing the examples of co-operation seen throughout nature to their immediate notice. The horrors of industrialisation and the worst features of factory life are made real by contrast with camping in the open fields under the health-giving rays of the sun and the mind-healing influence of a starry night. The creative facilities of youth are stimulated by the encouragement of handicraft and the self expression of the youth and the maiden is drawn out by art, music, poetry and literature.[72]

Additionally, as in the NWSA, there was a strong pacifist strain in the Folk — 'We hate war. We espouse peace.'[73] As such, opposition was mobilised against imperialist and military organisations like the Boy Scouts, though with the rise of fascism reports came in that conflict existed 'within the ranks of the Folk on our pacifist views'.[74] And in fact by the end of the thirties it was resolved that 'Groups have no right under Folk Law to expel solely for membership of the Territorials or other Organisations.'[75]

In the decade or so before the Second World War the Folk played an active part in working-class politics, achieving official support from the Labour Party National Executive in 1935.[76] Membership rose steadily from forty in 1925 to 721 in 1930 and 4,321 in 1938.[77] Even so, it must be added that there was some fear that the 1936 Public Order Act would be used against the Folk. Advice was sought from the Labour MP and future Chancellor of the Exchequer, the Sir Stafford Cripps, who cautioned that because the Folk was political in emphasis it could be prevented from wearing uniforms under the legislation.[78] It was therefore decided to play down the movement's political identity and stress its educational objectives as an 'organisation concerned for the future of the children in its care'; hence, 'the first serious crisis of its career' was resolved.[79] In fact, when it came to the wearing of uniforms at an International Camp at Rottingdean, near Brighton, the Home Secretary granted permission on the condition that political demonstrations were not patronised. As one far-sighted public official minuted: 'On the face of it, the P.O. (Public Order) Act cannot, without absurdity, be applied to a uniform worn by children under 15'.[80] In all, like the League of Youth and such bodies as the British Federation of Co-operative Youth, ILP Guild of Youth, Young Communist League, and local labour groupings – like the one in Bermondsey which organised annual children's sports catering for upwards of 1,000 participants – the Woodcraft Folk was an important element in a socialist totality, linking outdoor recreation and sociability to a human-inspired critique of industrial capitalism, with its alienating work process, ugly urban sprawl, individualism and competitive ethic.

At least for some union and socialist activists, sport was regarded as a means of recruiting both adult and young workers. Sport was a ploy 'by which the great masses of unorganised workers can be brought directly into the orbit of the Socialist Movement'.[81] Or as the joint secretary of the NWSA, Reg Underhill, put it in 1936: 'we feel our work is part of the organisational side of our Trade Union Movement. By our activities members can be imbued with interest in their branch, and such activities can be used as attractions for the recruitment of new members, especially amongst the young unorganised workers.'[82] The aim then was to use sport 'to attract people and keep them interested in the Labour Movement itself'.[83]

It must be acknowledged, however, that this objective was not always fulfilled and political assistance not as forthcoming as originally anticipated. In 1932, only four unions responded to an appeal for funds, while in 1936 and 1938 the shop assistants and transport workers refused to offer any financial help whatsoever.[84] Though some labour leaders appreciated, in Hugh Dalton's characteristically condescending terms, 'that we could only win power by the votes of the football crowds',[85] it should not be overlooked that in the ranks of, say, the Leeds labour movement were those who perceived sport as 'a remnant of barbarism used to stagnate the minds of the people'; it was the 'Opium of the Working Class' which needed to be replaced by 'real' political work – 'the serious business of life'.[86] Obviously such positions stifled workers' sport in its infancy.

Yet, despite the inclusion of caveats, the organic relationship between the NWSA and the wider workers' movement meant that labour sport was necessarily political. George Deacon, the Association's tennis secretary argued forcefully that sport was: 'a waste of time, unless it is approached as a piece of practical work. We are not interested in building up merely another sports organisation. For that reason it is most essential that the Association and its affiliated clubs are linked with existing industrial, political and Co-operative organisations which our working-class movement has built up'.[87] Clarion cyclists and sports activists thus provided political assistance during elections and May Day demonstrations.[88]

Turning now to the philosophy of the labour sports movement. At the outset there is a need to stress that the ideas and traditions which inspired the inter-war Labour Party and TUC were complex and extremely difficult to delineate. Of course, in organisational terms, the modern labour movement was far from monolithic, with different interests and identities – industrial, political, cultural. Distinctions can be made between socialist political parties, trade unions and co-operative societies, but even within these groupings divisions were real: the unions, for example, were split along craft, industrial and general lines. For analytical purposes, however, the historian can view the official labour and trade union movement as united by the broadly conceived ideology of labour socialism, a set of perspectives developed from, and in the process transforming, late nineteenth-century labourism, a position 'which accepted the possibility of social change within the existing framework of society'.[89] Without entering into the details, labour socialism provided the Labour Party and unions with a breadth of ideas and strategies as an alternative to British Marxism. Most of all, labour socialists or social democrats chose the Parliamentary road to socialism based on a constructive and idealistic view of the world, the need for educational change, spiritual renewal and social reform. Needless to say, this was in sharp contrast to the more systematic and critical position of Marxism, with its attention to historical materialism, the capitalist mode of production and the necessary correspondence between the economic base and superstructure, and above all its call for an oppositional political strategy, that of revolution. In general terms, the political approach of the NWSA and its supporting bodies was underpinned by labour socialism.

The attitudes and objectives of the labour sports movement were determined by a complex mix of internationalism, reformism and socialism. By the 1930s the leadership of the NWSA and CCC remained committed to the principles of international sport and peace. In a characteristically ethical and idealistic discourse – 'the spreading the more golden-glowing gospel of the Ideal' – Tom Groom could still talk about 'Peace through Sport', though more significantly even the extreme wing of the CCC believed in 'transferring international rivalries from the hate-compelling fields of Battle to the healthier atmosphere of the friendly fields of Sport'.[90] During its most militant phase, the belief in internationalism led the CCC to 'refuse to support any Capitalist War no matter whether it be organised by an Imperial British Government or the League of Nations'.[91] The NWSA also adopted the motto of 'Peace through Sport', and in this light numerous contributions from George Elvin promised that 'world comradeship of games is bound to promote peace and good feeling between nation and nation'.[92] In the NWSA's first pamphlet, *Labour and Sport*, some stress was laid on this aspect of labour socialism: 'Let the young people of all nations meet upon the playing field rather than upon the battlefield, and the Peace Mind will develop. Sport can become the link between the world's young by which international Peace can be secured.'[93] The internationalism of labour sport was also linked to the educational, even spiritual, fight for socialism – apparently, it

Newman University College
Library
Tel: 0121 476 1181 ext 1208

Renewed Items 11/01/2013 11:07
XXXX0428

Item Title	Due Date
* Sport, politics and the working class : organised labour and sport in inter-	01/02/2013 23:59:00
* social significance of sport : an introduction to the sociology of sport	01/02/2013 23:59:00

* Renewed today
Thank you for renewing your items
www.newman.ac.uk/library
library@newman.ac.uk

was possible to 'hasten forward the Co-operative Commonwealth' by 'playing for Socialism as well as working for it'.[94] Here also was a kind of verbal or linguistic symbolism threading sport to broader internationalist and socialist 'goals'; a means of consolidating the relationship between sport and political reform.

In distancing itself from the BWSF, labour sport rarely articulated a materialist critique of sport, though Clarion cyclists and the labour sports community in general were occasionally disparaging about certain aspects of the established order. There was, for instance, a genuine fear that 'unscrupulous employers', supported by 'organisations antagonistic to Trade Unionism and Socialism', would use company sport 'for their own ends'.[95] Notwithstanding Ernest Bevin's rabid anti-communism, which sometimes bordered on paranoia, he was quite aware that the 'great industrialists ' used sports clubs as a medium of expedience: 'I know of nothing that is used more against our Movement than the many sports organisations run by employers in the way of welfare clubs.'[96] Indeed, in 1929 Bevin's union, the Transport and General Workers' Union, discussed the essentials of opposing company sport.[97] Labour sport was thus regarded as a way to counteract welfarism and apply 'union won leisure for union-sponsored activity'.[98]

There was also criticism of commercialised leisure and the so-called 'Capitalist monopoly of sport', leading to the demand for 'working-class alternatives to the existing Capitalist sports organisations'.[99] Thus on occasions there was a more systematic overview of social life, ranging from a critical appraisal of religion and imperialism to a discussion of the structural elements of sports under capitalism.[100] One editorial in the admittedly left-wing *Clarion Cyclist* attempted a quasi-Marxist interpretation of bourgeois society: 'Pending the time when the means of production and distribution can be socialised, it is to the advantage of the worker to win as much of the surplus as possible. The workers can do this by carrying out successful strikes, building up the Co-operative movement, and demanding improved social and municipal amenities.'[101] Yet, possibly the clearest 'socialist' invective is contained in the pamphlet *Sport – Drug or Tonic?*, where sport is described as 'coloured by the kind of society in which it flourishes'. Under capitalist society, with its search for profit and capital accumulation, sport was assumed to act as a drug upon a great section of the people, turning them away from the important economic and social problems of the day.[102] In contrast, under workers' control, sport was felt to be a good, clean leisure activity which 'encouraged playing as against watching' and developed 'comradeship, healthy competition and the team spirit'.[103] In broad terms, when organised labour credited sport as tainted by the capitalist order, the conclusion was to take it over and re-make it for socialist purposes. After all, it has to be remembered that certain activists were on the left of the movement. To take but one example; George Elvin, when standing as Labour Parliamentary candidate at Weston-Super-Mare in 1935, declared that 'Labour will carry out a bold policy of Socialist reconstruction at home. That policy will include schemes of Public Ownership and control, in the national interest, of Banking, Coal and its produce, Transport, Electricity, Iron, Steel, and Cotton.'[104] Elvin may well have espoused the idealism of 'Peace through Sport', but this should not disguise his wider socialist commitment.

Superficially at least, labour socialists, like their communist antagonists, were critical of certain aspects of bourgeois sport and society. Even so, it is essential to add that the labour socialist conviction was never as dynamic or scientific as the Marxist one. Whereas the BWSF was overtly hostile to all forms of capitalist sport, the NWSA was not. The Association's opposition to capitalism was covert, and even when protests were made they were usually diluted and moderated. As activists themselves emphasised, labour socialists eschewed the Marxist approach of class-struggle sport with its 'rigid proletarian basis for every human activity';[105]

We in the British Labour Movement have never adopted a rigid doctrinaire Marxism, and we don't see the class struggle in every activity of life as do some of our Continental comrades. For instance, in our Workers Sports Movement we don't think it necessary to denounce the Olympic Games as 'bourgeois' because they are not Socialist, nor ... do we insist on a rigid proletarianism in everything from art to astronomy.[106]

Indeed, the Glasgow ILP paper, *Forward*, was openly scathing about the way in which the BWSF portrayed sport in terms of 'fascist' rugby, middle-class ruffians, and so on.[107] The BWSF would almost certainly have found it difficult to accept the view of that well-known author, journalist and associate editor of the *Daily Herald* (1919–22), Gerald Gould, that those who opposed professional sport were the most 'disgraceful and absurd of all'.[108] The main aim of the NWSA was not to discredit the overall capitalist arrangement or advance the class war, but to stimulate sport under working-class organisations.[109] Though labour socialists were not exactly advocates of the establishment, professional and established amateur sport was tolerated, even encouraged: the NWSA was therefore affiliated to the predominantly middle-class Amateur Athletic Association. There was even a reluctance by the Labour Party to publish a pamphlet on 'Socialism and Sport' because it was 'too propagandist'; apparently, the requirement was 'a bright pamphlet on sport only'.[110] It was this reformist position which led the NWSA to reject formal connections with organised communism.

As already noted, more likely than not, the BWSF was dissolved in order to give credence to the campaign for a united front against fascism. It is apparent that communist enthusiasts of sport wished to co-operate with the NWSA and, in fact, reports of the Association's activities began to appear in the *Daily Worker*. Writing in the paper, C. A. Quinn, a member of the management committee of the Labour Sports Association and also honorary secretary of the popular South London Sunday Football League, thus observed that there was a pressing need 'for a United Front of all peace-loving sports men and women'.[111] However, the strong anti-communist mood in the labour sports movement rendered it difficult for any form of agreement or *rapprochement*. As George Elvin proposed, under no conditions could the NWSA 'tolerate relations with Communist Sports organisations'.[112] In this he was merely toeing the line of his father, who had promised to 'appeal to the T.U.C. to combat the Communist propaganda of the B.W.S.F.'.[113] Hence, at the Association's annual meeting of 1935, complaints were pressed about the presence of members from the Young Communist League (YCL).[114] Moreover, the Association reaffirmed its opposition to the Red Sports International, while the TUC General Council 'rejected collaboration with the Communists'.[115]

Not all members of the labour sports movement were hostile to communist influence. There were radical Clarion cyclists, particularly in the Manchester area, who co-operated with and supported the BWSF.[116] In fact, militant pressure in the mid-1930s culminated in the disaffiliation of the Clarion from the ranks of the Workers' Sports Association 'until such 'time as the N.W.S.A. justifies itself'.[117] Though the Clarion reaffiliated in a short space of time, it continually prompted the Association into a more direct course of action, including alliance with communist bodies.[118] This kind of pressure on the labour leadership must have had some effect. True, no contacts were officially sealed, but an interesting report in the *Daily Worker* during 1936 implies that communists were beginning to operate within official labour channels: 'Without question a great change for the good has taken place since the latter half of 1935, when it was realised there is room for all worker sportsmen within the ranks of the N.W.S.A., and combined efforts show almost remarkable progress.'[119] There are further details to suggest that labour socialists were drawing closer to their communist rivals: Russian folk dancers were entertained at the athletic championships of 1935; Tom Groom gave a lecture on the Soviet Union; a tribute was paid to the *Daily Worker* for its services to labour sport; Reg Underhill wrote a series of articles for the YCL paper, *Challenge*; and a football match was staged against a Russian eleven, described as 'equal to most of the First Division teams of this country'.[120] As in other areas such as the Left Book Club and Unity Theatre, there was some reconciliation as labour socialists and Marxists came together to repel fascist tyranny and aggression. Obviously this was inextricably linked to events on the Continent, as chapter 7 of this study will discuss.

Conclusion

In conclusion, it would not be unfair to characterise the NWSA as first and foremost a sporting body. By co-ordinating labour sport various successes were achieved, ranging from the annual Workers' Wimbledon to participation in socialist Olympiads. Like the BWSF, however, the Association faced a profusion of difficulties. Throughout the 1930s, the labour sports movement was indeed on the margins of financial survival. The contributions made by organised labour at large were meagre and internal fund-raising was a major preoccupation. The lack of funds made even the most rudimentary of advances problematical: though activities were well-publicised in the *New Clarion* and then the TUC journal *Labour*, the only two labour sports papers, the *Clarion Cyclist* and the NWSA *Bulletin*, were sacrificed due to money worries. A certain degree of help was forthcoming from the Labour Party and the trade unions, but even then sport was perceived, rightly, as of marginal importance when set alongside wages, unemployment, the rise of fascism and other substantive issues. Indeed, the sports question has to be viewed in terms of the fundamental reorientation of labour policy in the 1930s. At a time when Labour was focusing on all manner of economic and social contingencies which would influence future electoral and class politics, it also seemed appropriate to take cognisance of the major working-class habit of sport. Nonetheless, Labour's influence in this regard was truncated, for sport was near the bottom of policy priorities.

It is easy to be critical of workers' sport, for there were many areas of seeming stagnation. As the secretary of the Lancashire and Cheshire Union of the CCC noted about the Liverpool branch: 'It appears to me to be almost a misnomer to call the section either Liverpool or a cycling club or in fact anything but a self satisfied collection of Clubhouse loungers.'[121] Yet given the breadth of financial, organisational and other constraints, growth was always going to be the central enigma. Even so, the thirties did witness the recovery of the CCC and the steady development of a viable labour sports movement. Within the sports sections of the NWSA, League of Youth, Woodcraft Folk, co-operative society, union branch and the rest, socialist ideas and policy were cultivated and nurtured. It is true that labour sport was usually provided exclusively for active trade unionists or Labour Party members, but it did represent a legitimate cultural formation which advanced the claims of the broad movement. Moreover, labour sportsmen and women, though concerned principally with sport, were not above politics. They enunciated a labour socialist critique of existing structures and, as the final chapters of the study will demonstrate, furthered the campaigns for improved sports facilities and global working-class solidarity. Such a conclusion again supports the hypothesis that even in societies, like inter-war Britain, where capitalist and bourgeois sports are dominant, there are spaces for resistance, and even opportunities for a type of counter-hegemonic project. In much the same way as Marxist activists, labour socialists were involved in the making of those contradictory forces which came together and shaped the inter-war sports agenda. Though the moment for an oppositional sports movement may well have passed by the end of the 1930s, by no means can the NWSA be considered a total failure.

Notes

1 S. Pollard, 'Trade union reactions to the economic crisis', *Journal of Contemporary History*, vol. 4 (1969).
2 S. Shaw, 'The Attitude of the Trades Union Congress Towards Unemployment in the Inter-War Period', PhD, University of Kent (1979), pp. 17, 31.
3 K. Middlemas, *Politics in Industrial Society: The Experience of the British System since 1911* (1979). R. M. Martin, *TUC: The Growth of a Pressure Group 1868-1976* (1980), pp. 205-43.
4 R. Lowe, *Adjusting to Democracy: The Role of the Ministry of Labour in British Politics 1916-1939* (Oxford, 1986), p. 119.
5 J. Saville, 'May Day 1937' in A. Briggs and J. Saville (eds), *Essays in Labour History 1920-1939* (1977), p. 238.
6 B. Pimlott, *Labour and the Left in the 1930s* (Cambridge, 1977). A. Booth, 'Essay in bibliography: the Labour Party and economics between the wars', *Bulletin of the Society for the Study of Labour History*, no. 47 (1983)

7 See E. Durbin, *New Jerusalems: The Labour Party and the Economics of Democratic Socialism* (1985). A. Marwick, 'The Labour Party and the welfare state in Britain 1900-48', *American Historical Review*, vol. 73 (1967-68).

8 Quoted in B. Donoughue and G. W. Jones, *Herbert Morrison: Portrait of a Politician* (1973), p. 71.

9 *North Tottenham Citizen*, Jan., May and July 1928. *Daily Herald*, 9 Oct. 1928. A similar point can be made about the Bermondsey Party. See F. Brockway, *Bermondsey Story: The Life of Alfred Salter* (1949), pp. 136, 191.

10 *London News*, Sept. and Dec. 1928. World Microfilms, London Trades Council Executive Committee Minutes, 25 Oct. and 28 Dec. 1928.

11 Labour Executive Mins, 19 Dec. 1928. TUC GC Mins, 27 March 1929. *London News*, March 1929. *Daily Herald*, 5 and 17 Aug. 1929.

12 *Daily Herald*, 9 and 13 Aug. 1929.

13 See *Labour Magazine*, Nov. 1922.

14 *Daily Herald*, 10 and 12 Aug. 1929.

15 National Trades Councils, *Annual Conference Report*, 1929, p. 10; TUC, *Annual Report*, 1929, p. 119. *The London Trade Union Handbook* (1930), p. 100. Cf. Donoughue and Jones, *Morrison*, p. 72.

16 *Daily Herald*, 21 Feb. 1930. *London News*, April 1930. There was a change of name in 1936 to the British Workers Sports Association (BWSA).

17 Labour Executive Mins, 27 March and 22 July 1930. Labour Party, *Annual Conference Report*, 1930, p. 28. TUC GC Mins, 26 March and 23 July 1930; TUC, *Annual Report*, 1930, p. 106.

18 Labour Party, *Annual Conference Report*, 1930, p. 301. Interestingly the Association's formation was even publicised in the German socialist paper, *Arbeitersport*. British Library of Political and Economic Science (hereafter BLPES), George Elvin Papers (hereafter Elvin papers), COLL MISC 685/1.

19 Labour Party, *Annual Conference Report*, 1932, p. 70. TUC, *Annual Report*, 1932, pp. 100-1. *New Clarion*, 20 Aug. 1932.

20 *Labour*, April 1934.

21 Labour Party, *Annual Conference Report*, 1936, p. 86. AEU, *Monthly Report*, Dec. 1936.

22 J. A. Fincher, 'The Clarion Movement: A Study of a Socialist Attempt to Implement the Co-operative Commonwealth in England 1891-1914', MA, University of Manchester (1971), pp. 168-9.

23 See Manchester Central Library Archives Department (hereafter MAD), deposit 016, records of CCC.

24 MAD, 016/ii/79, CCC, National Committee Report, 1937, p. 3.

25 NWSA, *5th Annual Report*, 1935, p. 14.

26 *Labour*, Oct. and Dec. 1933, Jan., April, June and Sept. 1935. Labour Party, *Annual Conference Report*, 1934, p. 21; 1935, p. 59.

27 AEU, *Monthly Journal*, July 1938. *Railway Service Journal*, Sept. 1938. TUC, *Annual Report*, 1939, p. 140. MAD, 016/i/32, Programme of the BWSA 7th Annual Athletics and Cycling Championships, 13 Aug. 1938.

28 *Co-operative News*, 21 July 1932.

29 *New Clarion*, 25 June 1932.

30 *Labour*, July 1938.

31 See J. Walvin, *The People's Game. A Social History of British Football* (1975), pp.

128-33.

32 G. Green, *The History of the Football Association* (1935), pp. 296, 340. *Sporting Chronicle and Athletic News*, 2 Dec. 1935.

33 *Labour*, March 1938. *Boost*, 14 to 21 May 1939. NWSA, *5th Annual Report*, 1935, p. 10.

34 *New Clarion*, 5, 12 and 19 Nov. 1932; MAD, 016/ii/79, CCC, National Committee Report, 1935, p. 7. *Daily Worker*, 11 Feb. and 20 April 1936. Labour Party, *Annual Conference Report*, 1940, p. 42. Workers' Film Association, *Annual Report*, 1939, p. 2.

35 NWSA, *5th Annual Report*, 1935, p. 10.

36 *New Dawn*, 10 Aug. 1935. Cf. *New Clarion*, 10 Sept. 1932.

37 See B. Nield, 'Elvin, Herbert Henry (1874-1949)', in J. M. Bellamy and J. Saville (eds), *Dictionary of Labour Biography*, vol. 6 (1982). For labour and temperance, see S. G. Jones, 'Labour, society and the drink question in Britain, 1918-1939', *Historical Journal*, vol. 30 (1987).

38 A. Clinton, *The Trade Union Rank and File: Trades Councils in Britain 1900-40* (Manchester, 1977), pp. 140, 165, 181.

39 Trades Councils, *Annual Conference Report*, 1933, p. 38.

40 R. C. Whiting, *The View from Cowley: The Impact of Industrialization upon Oxford 1918-1939* (Oxford, 1983), p. 176. EP Microform, Cambridge Trades Council and Labour Party Executive Committee Minutes, 5 April and 31 May 1937; Sheffield Trades and Labour Council Minutes, 7 Oct. 1930, 16 June 1931.

41 *New Clarion*, 29 Oct. 1932, 1 April 1933. NWSA, *5th Annual Report*, 1935, p. 3.

42 AEU, *National Committee Report*, 1936, pp. 154, 196; 1937, p. 110; 1938, pp. 153, 173; 1939, pp. 171, 213. *Railway Service Journal*, April and May 1937. University of Warwick Modern Records Centre (hereafter MRC), Mss 126/T&G/1/1/15, Minutes and Record of the 59th Statutory Meeting of the General Executive Council of the Transport and General Workers' Union, 4 March 1937. *Post*, 5 Nov. 1938, 25 Feb. 1939.

43 *Labour*, June 1937.

44 Labour Executive Mins, 27 April 1932.

45 See the *People's Year Book* and *Co-operative News*, passim.

46 National Union of Labour and Socialist Clubs, *Annual Bulletin*, 1932.

47 National Union of Labour and Socialist Clubs, *Annual Bulletin*, 1934.

48 National Union of Labour and Socialist Clubs, *Annual Bulletin*, 1935.

49 *Labour Magazine*, Feb. 1933; *Post*, 30 June 1934.

50 See *Daily Worker*, 17 April 1936. *Railway Service Journal*, Jan. 1938.

51 For details of the Associations, see R. H. Hayburn, 'The Responses to Unemployment in the 1930s, with particular reference to South-East Lancashire', PhD, University of Hull (1970), pp. 264-311. Shaw, 'Attitude of the Trades Union Congress', pp. 324-37. Clinton, *Trade Union Rank and File*, pp. 156-66.

52 TUC, *Annual Report*, 1932, p. 49.

53 *Daily Herald*, 27 Oct. 1932. *Labour*, Dec. 1938.

54 *New Clarion*, 16 July 1932.

55 *Lansbury's Labour Weekly*, April 1925. *Times*, 9 July 1925. TUC GC Mins, 28 Oct. 1928.

56 TUC and NPFA *Reports* for the 1930s.

57 NPFA, *Annual Report*, 1932-33, p. 21.
58 National Minority Movement, *Trade Union Congress and the Workers* (n.d., 1932?), p. 8.
59 Labour Executive Mins, 7 May 1919. Labour Party Organisation Sub-Committee Minutes, 3 June 1919.
60 Labour Party Organisation Sub-Committee Minutes, 5 Feb. and 13 Oct. 1920. J. Ferris, 'The Labour Party League of Youth 1924-1940', MA, University of Warwick (1977), pp. 17-39.
61 Labour Party, *Annual Conference Report*, 1924, p. 24.
62 Labour Party, *Annual Conference Report*, 1927, p. 190.
63 Labour Party, *Annual Conference Report*, 1924, p. 24.
64 Labour Party, *Annual Conference Report*, 1930, p. 28; 1931, p. 13. Labour Party League of Youth *Monthly Bulletin*, May 1931.
65 Ferris, 'League of Youth', p. 169.
66 P. Williams, *Hugh Gaitskell* (1979), p. 51.
67 Labour Party League of Youth, Conference Report, 9 Jan. 1932, pp. 4-5; League of Youth Advisory Committee Minutes, 10 Feb., 14 April and 20 Oct. 1935, 12 Jan. and 10 May 1936.
68 Leeds Archives Department, Acc. 2102 L.P./98, Leeds Labour Party League of Youth Advisory Committee Minutes, 13 March 1935, 14 Oct. and 9 Dec. 1936.
69 D. L. Prynn, 'The Socialist Sunday Schools, The Woodcraft Folk and Allied Movements: Their Moral Influence on the British Labour Movement since the 1890s'. MA, University of Sheffield (1971), p. 202. A partial summary of this excellent history is D. Prynn, 'The Woodcraft Folk and the Labour Movement 1925-70', *Journal of Contemporary History*, vol. 18 (1983).
70 BLPES, YMA/WF/259.
71 Prynn, 'Socialist Sunday Schools', pp. 263, 279. *New Leader*, 13 May 1932. *Co-operative News*, 31 March and 10 Nov. 1934. See also J. Attfield, *With Light of Knowledge: A Hundred Years of Education in the Royal Arsenal Co-operative Society, 1877-1977* (1981), pp. 102-23.
72 BLPES, YMA/WF/331, Herald of the Folk, March 1927.
73 *Ibid.*, May-June 1930.
74 BLPES, YMA/WF/333, Helper, Dec. 1936.
75 BLPES, YMA/WF/27, National Folk Council Minutes, 20 May 1939.
76 Prynn, 'Socialist Sunday Schools', pp. 289-90.
77 For membership data, see Year Books in BLPES, YMA/WF/3.
78 BLPES, YMA/WF/203, S. Cripps to L. Paul, 17 Nov. 1936.
79 BLPES, YMA/WF/26, National Folk Council Minutes, 30/31 Jan. 1937; YMA/WF/33, Helper, March 1937.
80 PRO MEPO 2/3103.
81 *Socialist Leaguer*, July-Aug. 1935.
82 AEU, *Monthly Journal*, Dec. 1936.
83 *Daily Herald*, 3 July 1933.
84 TUC, *Annual Report*, 1932, pp. 54-5. Union of Shop, Distributive and Allied Workers' Library, Manchester, National Amalgamated Union of Shop Assistants, Warehousemen and Clerks Executive Committee Minutes, 18 Oct. and 20 Dec. 1936. MRC, Mss 126/T & G/1/1/16, Minutes and Record of

the 64th Statutory Meeting of the General Executive Council of the Transport and General Workers' Union, 26 May 1938.

85 H. Dalton, *The Fateful Years: Memoirs 1931–1945* (1957), p. 421.
86 *Leeds Weekly Citizen*, 23 Aug. 1929, 25 Nov. and 23 Dec. 1932, 5 Jan. 1934.
87 *Daily Worker*, 8 Oct. 1937.
88 *Labour*, Dec. 1935, June 1936. *Clarion Cyclist*, July 1936, June 1937.
89 J. Saville, 'The ideology of labourism', in R. Benewick, R. N. Berki and B. Parekh (eds), *Knowledge and Belief in Politics: The Problem Of Ideology* (1973), p. 215.
90 *Clarion*, Jan. 1930, Jan. 1931. *Clarion Cyclist*, Jan. 1931.
91 MAD, 016/i/2, CCC AGM Mins, 12 April 1936.
92 *Daily Herald*, 3 July 1933.
93 NWSA, *Labour and Sport* (1934). See the interesting reviews in *Shop Assistant*, 25 Aug. 1934 and *Railway Service Journal*, Sept. 1934.
94 See the contributions of George Elvin: *New Clarion*, 22 Oct. 1932. *New Nation*, Dec. 1934. *Shop Assistant*, 2 Feb. 1935. *Bolton Citizen*, March 1935. *Labour*, July 1935. *People's Year Book*, 1936, p. 242.
95 TUC, *Annual Report*, 1936, p. 275. *Labour Magazine*, July 1933.
96 Labour Party, *Annual Conference Report*, 1928, p. 162. *Daily Herald*, 21 Feb. 1930.
97 Transport and General Workers' Union, *Delegate Conference Report*, 1929, p. 15.
98 *New Leader*, 1 Jan. 1937.
99 *Forward*, 24 Aug. 1929. *Clarion Cyclist*, Oct. 1930. *Labour Woman*, July 1933. Labour Party League of Youth, Conference Report, April 1936.
100 See *Clarion Cyclist*, Jan. 1931. *Labour*, Sept. 1934.
101 *Clarion Cyclist*, July 1930. Unsurprisingly, Tom Groom was anxious about the editorial line of the paper, which seemed to support communist policy. See *Clarion*, May 1931.
102 BWSA, *Sport – Drug or Tonic?* (1939).
103 See *North Tottenham Citizen*, Jan. 1928. *Shop Assistant*, 2 Dec. 1933. *Daily Worker*, 20 April 1936.
104 Elvin Papers, COLL MISC 685/4.
105 *Labour Woman*, July 1933.
106 *New Clarion*, 24 Dec. 1932.
107 *Forward*, 18 Oct. 1930.
108 *Daily Herald*, 23 July 1927.
109 *Times*, 21 Aug. 1930. *Labour Magazine*, Oct. 1930.
110 Labour Party Research and Publicity Committee Minutes, 22 June 1933.
111 *Daily Worker*, 21 May 1937.
112 *Labour*, Nov. 1934.
113 MAD, 016/ii/19, CCC Mins, 21/22 Jan. 1933.
114 Communist Party Archives, Report of NWSA Conference, 27 April 1935.
115 Communist Party Archives, NWSA Executive Sub-Committee Minutes, 8 May 1935. TUC GC Mins, 22 April 1936.
116 See *Daily Worker*, 19 Feb. 1930, 21 April 1933. *Clarion Cyclist*, 1930-31, *passim*. B. Rothman, interview with the author, 3 Aug. 1981.
117 Communist Party Archives, NWSA Executive Committee Minutes, 27 April 1935. *Daily Worker*, 30 April 1935. No doubt due to this action, the Labour Party advised the Falkirk Trades Council that the local branch of the CCC was not 'eligible for affiliation'. Labour Party Organisation Sub-Committee

Minutes, 3 Sept. 1935.

118 MAD, 016/i/2, CC AGM Mins, 12 April 1936; CCC Mins, 16/17 Jan. and 18/19 Sept. 1937; CCC, National Conference Mins. 28 March 1937. *Clarion Cyclist*, May 1937.

119 *Daily Worker*, 17 April 1936. During 1935, there were discussions within the NWSA of fusion with the BWSF. MAD, 016/ii/19, CCC Mins, 18/19 May 1935.

120 *Labour*, Aug. 1935. *Daily Worker*, 15 April 1936, 12 Feb. 1937. *Challenge*, June 1936. TUC, *Annual Report*, 1937, p. 257.

121 MAD, 016/i/4, Liverpool CCC Committee Minutes, 3 July 1938. In contrast, Harry Anslow – a member of the Communist Party and a *Daily Worker* agent – was critical of the Midlands section for being rowdy. *Clarion Cyclist*, Nov. 1936.

Chapter 6

The state, working-class politics and sport

Introduction

In a recent book, Lincoln Allison has argued that, although 'it would seem obvious that sport and politics impinge on one another ... Political science has lagged behind ... other social disciplines in its attempts to get to grips with sport'.[1] From a commonsensical point of view, however, there can be few doubts that sport in modern industrial society is a highly political question, structured as it is, for example, by East–West relations, apartheid, and goverment intervention in the areas of health, welfare and cultural life. Indeed, sport is very much part of the political process, for it is closely bounded by official policy formulation and implementation; that is, sport necessarily involves discussion, debate, even struggle, over physical resources, culture and ideological meanings. Sport is firmly situated in political society, though also constrained by specific kinds of socio-economic limits and pressures. Most of all, the agencies of the British state have impinged on the particular way sports have developed over time.

Social theorists drawn from a breadth of academic disciplines have focused in great detail on the forms and functions of the modern capitalist state. No longer can scholars view the state from general or simplistic Marxist or pluralist foundations, for reinterpretations have sought to refine existing models and introduce new ones. Hence, it is assumed that the capitalist state cannot be seen simply in terms of the crude Marxian focus on ruling-class interests or the pluralist focus on the (imperfect) democratic polity of 'free' elections and politically neutral governing institutions. Rather, following the insights of Gregor McLennan, the methodological approach to the state used in this chapter is that of 'pluralist Marxism'.[2] Here, though the account is still based on the neo-Marxian categories of the capitalist mode of production, exploitation, inequality, social conflict and especially the class character of sport, there is a more open-ended perspective of the state. Crucially, the methodology of 'pluralist Marxism' is very much premised by the need for historically informed analysis. Again, Richard Gruneau has expressed this cogently enough:

> Sports are historically constituted and contested features of human experience and their meanings, institutional shape, relations to class and the state are literally defined by the struggles that have characterized lived social experience at different historical moments. In this way it can be argued that the changing definition and organization of sport in the development of the capitalist societies is indissolubly connected to class conflicts and the conflicting cultural creations of different classes.[3]

In appreciating the need to relate political forms and functions to historically specific conditions of time and place, this chapter will show that as far as sport is concerned, the role of the inter-war state was not just one of facilitating bourgeois interests. The extent to which the state in the 1920s and 1930s could perform the functions of capitalist accumulation, reproduction and legitimation was contingent, shaped by tensions between the various complex institutions of the state – parliamentary assemblies, central and local government, the bureaucracy, the legal system, etc. – and changes in class relations. In brief, the state was not a unitary 'structure', rather an ensemble of practices and institutions which could be deconstructed depending upon the form of socialist or progressive politics. The chapter will argue that the various sporting reforms of the period were *won* from the capitalist state, in no small way due to the demands, campaigns and struggles of organised labour. This will be demonstrated with specific reference to the episodes of access to the countryside and urban sports provision. But first of all, the chapter must examine the salient features of the inter-war state.

The inter-war state and sport

Broadly speaking, the 1880s to the 1930s was a period of crisis for the British state. The sources of this crisis are of course familar, and would recognise the extension of the franchise, the role of organised socialism, industrial unrest, the women's movement, the Irish question and total war. All of this against the general backdrop of relative economic decline. In response to such domestic and external political difficulties, the British state was reconstituted, accommodating and adapting to a new economic and democratic age. Or as one excellent survey has put it: 'The issue at stake was how a new type of state could be constructed, capable of sustaining these new forces.'[4] Though older political and moral values were remarkably durable, the period witnessed the transition from individualism to collectivism. The economic ideology of *laissez-faire*, the individualist ethic and the Victorian moral code were recast and adapted to meet new trading realities, and a change in the balance of social, and indeed class, forces. To be sure, the First World War acted as a watershed, ushering in changes right across the economic and political terrain. Notwithstanding the deregulation of the economy and the drift back to market forces in the early post-war period, the bureaucratic experiments and the turn to new ideological perspectives would not be forgotten. The inter-war years saw a remarkable growth of state activity, be it at the institutional level in the civil service or the schools, or at the level of economic and social policy. It may well have been the case that neo-classical political economy retained its hegemonic position, yet economic and social ideology was the site of contestation, open to opposing viewpoints and perspectives. Though the Keynesian revolution would not happen until after the Second World War, there can be few doubts that Keynes and his followers were an influential voice in the corridors of Whitehall and Westminster, on the Economic Advisory Council, the Macmillan Committee and the like. Furthermore, as previously mentioned, it was in the 1930s that the Labour Party, already a political force that the establishment recognised, was drafting the blueprints for a new economic and social settlement, including nationalisation and socialised medicine. In fact, it was in this decade that the roots of a new policy discourse were laid. The abandonment of the Gold Standard in 1931 signalled the removal of a major policy constraint, and with this came expansionary monetary measures, protection, special areas legislation, more incentives for rationalisation, and a new approach to agriculture. At the same time, of course, a new consensus was evolving over industrial co-operation and planning, drawing in socialists, liberals and Conservatives. By the end of the thirties there was still much to do to consolidate such developments, but in the half-century or so after the so-called 'Great Victorian Boom' the position of the state in the life of the nation had surely been transformed.

Now, this transformation in the role of the state had a serious effect on leisure. The rise of collectivism and general shifts in the relationship of the state to civil society meant that sport and recreation were framed by novel political forces. Crucial here was the fact that as 'new' social disorders emerged – labour unrest, prostitution and juvenile delinquency – there was a tendency to set up new institutional apparatuses, including committees of inquiry, working parties, and even more permanent bureaucracies. By the same token, as leisure was recognised as a specific social problem, it was enclosed within a quite complex battery of rules and regulations. Certainly, the state had intervened in the people's leisure in a more or less ordered fashion from the days of the Industrial Revolution. Not only did the new police and judiciary try to outlaw a range of pre-industrial, often boisterous and undisciplined sports, but both central and local goverment, through legislative intervention, funding and admin-istrative control, provided open spaces, parks, swimming baths and the like. Although John Hargreaves and others have claimed that sport in the 1920s and 1930s 'remained remarkably free from state intervention',[5] in fact this period saw the state's sphere of influence widening. True, this was a function of broader centralising tendencies, but more specifically it was related to the ruling elite's perception of leisure's role in society as a whole, the influence of pressure group politics, and even the internationalisation of sport. These points will be returned to later in this study.

It would be tedious to rehearse all aspects of the state's involvement in sport, so what follows is meant to be suggestive rather than definitive. Government interference in sport in this country was not as systematic or politically motivated as in Soviet Russia, Fascist Italy or Nazi Germany.[6] Even so, it is apparent that in inter-war Britain there were two main forms of intervention in sport. First, the state provided facilities and services for sport as a political, and sometimes ambiguous response to both working-class demands and the wider requirements of social accommodation. Second, certain agencies of the state sought to regulate, even suppress, selected sporting activities. Before focusing on these two mutually reinforcing aspects of state intervention, it is also worthy of note that successive governments were especially sensitive to the question of sport when it had foreign policy implications, as we shall see in the next chapter.

First of all then, the role of the state was most conspicuous in the form of legislation. Intervention of this kind was official, for it seemingly had the support of Parliament and a variety of pressure groups – and so public legitimacy – so important in an age of mass democracy. Anyway, the 1920s and 1930s witnessed a stream of Bills dealing directly or indirectly with one facet of sport or another. Perhaps the most well known was the Physical Training and Recreation Act of 1937, but also important were the Education Act (1918), Public Health Act (1931), Right of Way Act (1932) and Access to the Mountains Act (1939). As a result, both central and local authorities were granted specific powers over sport and recreation.

At this point, it should come as no surprise that public funding for leisure was quite high. Legislative commitments ensured that resources would be made available for an array of amenities. Despite the wish of Treasury officials – most notably Sir Warren Fisher – to keep a tight grip of the public purse and to operate within the context of a balanced budget, the various sub-agencies of the state, particularly the municipalities, retained a considerable degree of autonomy.[7] This is a substantive point for, as two theorists of the local state have discussed, with a large degree of autonomy the potential exists for local political change, no doubt with implications for sport.[8] Relative independence at local level meant that it was difficult for the centre to stop, say, leisure finance from spiralling. Even taking into account the retrenchment campaigns of the immediate post-war years – a time of Rothermere's Anti-Waste Party, the People's League for Economy and Geddes 'axe' – and the early 1930s, evidence culled from the Ministry of Health reports shows that public spending on leisure rose significantly. Though only a fraction of total state spending, the annual current expenditure of local authorities in England and Wales on parks, pleasure gardens and open spaces increased from £1,643,000 in 1914 to £4,973,000 in 1929 and £6,294,000 in 1937; and for the same years, spending on baths, wash-houses and open bathing places rose from £877,000 to £1,896,000 and finally £2,814,000. Across the border in Scotland similar increases were recorded, outlays on public parks rising from £221,793 in 1914 to £742,272 in 1934. It is therefore unsurprising that by this latter date the Ministry of Health should refer to the fact that 'The importance of providing public open spaces and playing fields is being increasingly realised by Local Authorities.'[9] Certainly the social surveys of the period point to local public intervention in sport on a far greater scale than before, though it must be added that there was a dearth of facilities in parts of the country.[10] Even in London, where the County Council had 'attempted since the war to increase the facilities for playing games in the public parks under its control and to encourage borough councils within the County of London to follow its example', shortages were a problem as demand exceeded the grounds available.[11]

Also, from the mid-1930s the Ministry of Labour, through the Office of the Commissioner for the Special Areas, was channelling funds into sport for the unemployed of South Wales, the North-East, Cumberland and central Scotland. In stressing that 'Great importance should ... be attached to physical training and recreation as one of the measures most likely to improve the physique and maintain the morale of the unemployed', George Gillett, the Commissioner for the Special Areas Office established links with various voluntary recreational organisations.

For instance, in hoping 'to assist the development of hiking in the beautiful parts of the Special Areas [and so] bring purchasing power to them', the Youth Hostels Association was approached towards the end of 1935.[13] Though the Ministry of Labour wished for further details and the Treasury remained parsimonious, £10,000 was committed to funding construction of hostels.[14] On the other hand, it was the National Playing Fields Association which made the initial contact with the Special Areas Office, eventually producing the response that assistance would be given to playing field schemes operated by voluntary labour, but not those carried out by waged labour unless they had some overall economic value such as the removal of slag heaps 'which had the effect of repelling industrialists or even visitors from the area'.[15] Additionally, the Office, in collaboration with the National Council of Social Service, encouraged athletics, boxing, camping, cricket, cross country, cycling, football, rugby and walking, and provided equipment, kit and refreshments.[16] Characteristically then, voluntarism was to be an integral aspect of the collectivist approach as reflected in the triangular arrangements between the Special Areas Office, National Playing Fields Association and the Miners' Welfare Committee.[17] To be sure, vast sums were being granted to voluntary (and in some cases commercial) organisations under the ambit of the Special Areas legislation and the rest. Yet such intervention could be sinister, as in the case of the Ministry of Labour's Juvenile Instructional Centres which, though first set up in 1929 to provide some form of training, certainly justified the epithet of 'slave camps', with their compulsory games and physical recreation, as well as labouring work.[18]

This leads us on to our second area of concern, namely direct state regulation and suppression. Put simply, sport was undergoing a process of official bureaucratisation as more and more agencies of the state were being brought in to regulate specific sporting forms. Needless to say, the state was all pervasive in its influence on young people's sport through the educational system. As is well known, the Board of Education responded to the poor bodily condition of army recruits in the first two decades of the twentieth century by promoting physical training in elementary schools. Indeed, as early as 1905 the TUC was also recommending physical training as a 'necessary feature of school life', though military drill was firmly rejected. Despite the lack of specialist PT courses for men between 1923 and 1933, by the 1930s games and sports were an integral aspect of the curriculum. Judging from the Annual Reports of the Board of Education's Chief Medical officer, physical education was a salient question. Though recognising the financial difficulties of the early thirties which meant that 'additional expenditure is not immediately practicable', for the rest of the decade many secondary schools invested in gymnasia, playing fields and swimming pools. Furthermore, the number of 'elite' physical training organisers engaged by local authorities rose from 132 in 1920 to 163 in 1931 and 671 in 1938. There was also a progressive thrust to these developments, for it was women teachers who pioneered many school sports and gymnastics, no doubt challenging crude sexual stereotyping about the role of girls in sport.[19] By 1938 there were seven physical training colleges in England for women, but only three for men. Additionally, women played an important role in such bodies as the Ling (Physical Education) Association, Central Council of Recreative Physical Training (1935) and the National Fitness Council (1937). The Council of Recreative Physical Training, for example, established early contacts with the educational authorities, its grant from the Board of Education rising from £1,000 in 1937 to approximately £14,300 in the year ending March 1939.[20] Equally, the Cambridgeshire area committee of the National Fitness Council received 'exellent co-operation' from the local education authorities, as did the Lancashire and Cheshire committee – at least after some teething problems had been dealt with.[21] Arguably then, the 1930s represented 'the halcyon days of physical education', at least a time when 'the gospel spread further'.[22] Alternatively, the physical fitness movement may have been no more than a mere fad for health and beauty, as satirised nicely in the George Formby movie of 1937, *Keep Fit*. More seriously, the main point to grasp is that, in contrast to the permissive character of much official legislation, schools were acting as regulatory agents of the first order in the diffusion of *compulsory* sports. Even so, such regulation within the state could be progressive, as in the extension of facilities to working-class youth or the advance of female team sports like hockey.

Physical education was not the only sporting area for which public officials had a watching brief. For instance, the Racecourse Betting Control Board 'set a precedent for further state intervention which has enabled racing to survive'.[23] In addition, the fact that the government imposed an entertainment tax on spectator sport – football, cricket and racing – meant that commercial operators necessarily had contacts with customs and excise officers. Yet the best instance of state interference in the cultural and recreational life of the nation was, of course, the setting up of Britain's first public corporation, the British Broadcasting Corporation (BBC). It was the BBC which played such a vital role in both shaping and responding to the entertainment needs of the listening

uch, it is appropriate to note that the Corporation slowly but
ted to cover sports events, and in 1938 all stations began
g on physical education.[24]

Lastly, the so-called coercive agencies of the state were not far removed
from popular sports. Following a long battle of attrition in the Victorian
age, control agencies successfully stamped out traditional rural
recreations and blood sports, though residual elements like boister-
ousness were incorporated into their modern organised versions. By the
inter-war period the police continued to inspect public entertainment and
keep a close eye on the local community for illegal activity. Significantly,
the enforcers of the law were often called upon to patrol sports stadia,
particularly after the troubles surrounding the first Wembley FA Cup
Final in 1923. Aside from the fact that the final led to ground
improvements of some £50,000 to £60,000 and the suggestion that tickets
should be sold in advance,[25] it also resulted in the establishment of a
Departmental Committee on Crowds. The Committee, in stressing that
football 'appears to have the effect of rousing to a greater extent than any
other spectacle the excitement and partisan spirit of the spectators', noted
that it was 'especially important that arrangements for their control
should be as perfect as possible'.[26] Thereafter the police were a familiar
sight at sports grounds, performing a fairly successful peace-keeping role
in the case of horse-racing. And to take but one specific example; in May
1935 the Metropolitan Police deployed 1,167 officers (with total hours
duty of 7,047) at football matches, dog races and horse-race meetings,
though the fact that they were not willing to keep order at greyhound
tracks any longer is indicative of the pressure they were under.[27]

The local police and magistracy also sought to control the informal and
often irreverent sports and games of the street. In some ways the street
was becoming more prominent in the life of urban communities as
distribution and services expanded, and the growth of motor traffic
brought more accidents. Inevitably this created tensions between people
and authority, and also campaigns for more open spaces and facilities.
Even a cursory examination of newspaper sources show that working-
class youth – sometimes organised in street gangs – clashed with the local
state over boxing, fighting, football, pranks, swimming in canals, or
simply larking about.[28] Interestingly enough, despite the fact that a
century before the authorities had succeeded in outlawing pre-industrial
football, there are many press reports showing that young males were
being arrested for playing football in the streets, an activity not unrelated
to the lack of amenities, as well as a reaction against parental and state

authority. Kate Nicholas has discovered that in 1920s Middlesborough, footballing was by far the principal street offence – above damage to property, fighting, gaming, discharging missiles, prostitution and the rest.[29] In 1927, the Sheffield magistracy were also apparently perturbed to find that they had been unwittingly sending youths to prison for street football.[30] And in 1933, after six young Glaswegians had been imprisoned for 'conducting themselves in a disorderly manner while engaged in a game of football', their Labour MP, John McGovern, gave the question national significance when, because of vociferous and unremitting protests, he was suspended from the House of Commons.[31] The question of street games, together with the lack of facilities in some areas, was to be the kernel of Labour's campaign for improved provision.

Equally important as a site of class conflict and negotiation was street gambling. Despite the attempt to prohibit this unparalleled proletarian habit through the 1906 Street Betting Act, working-class communities continued to spawn a network of bookies, touts, croupiers, runners and scouts, often associated with sport. Above all, it is Jerry White's recent oral history of Campbell Road in North London which has drawn out the central importance of illegal betting in everyday life struggles, linked as it was to a hostile, and occasionally violent, relationship with the local state.[32] It is very probable that Campbell Bunk was not the only poor working-class neighbourhood to generate a fiercely independent street culture suspicious of outside interference. All in all, street sports and games, gambling and, of course, prostitution led to varying degrees of repressive intervention by police and judiciary alike.

Scholars have also recognised that in focusing on the forms and functions of the state the class origins, educational background and social contacts of policy advisors, public servants and the like are crucial. If Ralph Miliband is justified in arguing that the patterns of recruitment, world outlook and sympathies of state personnel have been politically biased in favour of capital and the ruling elite, then this would have structured the formulation and implementation of inter-war sports policy in a particular way.[33] Though the institutions of the state need not be working at the *behest* of the capitalist class, they may have been working on its *behalf*. Public officials would have had the opportunity to stress and support certain policy issues, whilst marginalising, even abandoning, others. Though there is plainly a need for more empirical research here, at least at central level the hierarchy of the inter-war state apparatus indisputably had close associations with the public schools, Oxbridge, and 'high' society in general. On the other hand, the state was, and is, a complex of institutions, each with it own traditions, priorities and, indeed, members, and it is likely that competing spaces, particularly at lower and local levels, facilitated the articulation of opposing perspectives. Also, even if it can be contended that the machinery of state is instrumentally connected to bourgeois interests, it does not necessarily follow that policy decisions will automatically support such interests. After all, the working classes were by no means politically impotent (as we shall see), whilst divisions within those sections of the dominant class conversant with sport meant that policy debate was conducted in a highly volatile, disordered and marginal way.

The discussion so far has attempted to outline the salient aspects of state intervention, as they impinged on working-class sport. Notwithstanding the rather sketchy coverage, it should be apparent that the sporting forms of the working class were shaped, if not determined, by the increasingly collectivist tendencies of the day. To some extent, by the inter-war period the fortunes of sport were closely intertwined with the policies of the government, the actions of bureaucracy and the preoccupations of the coercive agencies of the state. This said, it is now possible to focus on the ways in which the labour movement sought to defend and enhance the interests of the working class in sport. Let us now go on to analyse Labour's dealings with the state over the questions of, firstly, access to the countryside, and, secondly, urban sports provision.

Access to the Countryside

In focusing on history as a process of change, it is fair to say that continuity is often as real as the transformative elements. This is certainly so in the case of the British state. Despite the economic and political disruptions of industrialisation and the consolidation of capitalism, many of the pre-modern forms, traditions and rituals of the state remained intact. Of course, political systems gradually wither away and are supplanted by others, but elements survive and grow. To some, the rule of common law, money and tax, parliamentary monarchy, and the rights of the free-born Englishman are seen to be the properties of the Anglo-Saxon nation. To this list could be added the concept of English 'individualism', enfolded as it is by language, marriage, property, inheritance customs, and the rest. It is a matter for serious historical investigation whether or not the resilience of the British state in the post-medieval period owed something to the framework of Anglo-Saxon government. The Norman Conquest, the rise of the yeoman class in the fifteenth century and the English Civil War may have brought in the new, but older forms and patterns of political and socio-economic life endured. Similarly, the transition from feudalism to capitalism was for sure a dialectical process, involving tensions and contradictions between the old and the new. Thus various components of the pre-modern state survived the onset of capitalism. Most of all, the novel capitalist order accommodated older class structures and hierarchies. As both Marxist and non-Marxist scholars have observed, the ruling landed aristocracy, itself increasingly capitalist, maintained a political and cultural hegemony and was able to shape the emerging industrial bourgeoisie in its own image.[34] Now, although this interpretation of the renegotiation of political forms does not give enough space for the ways in which the popular classes used existing institutions like the law to fight for justice,[35] it is relevant for our consideration of access to the countryside.

The fact that the landed elite retained an ascendancy in the nineteenth century was vitally important in shaping the agenda for the development of sport, for the sports of the rural aristocracy enjoyed and conferred status. It has already been noted that the authorities attempted to control many of the more boisterous popular sports of the time. However, this could hardly be said for the sports of the upper classes. The hunting and killing of animals for fun by the wealthy continued unabated, as did their unashamedly intemperate bouts of gambling and drinking. Whilst cockfighting and bull-baiting were quite rightly outlawed, the equally uncivilised 'sports' of deerstalking, grouse shooting and fox and hare-hunting continue to this day. Like the British state, field sports and hunting have their origins in Anglo-Saxon method and Norman ritual, but it was Victorian ideology – hunting became embedded in the imperial experience – and the changing patterns of land ownership and demography wrought by the industrial and agricultural revolutions which determined their modern form. Game laws dating from the time of the Norman kings, together with the enclosure of common land, meant that access to large areas of the countryside was restricted to the rich and powerful. Thus by the nineteenth century the scene had been set for the popular classes' campaign for the greater access to Britain's mountains and moorland.

By late Victorian times there were clear signs of a burgeoning outdoor movement, with the formation of a wide range of botanical, camping, cycling and rambling clubs. Arguably, the demand for fresh air and the peace and solitude of the countryside was a reaction to an increasingly alienated work situation and polluted urban environment, though increased leisure time and pay may have been more substantive factors. However, as Howard Hill has shown, when the people's clubs began to venture into the countryside they found not only restricted routes, but also illegal closures of footpaths.[36] To a degree, the demand for access can be linked to the longer struggle over the rights to common land which dates back to the Norman Conquest. Even so, there was something new about the outdoor recreation movement of the nineteenth century as organised groupings began to legitimise and codify ancient rights in a directly political sense. In 1884, James Bryce, MP for South Aberdeen, introduced the first Access to Mountains Bill in the House of Commons, though like a number of similar Bills before the First World War, it was defeated. Despite such setbacks, struggle against a system which enslaved people in factories and slums, and then prevented them in the name of brutal aristocratic sports from enjoying the relative freedom of the countryside, was bound to continue.

Arguably, by the 1920s the hegemony of rural elites was increasingly contested. At one level, of course, the contribution of farming to the economy as a whole had steadily declined in the previous century. There was also a degree of rural disintegration as country estates were broken up due to personal factors and the rising burden of death and estate duties.[37] Obviously, such economic changes must have had significant cultural implications, especially in terms of the relationship between landed wealth and industrial and finance capital. Nevertheless, as far as field sports are concerned, traditional practices persisted. Despite the launching in 1924 of the avowedly anti-establishment League Against Cruel Sports, the setting up of the British Field Sports Society in 1930 was one reason why a series of anti-hunting Bills in the following years were rejected.

In fact, if anything, the conflict between outdoor enthusiasts and landed elites heightened in the post-war period. Landowners and officials were particularly hostile to ramblers, no doubt seduced by the popularly held belief that they were 'hooligans'. Even in 1942, the Committee on Land Utilisation in Rural Areas could refer to the 'exuberance' of the townsman's reintroduction to the countryside in the 1920s when 'his conduct there was often regrettable', whilst one work of 1946 was aptly called *The Untutored Townsman's Invasion of the Country*.[38] The rural communities' perennial fear of an urban takeover must have been thrown into even sharper relief by increased housebuilding, suburban growth, the advance of motor transport and the petrol station, electricity pylons, and the spread of the wireless and mass entertainment. At the same time, there was a proliferation of urban agencies catering for country recreation.

True, many voluntary organisations like the Commons, Open Spaces and Footpaths Preservation Society, the Council for the Preservation of Rural England, and the Camping Club of Great Britain did not escape the prejudices of their middlebrow origins and composition. Even so, the proletarian branches of the outdoor movement began to grow, and in certain localities took on a distinctly socialist perspective. Many of the rambling clubs had active links with labour groups as diverse as the Clarion, Independent Labour Party, Woodcraft Folk, Young Communist League, and the Co-op. Cyril Joad, the Oxford philospher, author and regular literary contributor to the ILP's *New Leader*, thus described the young people who joined the hiking clubs:

> They profess a love of the countryside, lament its ruin and regard motorists as their natural enemies. Most of them moreover, belong to the Labour Party and have Socialist opinions, including an objection to the private ownership of land and a contempt for keepers as a parasitic class, base minions of the rich. As for farmers, they consider them to be gross reactionaries who embrace diehard politics as an excuse for underpaying their labourers, and automatically oppose all movements for social betterment. Holding these views, it is not to be expected that the young people of to-day who walk through the countryside on Saturdays and Sundays should entertain an exaggerated respect for the rights of landowners.[39]

Perhaps more important than the socialist sympathies of young ramblers was the sheer growth of outdoor sport. At the height of what has been called the 'rambling craze' of the 1930s, there were probably some half a million enthusiasts of the open air. Some of them were grouped in national organisations, most notably the Holiday Fellowship, the National Council of Ramblers' Federations, the Workers' Travel Association (WTA) and the Youth Hostels Association. As such organisations mushroomed, something of a commercialised ancillary industry was stimulated. There was equipment such as climbing boots, rucksacks and tents, hostel and hotel accommodation, cheap rail and bus facilities, advertising, and literature of all kinds from specialist journals to fully-fledged commentaries, guidebooks and topographies. No doubt the relatively affluent ramblers, with their new rucksack, hostel ticket and copy of the latest journal, must have contrasted sharply with the unemployed hiker, often without the train or tram fare to get out to the countryside in the first place.[40] In aggregate terms, however, the proletarianisation of outdoor recreation in the 1930s underpinned the greater willingness to oppose the class position of the landowners.

It is evident that there were many protests at local level concerning the access question, yet at national level the campaign developed at a rather pedestrian pace. In May 1924, P. Gilchrist Thompson, the Liberal MP for Torquay, introduced a Bill in the Commons 'to secure to the public right of access to mountains and moorlands'. In stressing that the public were excluded from vast tracts of land in Scotland, as well as the Pennine range and Peak District, he sought to gain rights for recreational purposes. Yet in spite of apparent support from the rambling community, the Bill proceeded no further.[41] Much the same fate befell Private Members' Bills sponsored by that tireless defender of ramblers' rights and President of the Board of Education in the Labour Government of 1924, C. P. Trevelyan. Even during the office of the second Labour Government, Bills introduced first by Graham White and then Ellen Wilkinson were shelved. According to Ramsay MacDonald, the constraint was 'the congested state of business'.[42] In all, between 1924 and 1931 the six access Bills had done very little indeed to bother the Commons staff responsible for *Hansard*. Moreover, the report of the Labour-appointed National Parks Committee was rather timid – we are told that the landowners were generally liberal – and the position of such national bodies as the Council of Ramblers' Federations was still remarkably acquiescent.[43] The inertia at national level was yet a further pressure for militant local action.

Rambling was especially popular in the Manchester district, where workers sought release from material deprivation and unemployment. A Ramblers' Council was formed at the Clarion Café in 1919 and this joined forces three years later with a Federation of Rambling Clubs to create the Manchester and District Ramblers' Federation. By 1925, there were sixty-six affiliated clubs drawn from as far and wide as Blackpool, Leeds and Nottingham, and by the following year the Federation had been joined by a similar one in Sheffield.[44] Both the Manchester and Sheffield Federations were clearly sympathetic to radical thought and practice. In particular, G. H. B. Ward, as the founder of the Sheffield Clarion Ramblers in 1900, was a profound inspiration. Despite his depiction of the grouse shooter as 'the monarch who reigns despotically', he was convinced that the outdoor life could be used as a means of spreading the socialist gospel.[45] However, the socialist content of rambling could not alter the intransigent position of the landowners. This task was left to groups like the Manchester Ramblers' Rights Movement.

As previously noted, by the end of the 1920s a branch of the British Workers' Sports Federation (BWSF) had been established in the

Manchester area. Under the guidance of its communist secretary, Benny Rothman, it organised a variety of open-air activities and out of this came the Ramblers' Rights Movement. The aim of this movement was quite straightforward: to co-ordinate a mass trespass on Kinder Scout, an area of uncultivated moorland above the Derbyshire village of Hayfield. After considerable leafleting, publicity and, it must be said, opposition from the local press and Ramblers' Association, the mass trespass, perhaps 400-strong, was staged on 24 April 1932.[46]

Without entering into the details here, the trespass is a particularly good instance of class conflict in the recreational sphere, and perhaps the most famous single incident in the history of the movement for access to the countryside. John Lowerson has provided the most succinct, and the fairest, description of the trespass:

> After a 'mass rally' in the village at which they were exhorted to demand open access, low fares, non-militarism in rambling groups, cheap catering and the removal of restrictions on open-air singing, they marched to the top [of Kinder], to be met by temporary wardens. The pushing and shoving that followed saw only a few open fights; then they left. As they returned to Hayfield singing revolutionary songs, five of the 'ringleaders' [plus one other] were arrested and charged with violence and causing grievous bodily harm to one of the keepers.[47]

In a high degree, the trespass had shown that the forces of the state could be mobilised against worker sportsmen and women, not only the repressive agencies, but also, to use Louis Althusser's terms, the 'ideological apparatus' in the guise of the national and local press. After the six ramblers had been arrested by the police, they were sent to trial at Derby before a Grand Jury which comprised eleven country gentlemen, two brigadier-generals, three colonels, two majors, three captains, and two aldermen. The class bias of the judicial hearing is too obvious for further comment. Not only that the sympathies of the press were demonstrated by the fact that most reports of the trespass stressed, indeed exaggerated, its violent aspects, rather than the underlying causes.[48] Even pressure groups like the Commons, Open Spaces and Footpaths Preservation Society were quick to denounce the action.[49] As an editorial in the liberal *Oldham Chronicle* put it: 'The mass trespass movement seeks to take the ramblers' kingdom of heaven by force. The wiser and better way is to gain and keep that heaven by sweet reasonableness.'[50] Unsurprisingly, given this climate of opinion, though one defendant was discharged, the other five received prison sentences ranging from two to six months.

None of this is to argue, however, that the forces of reaction had it all their own way. Even at a time of mass unemployment and political setbacks, the organised working class was not without a voice in the affairs of state. At one level, it is material to bear in mind that a slightly different interpretation of the events appeared in the socialist press.[51] There was also active resistance to the arrests, protest meetings being held in London, the Midlands, the North, Scotland and Wales.[52] By the same token, further trespasses were organised in the North of England, as well as in Scotland and Wales, whilst in London, the Progressive Rambling Club, led by a communist, Philip Poole, was not averse to direct action.[53] As a number of commentators have argued, moreover, the mass trespass aroused a great deal of interest in, and changed perceptions of, the access question:

> it gained the cause of free access to mountains more sympathetic publicity in one day than the Ramblers' Federations had won for it in the previous thirty years ... it was 'The Battle for Kinder Scout' that lifted the movement from the level of 'private members' lobbying to that of mass politics. Its memory still echoes whenever the right to ramble or climb is threatened.[54]

It is true that at a time of 'Class Against Class' the Manchester branch of the BWSF marginalised its influence on the established open-air movement, describing it as militarist and a tool of 'the Capitalist masters' – interestingly, the National Workers' Sports Association did not seem to have a policy line on this particular issue. Even so, the action of militant working-class ramblers undoubtedly reshaped the policy agenda and gave further momentum to the access campaign. Appropriately, John Dower, in his well-known report on National Parks in 1945, referred to the conflict over Kinder Scout, observing that it was 'a special case and may call for a more drastic solution'.[55]

For the rest of the 1930s, certain labour activists continued to struggle for ramblers' rights. Regular demonstrations, for example, took place at Winnats Pass, near Castleton, and numerous supporting articles appeared in the labour press. Notably, in 1933, the socialist and rambling enthusiast, Tom Stephenson, left Transport House to act as a correspondent for the *Daily Herald* and to edit *Hiker and Camper*, a paper partly controlled by the TUC. After a period in jail in the Great War for his pacifist views, Stephenson founded a branch of the ILP in Dartford and then acted as a Labour Party agent. Though he failed to get a job in the Party's research department – the position went to Barbara Wootton – his experience in the directory and records department in the 1920s gave him an invaluable insight into labour politics and also convinced him that his future career did not lie in the House of Commons – 'too much sitting around, smoking and drinking'. Hence his decision to turn to journalism and the open-air movement; he combined his journalistic endeavours with that of leading Workers' Travel Association climbing and walking holidays. Though Stephenson is best remembered as the inventor of the Pennine Way – eventually completed in 1965 – he was generally a tireless countryside campaigner.[56] In 1936, for instance, he was advocating the need for national parks: 'In some districts of outstanding beauty no ordinary planning would suffice, and there is a growing demand that such areas should be scheduled as National Parks to be preserved for all time in their existing state for the enjoyment and recreation of the people.'[57] Obviously, there were many anonymous figures in the countryside movement, yet labour activists like Stephenson contributed immensely to the reforms eventually conceded.

By the mid-1930s, it appears that the authorities were slowly but surely moderating their previously hostile stand. Apparently, even the Peak District Landowners acknowledged 'that they are responsible for a system which operates with increasing unfairness to the community'.[58] Moreover, that most conservative of administrative institutions, the Treasury, was becoming more sympathetic to state involvement in outdoor recreation.[59] This is a cardinal point for the Treasury, as the pivot of modern government finance was able to exert considerable pressure, at least at the centre. As John Sheail wisely comments: 'By the late 1930s the need for some kind of national land-use policy was beginning to be recognized.'[60] This is transparent in the campaign for a National Park in the Lake District,[61] and also in the debates dealing with the Access to Mountains Bill in 1938 and 1939.

The sponsor of the final Mountains Bill of the 1930s was Arthur Creech Jones, Labour MP for Shipley. By way of background, it is interesting to note that he served on both the Executive Committee of the London Labour Party during its 'cultural' phase of the mid-1920s, and the Management Committee of the WTA, having responsibility for a walking and climbing 'knapsack holiday' in the Swiss Alps in 1925. In his opening speech, Creech Jones attempted to relate the demand for access to wider recreational developments, the growth of the Youth Hostels Association, the work of the Forestry Commission, the physical fitness movement and the spread of paid holidays. But above all else, he claimed that the working class should have the opportunity to benefit from the beauty of the open countryside. After all, as one of his supporters remarked, 'How are you to preach your Keep Fit Campaign in smoky Sheffield and Manchester if those to whom you preach are denied access to their native open spaces?' Despite the 'reasonableness and moderation' of the Bill, a point emphasised by Geoffrey Lloyd, the Under-Secretary of State at the Home Office, certain Conservative members rose in opposition. As representatives of the landed interest, they argued that not only was the proposed measure 'a direct attack on the rights of property', but also an attack on deerstalking and grouse shooting. The ironic response of Fred Marshall, Labour MP for Sheffield Brightside, was more to the point: 'HON. Members opposite talk about sporting rights and about grouse. Who eats the grouse? The working men of Sheffield do not eat the grouse. They have a grouse, of course, but it is a mental grouse.'[62] In the end, though the Bill was read a second time, it underwent considerable dilution at committee stage: little wonder then that, despite references to 'offenders against good taste', 'poachers', 'tramps' and the 'ill-behaved rambler', it emerged from the House of Lords relatively unscathed.[63]

The Access to the Mountains Act of 1939 was therefore a weak measure, described by Howard Hill as a 'landowners' protection bill' rather than a 'Ramblers' Charter'.[64] True, the imposition of the infamous trespass clause, which enabled the criminal law to be used against ramblers on wild moorland, was draconian. Yet the Act granted access to limited areas, something which the state had not done before. Most of all, the legislation was important in a symbolic sense as a clear sign that attitudes were changing and that the working class was entitled to certain elementary rights of outdoor recreation. Arguably, it was a necessary step on the way to the more radical and satisfactory National Parks and Access to the Countryside Act of 1949. Also, the 1939 Act should not be discussed in isolation. It has to be seen alongside wider changes in the balance of class forces and structures of the state, and as part of a more general reform movement which included the Ancient Monuments Act of 1931, National Parks in Argyllshire (1936), Forest of Dean (1939) and Snowdonia (1940), legislative concessions over camping, and, as the next section will discuss, urban recreational provision.

Urban sports provision

Chris Waters has shown that from the late nineteenth century socialists in the Fabian tradition pioneered the provision of recreational facilities at municipal level.[65] The Labour Party was therefore following established doctrine when in 1918, in its provocative and radical document, *Labour and the New Social Order*, it put the extension of public enterprise in the organisation of popular recreation in the policy limelight; similarly at the TUC conference of that year, demands were made for organised games, playing fields and school baths – labour was to be the 'players' party too'.[66] From then on, the labour movement on both national and local platforms was to make repeated claims for public sports provision. In 1933, for instance, Labour's National Executive agreed that labour representatives should seek to enter appropriate positions of responsibility in local authorities in order to extend the provision of playing facilities under the 1931 Public Health Act.[67] In fact, labour-controlled councils attached some weight to sports provision. By 1937, leisure appeared in the Party's important policy blueprint, *Labour's Immediate Programme*, as one of the so-called 'four great benefits'.[68] At a time when labour was discussing fundamental questions of social and economic reconstruction, it is significant that sport and leisure were not neglected. Above all, though, policy was essentially reformist, seeking to prise as many benefits as possible out of the capitalist system.

More specifically, labour was concerned that urbanisation had reduced the number of sports grounds. 'The city is gradually encroaching on the land', as Percy Alden, Labour MP for Tottenham South, put it.[69] In the early post-war period, the rather eccentric Labour MP, Jack Jones, quite rightly protested that it was essential to 'preserve the present recreation and sports grounds, and to release more space in parks, so that the young people may indulge in their weekly sports'.[70] Another Labour MP, Robert Richardson, similarly claimed that sports clubs in all parts of the country had difficulty in securing playing space.[71] Now, although some local authorities were providing greater levels of sports amenity, there were still shortages and a reluctance by central government to take initiatives. By the 1920s the role of the state can be viewed as increasingly collectivist, yet *laissez-faire* precepts remained, especially in terms of financial orthodoxy and the requirements of a balanced budget. Clearly the economic ideology of the time was a principal constraint on the emergence of a more dynamic sports policy. As the Conservative Parliamentary Secretary of Health, Sir Kingsley Wood, said on more than one occasion, the provision of sports grounds would be delayed by 'the present need for economy'.[72] Predictably, therefore, a handful of Private Members Bills dealing with open spaces foundered. However, the situation was not static; pressure groups like the National Playing Fields Association, which had links with the TUC, played a vital campaigning role and helped to 'educate' and galvanise public opinion. It was even suggested that the government raid the road fund for resources for sport, though no doubt the parsimonious Treasury official must have been somewhat amused. Besides this, with the election of a Labour Government official policy positions could change.

Bearing in mind that the administrative institutions of the central state retained their crucial leverage over the policy-making process, the Labour Government of 1929-31 supported certain recreational reforms – 'this modest field of Labour endeavour' as Ernest Thurtle expressed it.[73] The new 'socialist' Minister of Health, Arthur Greenwood, may have reaffirmed official policy when suggesting to P. J. Noel Baker that such measures as housing and unemployment would have to take precedence over playing fields in the allocation of scarce public funds,[74] but in fact George Lansbury, as Commissioner of Works, sponsored a 'Brighter Britain' campaign. Despite opposition from the puritan lobby, often using the correspondence columns of *The Times* as their mouthpiece, a range of facilities were introduced in London parks, from boating ponds to sandpits and mixed bathing. In fact, Lansbury thought that the first plunge in the newly-constructed Lido on the Serpentine in Hyde Park should be taken by the Conservative MP for Epping – none other than Winston Churchill![75] Towards the end of 1930, Sir Kingsley Wood referred to mixed bathing in the Serpentine: 'Is this the greatest achievement of the Labour Government?', he asked. According to Lansbury, 'it is certainly one of the most popular in London.'[76] Indeed, not only was 'Lansbury's Lido' to be the best known legacy of Labour's time in office, but also an element in a wider transformation of popular opinion. Changes in the public's imagination are frequently imperceptible and difficult to trace, but presumably the prominence given to play by Lansbury at this time shifted and advanced the possibilities for a more democratic access to sport. Lansbury became known as the Minister of the Open Air, and as such was even able to extract resources from the Treasury. Furthermore, he envisaged a more radical programme of reform, whereby factories would be rebuilt in the countryside with gardens, tennis-courts and playing fields, and Sundays 'thrown open' to the public for pleasure and sport. As ever, ethical socialism pervaded his thought, and like many public school masters before him he wished Britain to 'Pay up and play the game!': 'In the free pure air and sunshine of the seaside or countryside, enjoy all that the beauties of nature can give you, but remember always that life should and will be one glad sweet song when we have each learnt to discipline our own life and conduct . . .

This in turn means comradeship, brotherhood and love'.[77] Unfortunately, the Labour administration fell from power before Lansbury was able to draft detailed plans.

On the broader front, the labour sports movement was also concerned about the question of public sports provision. Given the widely-supported view of one Clarion cyclist that 'the glaring injustice of the lack of proper sports amenities ... should be made the basis of our policy', it is not surprising that demands were made upon Town Councils to provide playing fields, running and cycle tracks, open spaces, gymnasia, and swimming baths.[78] To take but one example. In the mid-1930s the National Government proposed to introduce cycle paths and, as in the previous decade, the compulsory fixture of rear lights to cycles. The CCC and other cycling organisations were against these proposals on the grounds that they infringed the liberties and rights of cyclists. A number of steps were taken: letters of protest and a petition were forwarded to the Ministry of Transport, a campaign committee was formed for the purpose of protecting cyclists against the threatened legislation, and a mass demonstration took place in London.[79] Though the Labour Party was reluctant to make an issue of the cyclists' grievances, by the end of the thirties the campaign had spawned cyclists' defence committees and was even expressed in terms of the class struggle, part of 'the fight for Workers' Power and Socialism'.[80] Indeed, the cyclists' pressure group activity, together with certain administrative and technical constraints, meant that few cycle tracks were built in the period: by March 1938 only forty-one miles of track had been laid, and a further fifty-seven and a half miles were under construction.[81]

Moreover, it is essential to recall that the political role of the communist-inspired BWSF extended to militancy in sport. The revolutionary posturing of certain communists did not preclude the fight for piecemeal reform. Marxists believed that under a communist system of society, the quality of working-class sport would inevitably improve, yet, in the meantime, it was further assumed that there must be a struggle within capitalism for intermediate benefits. Even during the sectarian period of 'Class Against Class' the CP's industrial satellite, the National Minority Movement, called for 'Free sports grounds and gymnasiums for worker sportsmen, with adequate equipment'.[82] Yet it was with the onset of the united front against fascism in the mid-1930s that the British communist movement began to advocate a range of social reforms embracing sport. The CP's notable policy document, *For Soviet Britain* (1935), thus noted that sports facilities under workers' control would make 'it easy for workers to keep fit and enjoy their increasing leisure'.[83] Additionally, in the localities, CP branches like the one at Southall in London were calling for municipal provision:

> Take a walk along the Broadway almost any night in the week. There are always a large number of youths promenading up and down. We hold the view that immediate steps must be taken to provide these young people with proper facilities for recreation, physical culture, etc., and propose that a MUNICIPAL GYMNASIUM should be built in or near the Spikes Bridge Ground. The Labour majority certainly did a very good piece of work when it provided this opportunity for the youth of Southall to take part in open-air sports, under ideal conditions and at a minimum cost, but the long winter evenings still have to be catered for. A fully-equipped Gymnasium, with properly trained instructors in attendance is an additional need which the best interests of the Borough demand should receive immediate attention.[84]

The Young Communist League followed such examples, articulating a programme of sporting demands in its 'Charter of Youth Rights'.[85] And if anything, interest in the sports question increased towards the end of the decade, the newly-elected National Council of the YCL being requested by the annual conference of 1938 to 'study the whole question more deeply and issue a thorough statement of policy'.[86]

Turning to the policy position of the BWSF, it is fair to say that campaigns were organised around the issue of access to the countryside (as already discussed), improved sports provision in inner city areas, and Sunday games. The objects of the Federation thus stressed 'struggle for the provision of better playing and recreational facilities from local and national authorities'.[87] Apparently, sporting campaigns would not be 'isolated from the general economic struggles of the workers'; they would be linked to the issues of the rationalisation, unemployment and the like.[88]

Various sections of the BWSF sought to make recreational gains: not only the Ramblers' Rights Movement in Manchester, but also those clubs in Glasgow as at Bridgetown, Springburn and Townhead which urged the local Parks Committee to improve the city's sports amenities.[89] Yet it was in London that worker sportsmen and women proceeded with most success. It is therefore appropriate here to use the BWSF's struggle within the channels of the London County Council (LCC) for organised Sunday football as a detailed case study of communist-inspired initiatives in the sporting domain.

Members of the BWSF followed the line of Marxist writers like Allen Hutt, who insisted in 1933 that due to the 'parasitic claims of rent, interest and profit' there was a definite paucity of recreational facilities in the capital: 'The provision of sports grounds is not merely scandalously below the need, but is far worse to-day than it was a score of years ago.'[90] To be sure, there was more than a pinch of polemic in this. Yet, notwithstanding the improvements that had been achieved in certain inner London boroughs, there can be few doubts that impoverishment in sport was a fact of life for many workers. Apparently, areas such as Finsbury, Islington, Shoreditch, Southwark and Walthamstow were particularly hard hit, and at a time of Treasury-induced economy campaigns vulnerable to public expenditure cuts. Above all, Michael Condon of the BWSF exposed the kind of society that expected working-class youth to play sport in the streets with little or no equipment, the fear of traffic accidents, and the possible intervention of the police and courts. In examining the lack of decent playing areas, dressing accommodation, sanitary conveniences and even first aid, he emphasised the high cost of the LCC football pitches, the dearth of open spaces and especially the restrictions on Sunday sport, 'the one full day, for many the only day, when they can play games'.[91] Given that Sunday sport helped to mobilise working-class interests, it will serve to provide a focus for the narrative.

Put simply, despite the decision of Eric Liddell, the Presbyterian missionary and Olympic sprinter, to withdraw from the Sunday heats of the Paris Olympics in 1924, and the sustained operations of the Lord's Day Observance Society, the inter-war period witnessed a growth of Sunday sport. Already by the latter nineteenth century, the middle classes had begun to cultivate an interest in Sunday boating, cycling and golf.[92] And true, in the early 1920s, Labour members of the LCC, such as Harry Gosling, who became known as the 'Killer of Kill-joys', succeeded in opening up London parks for unorganised games of cricket, football, hockey and lawn tennis; athletics, bathing, boating, fishing and sailing were already permitted.[93] Even so, the working class found it difficult to participate in club competition on Sundays as the LCC had decided in 1922 to outlaw organised games from Council pitches.[94] As Montague Cox, the County Clerk, reported the decision to the Office of Works: 'The conditions are that no paid caddies or scouts shall be employed by those playing golf and lawn tennis respectively, and that permits for reserved cricket, football and hockey grounds shall not be available for matches in any league, cup or similar competitions'.[95] Interestingly, given the fear that organised Sunday sport would lead to crowds, betting, the exploitation of labour, and above all the emasculation of the Sabbath, the policy of the LCC was imitated by the Office of Works with regard to the

Royal Parks.[96] It was these rulings which lay behind the action of the BWSF.

At the outset, it should be noted that Sabbatarian sentiment had an influence in the labour movement.[97] Needless to say, however, such feelings did not moderate the demands of the BWSF for organised Sunday sport. In the wake of a successful rearguard action against Sabbatarianism in Tottenham in 1930 and 1931, the BWSF turned its attention to the policy stand of the LCC's Parks and Open Spaces Committee.

At this time some twenty-seven football clubs played in the London Workers' Sunday League, thereby infringing the Council's rules on organised games. Interestingly, though such rules had been introduced to stop rowdyism and betting, Brigadier-General Philip Maud, the chief officer of the parks department (1911-35), reported that they were largely irrelevant and should be dropped in the case of the Workers' Sunday League for 'no inconvenience to the public or disorderly conduct on the part of the players or spectators has resulted from these games taking place'.[98] Somewhat curiously, therefore, at least one public servant with flawless establishment credentials – Maud was the son of a vicar and had an impeccable military record with service in India and East Africa – seemed to be siding with the workers' case. Yet despite Maud's continued positive responses, the Conservative-dominated Council decided that all the teams affiliated to the League 'be struck off the register of clubs for whom reserved football pitches are made available', and that their one-guinea deposits be forfeited.[99] Now, given the fact that all of these clubs had links with the BWSF, it is hardly amazing that the Federation should act on their behalf.

Condon, as a leading light in the BWSF and secretary of the London Workers' Football Council, publicised the case in the working-class press and co-ordinated the campaign for organised Sunday football and improved facilities.[100] In pointing out that the Football Council was a body of representatives from 150 football, sports and social clubs, Condon and A. C. Brown of the Tooting Workers' Sporting Club protested that organised football meant 'disciplined orderly football' and democratic control whereby Committees had the 'power to expel or suspend objectionable persons'.[101] However, the Parks and Open Spaces Committee was not impressed: they would not receive a deputation from the Workers' Football Council, a fact not changed by a delegate conference of 105 workers' clubs at Shoreditch Town Hall in August.[102] Slowly but surely, though, due to pressure exerted by Labour members of the LCC, the tone of 'expert' advice, and the growing momentum of the campaign –

which seemingly had the support of 585 teams and the sympathy of perhaps over 1,000 teams by the beginning of 1933 – the Parks Committee relented.[103] As the *Daily Worker* tartly observed: 'it is only after months of agitation that the BWSF has been able to force the Parks and Open Spaces Committee to meet the deputation'.[104] The deputation was received in February 1933, Condon making a passionate speech for the rights and needs of workers' sport.[105] Once again good feeling was evinced by the parks department, and indeed certain concessions were granted: a number of recreation grounds were added to the list of places where Sunday football was allowed.[106] Indeed, central government recognised that 'in view of the present trend of public opinion, we need not object to Sunday play'.[107] Even so, the Parks Committee was still intransigent on the question of *organised* Sunday football – to some extent this decision is unsurprising when it is appreciated that even the Football Association, under its rather conservative leadership, was against Sunday fixtures.[108]

As a result of the Council's failure to compromise, various football clubs in the North Kensington, Regent's Park and West London Sunday Leagues had few options but to continue to participate in organised competitions, as did some unregistered clubs using facilities at Hackney Marsh and Wormwood Scrubs.[109] In addition, by the summer of 1934 the campaign had widened its sphere of influence, culminating in the formation of the Sunday League Football Campaign Committee, with George Sinfield as secretary, and support from the National Sunday Football Association, Workers' Football Advisory Board and a variety of Football Leagues.[110] In fact, at a deputation demanding reduced charges, increased provision of pitches and dressing rooms, washing and accident facilities, Sinfield claimed that the Campaign Committee had the backing of thirty active Leagues, with approximately 25,000 members.[111] Crucially, at the same time the movement was growing, the fact that Labour emerged from the municipal elections of 1934 with a clear majority meant that the LCC could respond to this heightened interest more positively. Side stepping the enraged Sabbatarian lobby, the Parks Committee, with the bricklayer trade unionist, Richard Coppock, in the chair, was 'in no doubt that there is an ardent desire on the part of many hundreds of people in London to play organised competition football on Sundays, and that the large majority of Sunday players is labouring under a deep sense of grievance on account of the action of the Council in prohibiting games of this character'.[112] Hence the decision to rescind all bans on organised Sunday football, cricket and hockey.

Obviously, Labour's electoral victory was instrumental in bringing to fruition a longstanding demand. Even so, the fact that the grievances of worker footballers had been articulated and publicised by campaign organisations under a predominantly communist leadership should be acknowledged. The BWSF and like-minded groups were a force in promoting working-class aspirations and influencing the terms of policy formulation and debate. Though it is not always easy to agree with the statements of the *Daily Worker*, in the case of its sports summary of October 1934 there is no such compunction: 'Sunday football in London is definitely on the map, and is making great progress. The credit for this is very largely due to the British Workers' Sports Federation, who organised the campaign to legalise the playing of League and Cup matches on Sundays on public pitches'.[113] Indeed, not only did the Sunday League Football Campaign Committee achieve further concessions from the LCC, namely additional open spaces – 500 acres during 1934 – and improved amenities, but also was able to conduct its affairs in a peaceable manner; despite increased attendances at Sunday fixtures 'no difficulty had been found in dealing with the public, and that there had been no reports of disturbances and no complaints from the public'.[114] At the same time, the LCC announced its intention to preserve a green belt of open spaces at a cost of £2 million.

Conclusion

This chapter has claimed that as far as the sports question is concerned, organised labour was able to make inputs into the policy-making process and help shape the patterns of policy formulation and implementation. Certainly the evidence suggests that the workers' sports movement was by no means above politics; it was prepared to use direct action, as in the case of the mass trespass, and formal channels of persuasion within the national and local state, as demonstrated by the negotiations entered into with the LCC. Underpinning all of this were the demands for reform made by both Labour and Communist Parties. However, simple reference to demands and political programmes does little to highlight their relevance, specificity or effectiveness. In other words, there has to be some attempt to show the links between labour politics and the concessions made. This is a theoretical and empirical question.

The particular approach to the state taken in this chapter of 'pluralist Marxism' has important implications for the question of Labour's ability to transform the political agenda. Palpably, access to and influence in the institutions of state was structured by an unequal distribution of resources and power within and between social classes. The landed elite, owing to its ability to preserve a negotiated cultural leadership of the bourgeoisie, brought undue pressure on the related issues of field sports and access to the countryside. Through a complex interaction of economic, political and cultural influences, ruling bourgeois interests were able to set the limits and possibilities of policy discourse and concessions. However, these limits and possibilities were historically constituted, dependent on shifting class forces, as well as institutional and political changes within the state. Organised labour as historical agent and political actor was able to find spaces within these (unspecified) boundaries to advance working-class demands. But in what ways?

At one level, in an age of mass political democracy, the representatives of the workers were able to 'capture' perhaps the essential instrument of the modern state – government. The quest for sporting reforms was enhanced in 1929 by the election of a Labour administration, which under George Lansbury's inspiration established some well-known sporting landmarks. By the same token, labour made advances in local politics. After the 1934 local elections, for example, labour controlled fifteen of the metropolitan boroughs, twenty-one county boroughs and eighteen non-county boroughs. Though there is a pressing need for further research into the character of municipal intervention, it can be postulated that labour-dominated councils were a force behind the improvements made in sports provision. After all, sport was an issue which concerned local Labour Parties from Glasgow to Bolton, Pontypridd to London. And, of course, it was a Labour LCC which sanctioned organised Sunday sport and the rest. At least on the surface, some validity lies behind Professor Percy Ford's rather optimistic view of 1939 that 'Pressed by democratic votes, the State has aimed at bringing all this leisure equipment to workers with low incomes.'[115]

At a slightly different level, arguably state personnel, though generally of a conservative disposition and certainly not politically neutral, could advance or support quite progressive claims. Rather than serving ruling class interests all the time or even in the last instance, the state, with its 'plurality of institutions' and its own 'specific privileges', could be an instigator of, as well as an obstacle to, reform and change. E. P. Thompson is surely right to argue that governing 'institutions operate with a good deal of autonomy and sometimes with distinct interests of their own'.[116] The fact is, as Bob Jessop has been at pains to stress, struggles in the state apparatus take place within the overall context of 'structural constraints' and 'conjunctural opportunities'.[117] Hence, within the inner sanctuaries of Whitehall, public servants at the Board of Education, Ministry of Labour, Office of Works and the Treasury discussed, debated and disagreed over a range of recreational questions from the funding of projects to relations with voluntary groups, and the management and regulation of recreation grounds. Significantly here, the relevant central departments of state often delegated their responsibilities for recreation to advisory bodies or quangos. For example, the National Fitness Council, nominally attached to the Board of Education, had considerable executive powers, which allowed it to improve the profile of recreation as a public issue. Underpinning this is the fact that between 1937 and 1939 the permanent staff of the Council, together with the associated Grants Committee, increased from seven to eighty. Moreover, given the relative independence of the local state from the centre, and so the financial and moral dictates of the Treasury, micro-bureaucracies could be architects of reform; thus the favourable reception to the idea of organised Sunday games by the Parks Department of the LCC.

It is also too easy to depict the police and the courts as repressive agencies. Such agencies, repressive or not, were manned by 'real' people in 'real' situations, and the particular style of their intervention in the sporting domain was shaped, however painstakingly and marginally, by attitudes to community policing, the political complexity of the local legal system, and the relations between the people and authority. The views of John Maxwell, the chief constable of Manchester, are revealing. Though in no sense a 'progressive', Maxwell was particularly sensitive to the need for community policing. He believed that the police could not apply undue pressure against illegal street betting because unlike most offences it enjoyed 'the sympathy of the major portion of the public'. By the same token, in order to reduce the number of traffic accidents involving children, Maxwell supported the demand for play areas and other recreational facilities.[118] Furthermore, suppression of street football may have been a direct response to the wishes of local employers, traders, educationalists and other elites, but it may also have been motivated by working-class neighbourhoods themselves, fed up by boisterous behaviour and damage to property. Again, these points need to be followed up by detailed research.

Lastly, the workers' sports campaign fed into ideological construction and helped forge new possibilities for the development of sport. At the very least, Labour articulated people's expectations and in turn gave them further momentum. By the 1930s the 'people' seemed more willing to press forward their demands, and politicians and officials more aware of the significance of sport. One small indication of this is the fact that popular newspapers such as the *Daily Mirror* carried numerous articles and reports on the need for cheaper sport. Interestingly enough, the *Daily Herald* launched a Playing Fields Slogan competition in the mid-1930s; in the end, H. R. Maynard, a civil servant from Kent, won the £5,000 prize for his line 'They live in the shadow – let them play in the sun.'[119]

Moreover, the National Government's Physical Training and Recreation Bill of 1937 was partially a response to the growing assertiveness of the working class in this particular area of social life. Aneurin Bevan, the left-wing Labour MP for Ebbw Vale, criticised the puritanical attitude to sport and the implications for organised recreation contained in the Bill, but like the rest of the Parliamentary Labour Party was appreciative of the need for increased facilities. Labour members acquiesced to the legislative initiative which sanctioned £2 million to begin a national fitness campaign, and the TUC endorsed the objectives of the Advisory Council for Physical Training and Recreation.[120] Having said this, the attempt on the part of the government to promote recreation was considered somewhat hypocritical in the light of poor standards of health – even malnutrition – low wages, unemployment and poverty, whilst at a time of rearmament critics pointed to the military aspects of the fitness programme.[121] As one activist observed, if the government was really concerned about recreation it would have tried to improve the people's health by shortening working hours and furnishing even more resources for sport.[122] Besides, as both the Association of Municipal Corporations and the Metropolitan Boroughs' Standing Joint Committee noted, many local authorities had already pioneered recreation in anticipation of the powers conferred by the Physical Training legislation.[123]

In 1940, the Royal Commission on the Distribution of the Industrial Population reported that urbanisation and industrialisation had made it difficult to preserve public open spaces for amenity and recreation.[124] Nonetheless, whilst recognising the lack of hard evidence on rural and urban local government, the argument of this chapter is that organised labour attempted to rectify such deficiencies with particular reference to access to the countryside and urban sports provision. The campaigns and policy debates of the inter-war period led to short-term gains and laid the foundation for future advances. Indeed, the fact that the Labour and Communist Parties raised the leisure question at the 1945 election was an outcome of the positions taken up before the war. Not only did the inter-war initiatives feed into the radical programme of the post-1945

Labour Government, but they were also connected to wider state involvement in sport. This is especially important in terms of the decommodification of sport. At a time when commerce was exploiting many sporting forms, the regulation of private economic interests and the establishment of public facilities were necessary counters to the spread of commodity capitalism. Significantly, though, it may have been the case that the demand for public sports provision imposed new limits to socialist self-help and labour's creational project by reinforcing the established patterns of domination and subordination within state and society. Furthermore, even in the 1970s socialists like Jimmy Reid were justified in protesting that the lack of sports facilities was a 'scandal'.[125] Labour activists may well have been instrumental in gaining improvements, yet recent history under the Thatcher administration demonstrates that economy campaigns can threaten such improvements.

Notes

1 L. Allison, 'Sport and politics', in L. Allison (ed.), *The Politics of Sport* (Manchester, 1986), pp. 12, 23.
2 G. McLennan, 'Capitalist state or democratic polity? Recent developments in Marxist and pluralist theory', in G. McLennan, D. Held and S. Hall (eds), *The Idea of the Modern State* (Milton Keynes, 1984). See also B. Jessop, *The Capitalist State: Marxist Theories and Methods* (Oxford, 1982). L. Johnston, *Marxism, Class Ananlysis and Socialist Pluralism* (1986).
3 R. Gruneau, 'Sport and the debate on the state', in H. Cantelon and R. Gruneau (eds), *Sport, Culture and Modern State* (Toronto, 1982), pp. 27-8.
4 S. Hall and B. Schwarz, 'State and society, 1880-1930', in M. Langan and B. Schwarz (eds), *Crises in the British State, 1880-1930* (1985), p. 16.
5 J. Hargreaves, 'The state and sport: programmed and non-programmed intervention in Britain', in Allison, *Politics of Sport*, pp. 247-8.
6 See J. Riordan, *Sport in Soviet Society: Development of Sport and Physical Education in Russia and the USSR* (Cambridge, 1977). V. de Grazia, *The Culture of Consent: Mass organization of leisure in fascist Italy* (Cambridge, 1981). A Kruger, 'The influence of the state sport of fascist Italy on Nazi Germany. 1928-1936', in J. A. Mangan and R. B. Small (eds), *Sport, Culture and Society: International historical and sociological perspectives* (1986).
7 R. Middleton, *Towards the Managed Economy: Keynes, the Treasury and the fiscal policy debate of the 1930s* (1985), pp. 44, 51-2.
8 G. L. Clark and M. Dear, *State Apparatus: Structures and Language of Legitimacy* (1984), p. 131.
9 Ministry of Health, *Annual Report*, 1934-35, p. 40. S. G. Jones, 'State intervention in sport and leisure in Britain between the wars', *Journal of Contemporary History*, vol. 22 (1987), pp. 177-8.
10 S. G. Jones, *Workers At Play: A Social and Economic History of Leisure 1918-1939* (1986), pp. 94-7.

11 International Labour Office, *Recreation and Education* (1936), p. 99.
12 *Report of the Commissioner for the Special Areas in England and Wales*, Nov. 1937, cmd. 5595, p. 112.
13 PRO LAB 23/125, F. N. Tribe to J. J. Mallon, 11 Nov. 1935.
14 PRO LAB 23/125, F. N. Tribe to C. C. Allen, 23 Nov. 1935; C. C. Allen to F. N. Tribe, 2 Dec. 1935; B. W. Gilbert to F. N. Tribe, 26 March 1936; Notes of Youth Hostels deputation, 11 July 1936. See also Youth Hostels Association, *Annual Report*, 1936, pp. 13–14. *Report of the Commissioner for the Special Areas (England and Wales)*, Feb. 1936, cmd. 5090, p. 95. *Report of the Commissioner*, Nov. 1937, p. 176.
15 PRO LAB 23/26, Sir Thomas Inskip to P. M. Stewart, 29 Nov. 1934; Sir Lawrence Chubb to R. N. [sic] Stewart, 5 Dec. 1934; Minute of 21 Nov. 1935.
16 *Report of the Commissioner for the Special Areas (England and Wales)*, Nov. 1936, cmd. 5303, pp. 81–2. See also PRO LAB 23/1–19.
17 PRO LAB 23/27.
18 See W. Hannington, *The Problem of the Distressed Areas* (1937), ch. 7. D. Colledge and J. Field, '"To recondition human material ...": an account of a British labour camp in the 1930s. An interview with William Heard', *History Workshop Journal*, no. 15 (1983).
19 S. Fletcher, *Women First: The Female Tradition in England Physical Education 1880–1980* (1984), ch. 5.
20 Central Council of Recreative Physical Training, *Annual Report*, 1935–36, p. 11; 1936–37, p. 40; 1938–39, p. 45. See also H. Justin Evans, *Service to Sport: The Story of the CCPR 1935 to 1972* (1974), chs 2–3.
21 PRO ED 113/1, 8.
22 A. L. Stevenson, 'The Development of Physical Education in the State Schools of Scotland 1900–1960', M Litt, University of Aberdeen (1978), p. 295. Fletcher, *Women First*, p. 86.
23 W. Vamplew, *The Turf: A Social and Economic History of Horse Racing* (1976), pp. 224–31.
24 M. Pegg, *Broadcasting and Society 1918–1939* (1983), pp. 214–15. Stevenson, 'Development of Physical Education', p. 197.
25 PRO HO 45/11627, Sir Travers Clarke to Sir John Anderson, 28 Jan. 1924; Sir William Horwood to Sir John Anderson, 1 Feb. 1924.
26 *Report of the Departmental Committee on Crowds*, (1924) cmd. 2088, pp. 6–7.
27 Figures calculated from data in PRO MEPO 2/3283.
28 See S. Humphries, *Hooligans or Rebels? An Oral History of Working-Class Childhood and Youth 1889–1939* (Oxford, 1981), pp. 121–49.
29 K. Nicholas, *The Social Effects of Unemployment on Teesside, 1919–39* (Manchester, 1986), p. 121.
30 *Sunday Worker*, 4 Dec. 1927.
31 *House of Commons Debates*, 20 July 1933, cols 1994–6. For the general background to inter-war Glasgow street life, see B. Murray, *The Old Firm: Sectarianism, Sport and Society in Scotland* (Edinburgh, 1984), pp. 143–54.
32 J. White, *The Worst Street in North London: Campbell Bunk, Islington, Between the Wars* (1986), *passim*. Cf. Nicholas, *Social Effects*, pp. 123–4, 185–6.
33 R. Miliband, *The State in Capitalist Society* (1969).
34 See P. Anderson, 'The origins of the present crisis', *New Left Review*, no. 23

(1964). M. J. Weiner, *English Culture and the Decline of the Industrial Spirit 1850–1980* (1981).

35 See S. Hall, 'Popular culture and the state', in T. Bennett, C. Mercer and J. Woollacott (eds), *Popular Culture and Social Relations* (Milton Keynes, 1986), pp. 27–31.

36 H. Hill, *Freedom to Roam: The Struggle For Access to Britain's Moors and Mountains* (Ashbourne, 1980), pp. 18–49.

37 See J. Sheail, *Rural Conservation in Inter-War Britain* (Oxford, 1981), pp. 21–47.

38 *Report of the Committee on Land Utilisation in Rural Areas* (1942), cmd. 6378, pp. 26–7. C. E. M. Joad, *The Untutored Townsman's Invasion of the Country* (1946). A. Holt, 'Hikers and ramblers; surviving a thirties' fashion', *International Journal of the History of Sport*, vol. 4 (1987), pp. 64–6.

39 C. E. M. Joad, *The Horrors of the Countryside* (1931), p. 31.

40 Bernard Rothman, interview with the author, 3 Aug. 1981. See also Hill, *Freedom to Roam*, pp. 50–61. J. Lowerson, 'Battles for the countryside', in F. Gloversmith (ed.), *Class, Culture and Social Change: A New View of the 1930s* (Brighton, 1980). H. Walker, 'The popularisation of the outdoor movement, 1900–1940', *British Journal of Sports History*, vol. 2 (1985). Holt, 'Hikers'.

41 *House of Commons Debates*, 13 May 1924, cols 1152–4; 25 June 1924, col. 538.

42 *House of Commons Debates*, 12 Feb. 1930, cols 419–21; 13 May 1931, col. 1192; 14 May 1931, cols 1357–8.

43 *Report of the National Parks Committee* (1931), cmd. 3851, pp. 10, 40. *Out-O'-Doors*, Nov. 1931.

44 A. W. Hewitt, *The Ramblers Federation: Nineteen Years of Progress in Manchester* (Manchester, 1938).

45 EP Microform, G. H. B. Ward Correspondence, G. H. B. Ward, Memorandum in Regard to Mountains and Moorlands (n.d.), p. 3; G. H. B. Ward to J. S. Middleton, n.d.

46 See B. Rothman, *The 1932 Kinder Trespass: A personal view of the Kinder Scout Mass Trespass* (Timperley, 1982).

47 Lowerson, 'Battles', p. 276. Cf. Rothman, *Kinder Trespass*, pp. 23–38. Hill, *Freedom to Roam*, pp. 62–9. D. Cook, 'The battle for Kinder Scout', *Marxism Today*, vol. 21 (1977).

48 See the following papers for 25 April 1932: *Daily Express, Daily Mirror, Manchester Evening Chronicle, Manchester Evening News, Manchester Guardian*.

49 *Journal of the Commons, Open Spaces and Footpaths Preservation Society*, July 1932.

50 *Oldham Chronicle*, 14 May 1932.

51 See *Daily Herald*, 25 April 1932. *Daily Worker*, 26 April 1932. *Worker Sportsman*, 1 May 1932.

52 M. Jenkins, 'Salute to "riotous ramblers"', *Morning Star*, 5 July 1969.

53 Hill, *Freedom to Roam*, pp. 69–75. *Daily Worker*, 18 June 1932. *Young Worker*, 27 Aug. 1932.

54 Cook, 'Battle', P. 243.

55 Ministry of Town and Country Planning, *National Parks in England and Wales. Report by John Dower* (1945), cmd. 6628, pp. 32–3.

56 See D. Rubinstein, 'An interview with Tom Stephenson' *Bulletin of the Society for the Study of Labour History*, no. 25 (1972). *Guardian*, 12 Feb. 1986.

57 *Labour*, Feb. 1936.

58 *Northern Rambler*, May 1936.
59 Sheail, *Rural Conservatism*, p. 184.
60 *Ibid.*, p. 170.
61 F. R. Sandbach, 'The early campaign for a National Park in the Lake District', *Transactions Institute of British Geographers*, vol. 3 (1978).
62 For the debate, see *House of Commons Debates*, 2 Dec. 1938, cols 747–829.
63 See *House of Commons Debates*, 21 April 1939, cols 697–753. *House of Lords Debates*, 9 May 1939, cols 969–97.
64 Hill, *Freedom to Roam*, p. 81.
65 C. Waters, 'Socialism and the Politics of Popular Culture in Britain, 1884–1914', PhD, University of Harvard (1985), ch. 5.
66 Labour Party, *Labour and the New Social Order: A Report on Reconstruction* (1918), p. 5. TUC, *Annual Report*, 1918, p. 391. *Daily Herald*, 2 July 1920.
67 Labour Party, *Annual Conference Report*, 1933, p. 235.
68 Labour Party, *Labour's Immediate Programme* (1937), p. 6.
69 *House of Commons Debates*, 8 July 1924, col. 1974.
70 *Daily Herald*, 20 May 1919.
71 *House of Commons Debates*, 21 June 1920, cols 1741–2.
72 *House of Commons Debates*, 22 March 1926, col. 862; 9 June 1926, col. 1471.
73 *Labour Magazine*, Oct. 1929.
74 PRO HLG 51/49. A. Greenwood to P. J. Noel Baker, 6 Aug. 1929.
75 *House of Commons Debates*, 2 June 1930, col. 1766.
76 *House of Commons Debates*, 3 Nov. 1930, col. 477.
77 *Labour Magazine*, Aug. 1931. *Daily Herald*. 31 Aug. 1931.
78 *Clarion Cyclist*, July 1930, Jan. 1931. *Labour*, Jan. 1937. BWSA, *Sport – Drug or Tonic?*, (n.d. 1939?). Cf. *Daily Worker*, 24 Sept. 1937.
79 See Manchester Central Library Archives Department (hereafter MAD), 016/ii/19, CCC AGM Mins, 17 April 1927; 016/i/4, Liverpool CCC Committee Minutes, 24 Feb. 1935; 016/ii/79, CCC, National Committee Report, 1936, p. 4. PRO MT 39/127, Letters from the Rochdale and Bolton sections and Yorkshire Union of the CCC to the Minister of Transport, 14 March, 3 and 8 Dec. 1934. *Challenge*, 23 March 1935. *Daily Worker*, 26 Aug. 1935. *Clarion Cyclist*, Aug. 1936.
80 Labour Executive Mins, 29 Sept. 1935, 26 Feb. 1936. *Challenge*, 6 Jan. 1938. *New Leader*, 28 Jan. 1938.
81 PRO MT 39/127, A. Y. Y. Robinson to H. R. Watling, 20 Jan. 1939.
82 *Worker*, 4 April 1931.
83 CP, *For Soviet Britain* (1935), p. 39.
84 Southall CP, *Communist Plan For Southall* (n.d. 1937?), pp. 7–8.
85 See *Challenge*, Dec. 1936.
86 *Our Youth: Discussion Magazine of the YCL*, May 1938, April 1939.
87 *Sport and Games*, Jan. 1932.
88 Programme of Demands of the BWSF, n.d.
89 See *Daily Worker*, 22 Aug. and 5 Sept. 1931, 22 Nov. 1932. *Worker Sportsman*, 1 May and Aug. 1932.
90 A. Hutt, *The Condition of the Working Class in Britain* (1933), pp. 175–6.
91 T. M. Condon, *The Fight for the Workers' Playing Fields* (n.d., 1931?).
92 See J. Lowerson, 'Sport and the Victorian Sunday: the beginning of middle-

class apostasy', *British Journal of Sports History*, vol. 1 (1984).
93 See *Times*, 10 and 12 July 1922. *Record*, 12 July 1922. H. Gosling *Up and Down Stream* (1927), pp. 102–3. H. Snell, *The Case for Sunday Games, Against Sabbatarian Prejudice* (1923).
94 *Times*, 24 July 1922.
95 PRO WORK 16/559, M. Cox to the Secretary HM Office of Works, 18 Sept. 1922.
96 PRO WORK 16/559, E. H. Bright to M. Cox, 3 Oct. 1922; Notes of a conference on the subject of Sunday games, 17 Oct. 1922. The Office of Works thus refused to allocate ground in Regent's Park on Sundays to the hockey team of the West Central Jewish Girls' Institute. H. Bird to Miss L. H. Montagu, 8 Nov. 1922.
97 See S. G. Jones, *The British Labour Movement and Film, 1918–1939* (1987), pp. 130–4.
98 Greater London Record Office (hereafter GLRO), LCC Parks and Open Spaces Committee Papers, 22 April 1932, no. 28, Report from P. Maud, 11 April 1932.
100 *Daily Worker*, 6 June 1932. *Worker Sportsman*, July 1932. *Young Worker*, 27 Aug. 1932. Interestingly, there seems to have been some opposition to the BWSF in the London Workers' Football Council. BWSF Mins, 29 July 1932.
101 GLRO, Parks and Open Spaces Committee Papers, 17 June and 15 July 1932, T. M. Condon to LCC, 4 June 1932; A. C. Brown to LCC, 18 June 1932.
102 GLRO, LCC Parks and Open Spaces Committee Mins, 17 June 1932; Parks and Open Spaces Committee Papers, 21 Oct. 1932, T. M. Condon to LCC, 1 Sept. 1932. *Daily Worker*, 16 Aug. 1932.
103 GLRO, LCC Mins, 1 Nov. 1932; LCC Parks and Open Spaces Committee Mins, 18 Nov. 1932, 27 Jan. 1933; Parks and Open Spaces Committee Papers, 27 Jan. 1933, T. M. Condon to LCC, 21 Jan. 1933.
104 *Daily Worker*, 1 March 1933.
105 See T. M. Condon, *The Case For Organised Sunday Football* (1933).
106 GLRO, Parks and Open Spaces Committee Papers, 10 March 1933, Report of P. Maud; LCC Parks and Open Spaces Committee Mins, 10 March 1933.
107 PRO WORK 16/559, Memoranda, 19 May 1933.
108 GLRO, LCC Parks and Open Spaces Committee Mins, 24 March 1933; LCC Mins, 4 April 1933. For the FA and Sunday football, see S. Inglis, *Soccer in the Dock: A History of British Football Scandals 1900 to 1965* (1985), ch. 9.
109 GLRO, Parks and Open Spaces Committee Papers, 8 Dec. 1933, Report by P. Maud.
110 GLRO, Parks and Open Spaces Committee Papers, 15 June 1934, F. Terry and G. Sinfield to LCC, n.d.
111 *Daily Worker*, 15 June 1934.
112 GLRO, LCC Mins, 10 July 1934.
113 *Daily Worker*, 16 Oct. 1934.
114 GLRO, LCC Parks and Open Spaces Committee Mins, 19 Oct. 1934, 31 May 1935; LCC Mins, 30 Oct. 1934.
115 *Listener*, 1 June 1939.
116 E. P. Thompson, *The Poverty of Theory and other Essays* (1978), p. 48.
117 See Jessop, *Capitalist State*.

118 See, for example, *Minutes of Evidence Taken Before the Royal Commission on Lotteries and Betting* (1932), pp. 51–62. Johnston, *Marxism*.
119 *Daily Herald*, 20 Aug., 2 and 14 Sept., 3 and 19 Oct., and 18 and 30 Nov. 1935. National Playing Fields Association, *Annual Report*, 1935–36, p. 26.
120 *House of Commons Debates*, 7 April 1937, cols 193–284. TUC, *Annual Report*, 1938, p. 238, See also PRO ED 113/1–85.
121 *Labour*, Dec. 1936, Feb. 1937. *Daily Worker*, 12 Feb. 1937. British Library of Political and Economic Science, George Elvin Papers, COLL MISC 685/2, Manifesto of the London Labour Sports Association in Connection with the Physical Culture Proposals of the Government.
122 *Challenge*, 14 April 1938.
123 See PRO HLG 52/902.
124 *Royal Commission on the Distribution of the Industrial Population: Report* (1940), cmd. 6153, pp. 76–7.
125 J. Reid, *Reflections of a Clyde-Built Man* (1977), pp. 153–4.

Chapter 7

'Sport under red flags': the working class and international sport

Introduction

Preceding chapters of this study have focused on the domestic dimensions of the working-classes' relationship to sport. It is appropriate, however, to widen the discussion to include the international perspective. After all, like the economy in terms of overseas trade and politics in the context of international relations, sport is a global phenomenon. Indeed, sport itself is inextricably linked to world trade and world politics. The Olympics as the apotheosis of the international sports movement have continually demonstrated their link with commerce and politics ever since the modern Games were launched in Athens in 1896. Hence the 1900 Paris Games were an integral aspect of the Great Exhibition, whilst the St Louis Games four years later were held in conjunction with the World Fair. More generally, given that the Olympics were reconstituted in an atmosphere where national chauvinism gained expression through culture, as well as economic, political and military forms, they were bounded from the outset by international politics.[1] Or as one commentator has put it, 'the Games were seen as a proving-ground for national prestige; a country's organisational capacity and financial endowment were tested by its ability to host the Games'.[2] What this means, of course, is that analyses of sport which neglect the international scene do so at their peril. Before moving on to discuss the international side of the workers' sport movement, there is a need first to provide a brief discussion of Britain's role in the evolution of world sport.

British sport has exerted significant pressure on, and also been influenced by, developments at the global level. Needless to say, in sports dominated by the middle classes, Britain has been the home of major events, the Open in golf and Wimbledon in lawn tennis being the premier examples. And in other sports too, the British have been involved in a substantial export initiative. The people's game of association football is a particularly good instance of a sport diffused abroad by English and Scots at play. Though Britain was not the only force behind the spread of

164

football, British commerce, education and the army were vital influences in the introduction of the game to all parts of the globe. The game as developed in such countries as Argentina, Brazil, Rumania, Russia, Spain and the colonies benefited from enthusiasts drawn from British bankers and businessmen, clerks and manual workers, teachers and officers.[3]

Cricket, golf, horse-racing – the 'sport of kings' – hockey, rugby, tennis and even the genteel sport of croquet have also been transplanted overseas, often the more acceptable face of brutal Empire-building. In a stimulating essay, Brian Stoddart has claimed that sport was a potent element in the construction of what he terms imperial 'cultural power'. Sport, together with education and religion – which themselves actually helped to instil the games ethic – was a cultural support to the exercise of military authority, often defusing discontent and pre-empting the need for coercion. From Australia to South Africa, India to the West Indies, sport apparently consolidated the British power network through its heirarchical organisation, patronage, patterns of participation and exclusion, Empire Games, and the centralisation of authority in London.[4]

This is not to enter into an ethnocentric or Anglocentric history of the world, for clearly many so-called Third World countries have developed their own games, pastimes and traditions – some stamped out by the colonising process – and also taken over and recast British and European sports. It is indeed salutary to read the work of C. L. R. James to see the way in which the West Indies has used cricket in accordance with their own culture, institutions and values.[5] Thus, though Richard Burton has tentatively raised the point that cricket in the Caribbean may act as a kind of safety valve for popular grievances, more persuasively he demonstrates that the game has evolved not merely as a cultural imposition from above by imperial and planter elites, but also out of the lived experiences of the black population, through the play and sociability of slave resistance, carnival, games like stick-fighting, and male street culture.[6] Moreover, cricket and other games could be a clear sign of incipient nationalism and a new assertiveness, especially when the defeat of English touring sides symbolised colonial parity, even supremacy. Though at a time when the independence movement was beginning to gain ground in the 1930s sport may have played an important role in cementing Empire, its political manifestations as a symbolic form of domination or emancipation and a diplomatic bargaining ploy were apparent for all to see. Lastly here, it has to be recalled that by the inter-war period, Britain actually imported sports such as speedway from Australia, and black cricketers like George Headley and Learie Constantine – who in his autobiography was critical of the established order in English cricket.[7] Britain as the first industrial nation with an Empire at one time spanning five continents played a starring role in the development of world sport, but even under imperial domination sports could display an urgent transformative impulse.

This discussion of Britain's place in the history of world sport has some relevance to this study. It is as well to remember that international sport as reflected in the Olympics and Empire was, and is, of such importance as to influence workers' views on sport. Also, the exploitative institutions and relationships of Empire were to some extent behind the rise of alternative labour movements, including those dealing with workers' sports. True, the pioneers of the international workers' sports movement were found across the Channel. For socialist sport in Britain before the Great War was vitiated partially by the economism of the labour movement, together with the fact that commerce and bourgeois amateurism were able to exercise levels of authority over certain major sports. Notwithstanding the recreational activities associated with the Clarion and other socialist groupings, the Continental labour movement, especially in Germany, paid much more attention to sport. However, the fact that the international workers' sports movement centred on the Continent should not lead us to believe that British socialists were redundant in this sphere. It is the purpose of this chapter to show that the British labour movement played a part in international sport. The chapter will focus on the inter-war position of the European workers' sports movement, and the sporting and political points of contact with the organised working class in Britain.

The European workers' sports movement

The origins of organised workers' sport on the Continent can be traced to the end of the nineteenth century. Most crucially, 1893 saw the formation of what was to become the largest workers' sports organisation, the German Workers' Sports and Gymnastic League. The League had been founded as a consequence of the anti-socialistic laws which led to the expulsion of social-democratic clubs from the bourgeois Gymnasts' Association.[8] Yet the initiative for independent working-class sport also came from the labour and socialist movement itself. As has been well chronicled, German labour sponsored a thriving workers' culture movement; that is, a kind of sub-culture, consisting of education, music, theatre and even photography. In late nineteenth-century Düsseldorf, for example, the socialists established singing clubs, a theatre association, a bowling club and a stenographers' group. Sport was of course included in all of this, so that by 1914 Düsseldorf had a popular socialist athletic club, as well as a variety of recreation societies catering for cycling, football, swimming and the rest.[9] Nationally, the workers' sports movement attracted thousands of supporters before the First World War.[10]

At this time workers' sport also became popular in other central European nations, especially the Czech lands of the Austro-Hungarian Empire. In addition, by the early twentieth century groups had been set up in Austria, Belgium, France, Switzerland and, as already discussed, Britain.[11] Indeed, in August 1912, the second Socialist International discussed workers' sport, undertaking a survey among member sections. And in the following year representatives of the European workers' sports movement met in Ghent to form the short-lived Socialistic International for Physical Education. Given that European socialists then believed that an impending war would be averted by proletarian solidarity and the refusal of the working class in each country to take up arms, the new International was to be an agency for promoting such beliefs. With some notable exceptions, however, when war came in August 1914 socialists supported the position of their respective national governments and were swept along on a wave of patriotic fervour. Nonetheless, though the outbreak of military conflict cut short the activities of the International, a start had been made in uniting the various national sporting organisations. After the war, against the general backdrop of international reconstruction, the notion of working-class solidarity on and through the sports field revived, and a further conference in Lucerne in September 1920 created the International Union for Physical Education and Workers' Sport, later renamed the Socialist Workers' Sports International (SWSI). The aims of the reconstituted Sports International, which was essentially social democratic in emphasis, 'were to re-create among worker sportsmen the unity which had been shattered by the war, to develop the national workers' sports movements and to generate among workers sport activity that was truly international'.[12]

Throughout the inter-war period social democratic sportsmen and women stressed the principles of pacifism and internationalism, drafting statements that sport could function as a form of world brotherhood and part of the struggle against the evils of nationalism and militarism. As Fritz Wildung, a socialist sport ideologist, declared at the third congress of the SWSI in 1922:

Our International Association for Sport and Physical Culture differs from the political and trade union internationals in that it brings its members together to action ... In our sporting events we must face each other eye to eye and get to know that none of the others is an enemy, but rather that all men are brothers ... We have the most powerful interest that the great world-wide lies spread by capitalism finally be destroyed, that the people learn that they are a thousand times more unified than divided.[13]

The social democratic wing of the movement was essentially reformist, seeking to build sporting and political alliances between the main European nations. The emphasis was on co-operation with the Continental working class and conciliation with Continental nations in general.

Following on from this, the movement believed that competitive games were less important than pursuits like cross-country running, gymnastic displays and rambling, in which large numbers of people could participate. True, competitive sports were well supported by workers, a fact appreciated by Wildung:

> We are still living in the social order of the bourgeoisie, and to some extent we are still captive to its spirit. Public taste is not oriented toward finding serious educational benefits in physical exercises, but rather sensationalism in competitive sport; one need only think of boxing matches or six-day bicycle races. Very large numbers of workers are still devoted to these sensational sporting events and make up a large part of their spectators.

No doubt reflecting the popularity of boxing, football and the like, but also the view that competition was legitimate, if edifying and disciplined by society, the workers' sports movement also sponsored competitive games.[14] Yet, at least on the surface, workers' sport would encourage those endeavours which were less competitive. Sporting fellowship was to be stimulated at the expense of training talented individuals and prioritising outstanding performances. In some ways this reflects the fact that social democratic precepts of sport were not divorced from socialism. That is to say, there was more about the philosophy of sport peculiar to socialists than notions of international peace and brotherhood. In brief, socialists outside the communist movement also believed that workers' sport could be an avenue by which bourgeois ideology and culture could be challenged and ultimately undermined. There was a pressing need for a socialist alternative to counter the evils of capitalist society and serve the interests of the working class. If 'Peace through Sport' was the dominant element in the labour movement approach, then this was informed in a rather complex and contradictory way by an opposition to bourgeois society, sport and leisure.

By the early 1920s the European workers' sports movement was split between the social democratic International and the communist-sponsored Red Sports International (RSI). The RSI was formed in Moscow in 1921, and in contrast to the SWSI was revolutionary in emphasis:

> The formation of workers' gymnastic and sport organisations is necessary in order to make the toiler, and especially the toiling youth, physically capable of the efforts demanded by the proletarian class struggle, and in order to draw them away from the bourgeois gymnastic and sport organisations. Sport organisations are not, and cannot be, politically neutral bodies. For the bourgeoisie, as well as for the working class, they are a means for the carrying out of the definite tasks in the class struggle.[15]

Indeed, there was a strong belief that so-called 'toiling youth' were being brought under the influence of bourgeois ideology through capitalist sports propaganda in the press and increasing sports provision in middle-class associations, companies, schools, the armed forces and the rest.[16] Yet, at least initially, it was quite rightly recognised that because working-class youth often preferred sport to politics there was a need for revolutionaries to combine their own political outlook with the more spontaneous inclinations of the masses.[17] In reality, however, there was little attempt to understand working-class culture at anything other than a cosmetic level; rather, initiatives took place under the grip of Soviet power and ideology. Though the Communist International (formed in 1919) did not play a leading role in the foundation of the RSI and failed to deal with sport until its fifth congress in 1925, the fact that the RSI had a centralised structure of organisation undoubtedly was witness to the wider needs of Moscow. In contrast to the relatively decentralised SWSI, whose national sections had a great deal of autonomy and whose international bureau met in numerous European cities, the activities of the RSI were invariably centred on Moscow, though Berlin, Copenhagen, and finally Prague were to act as headquarters in the 1930s. In any case, the RSI was close to the Communist Youth International and to the development of physical culture within the USSR itself.[18]

Accepting the constraints imposed by the fragile economic environment of War Communism and then the New Economic Policy, sport was important to the fledgling Soviet system, for according to Lenin 'a nation cannot be strong, unless it is strong in sports'.[19] In 1925, the central committee of the Russian Communist Party further appreciated that sporting contact would 'strengthen the international labour front'.[20]

However, it must be stressed that the emergence of reformist and Marxist sport factions actually divided the international movement. Despite the repeated calls of the RSI for unity in sport, at least until the end of the 1920s, a move towards reconciliation came only with the united front against fascism in the late 1930s. Indeed, during the infamous third period of the Communist International from about 1929 to 1935, when the strategy of 'Class Against Class' operated, the RSI branded the SWSI as 'social fascist' in character and policy. In brief, workers' sport was intimately related to wider political developments and ideological shifts in the socialist movement.

It is appropriate here to stress the main difference between the SWSI and the RSI. As noted above, the RSI perceived sport as a force in the class struggle, an avenue by which European workers could be united in a revolutionary offensive against imperialism and the world's ruling elites, rather than an expression of internationalism and pacificism. The SWSI, in contrast, wished to create better sports provision for the working class within the existing capitalist arrangement. Now, it is true that communists and social democrats agreed in opposing capitalism and militarism, yet there were differences over strategy. Thus to take but one example; a distinction arose between communist and social democratic conceptions of sport and defence; for the former sport was to be one means of attack in the abridgement of the class struggle, for the latter only a means of defence in breaking violence directed against the working class.

Notwithstanding the divisions in the European workers' sports movement, however, it did record considerable growth and was able to organise many sporting events. In 1927, the SWSI had 1.3 million members in eighteen national constituencies, the largest of which were in Germany with 913,786 members, Czechoslovakia with 153,188 and Austria with 144,016.[21] The RSI also expanded with affiliated sections throughout the world; there were 3,750,000 members in 1928, though ninety-five percent of these were Russian.[22] By the close of the 1920s the two sports Internationals had a combined membership probably in excess of five million, making sport the most popular recreational and cultural activity in the socialist movement. It is true that the Nazis disbanded the German organisation in 1933, but workers' sports continued to flourish in other countries during the 1930s.

At this point it is necessary to focus on the relationship between the workers' sports movement and the wider culture of which it was a part. It is now almost twenty-five years since Gunther Roth coined the phrase 'negative integration' to express the function of the German social-democratic sub-culture, namely its inability to pose a revolutionary threat to the imperial order.[23] Today, many commentators on German Labour movement culture have rejected Roth's thesis. Without detailing the debate, as Vernon Lidtke has protested, there were many aspects of labour's social–cultural milieu which were destabilising forces. Also, it is acknowledged that a need exists to consider the positive links between the social and cultural endeavours of organised labour and the rest of society.[24] Here, Richard Evans has perceptively distinguished between labour movement culture and the working-class culture of everyday life in the workplace, the community and the home. He suggests that labour movement culture, like workers' sport, was formed around and catered specifically for labour activists in political parties and trade unions, and never 'played such a central role in working class life or encompassed a majority of the working class'.[25] This is certainly true of many sections of the European proletariat. Research carried out by Lidtke, Steinberg, Wheeler and others has pointed to the fact that labour culture was held together by such influences as occupational identification, class awareness, and a broad socialist ideology. Yet, though it cannot be doubted that the European workers' sports movement was a pulsating expression of proletarian associational life and creativity, it did not have the same levels of political and cultural significance as did the non-socialist voluntary organisations. Despite variations in estimates of membership, in the immediate pre-war period the Arbeiter-Turnerbund (Workers' Gymnastic Federation) had 153,000 members compared to the 1,340,000 on the rolls of the bourgeois Deutsche Turnerschaft (German Gymnastic League).[26] At the same time it is likely that the German masses were enthusiastic consumers of commercialised culture: on the eve of the war there were 2,446 permanent cinemas in the Reich, and many successful forms of low-grade literature or *schund* (trash).[27] Again in the post-war world, the workers' sports movement did not attract the same numbers as did non-socialist groupings.

Soon after the war the majority of West European nations introduced the eight-hour day or forty-eight hour week. Between the armistice of November 1918 and the end of 1919 legislation and collective agreements dealing with the eight-hour day were finalised in many countries. And at the global level the newly formed International Labour Organisation was actively involved in the question, having drafted a worthy Hours Convention in 1919. By 1922 the forty-eight hour week was a norm for a preponderance of European industrial workers.[28] More specifically, the

French eight-hour law was enacted in April 1919 in the wake of strikes throughout Europe for shorter hours and the threat of industrial action by the French Trade Union Confederation (CGT).[29] Yet the legislation was more than a response to trade union pressure. It provided a respite from industrial fatigue, and an acknowledgement that reduced working time could help to improve productivity and facilitate greater employment.[30] But most of all, as Gary Cross has cogently argued, the movement for the eight-hour day must be seen in the context of 'a quest for leisure'.[31]

Without doubt, the working time reductions of the early 1920s had broad implications for leisure behaviour. It is even possible that they acted as a catalyst in the development of new forms of sport and leisure. Before the war the average working week in Western Europe was about fifty-four hours, but by the early 1920s it had come down to approximately forty-eight. Also important here is the fact that overtime working did not seem to present much of a problem, at least in some countries.[32] Under such circumstances sports flourished.

Eugen Weber has argued that prior to 1919 there was not a great deal of free time for sport in France, and consequently organised sport was narrow in scope.[33] However, after the eight-hour legislation there was 'a phenomenal upsurge in lower-class sport', and all in all the twenties and thirties witnessed a considerable rise in those participant sports formerly restricted to the affluent.[34] The number of football clubs, for example, rose from 659 in 1919 (when the Football Federation was founded) to 3,983 in 1923.[35] Furthermore, as the French Ministry of Labour discovered, reduced hours of work had not led to an increase in drinking; on the contrary, it was sport and gardening which benefited.[36]

In other West European countries the shorter day was said to have had a fundamental impact. In Germany, such sports as rowing, tennis, and especially soccer were taken over by the masses following the eight-hour law of 1918. The membership of the German Soccer Association, for example, increased from 150,000 in 1919 to over one million a year later.[37] Little wonder then that Gerhard Ritter has claimed that organised mass sport in Germany became 'of major importance after the first world war'.[38] Similarly, in Austria and Finland the eight-hour day served as the basis for a marked expansion of games and pastimes whilst in the Netherlands there was 'astonishing growth around 1920': between 1910 and 1920 the number of football clubs rose from 7,500 to 48,000, gymnastic clubs from 6,000 to 8,000 and swimming clubs from 2,000 to 6,000.[39] In Sweden as well, the hours legislation of 1919, which came into operation in 1920 and brought down net working hours from fifty-five to forty-eight a week, helped to popularise sport among the working classes. Skiing became the main winter sport, and football the main summer sport. In 1918, the National Federation of Swedish Gymnastic and Sports Societies had 80,000 members on its rolls, but by 1923 it had 140,000 members. The Federation itself was definitely of the opinion that the shorter working day had aided the vigorous development of sport:

> Hours of work must be considered to have an important influence on the practice of sport in this country, not only on account of the real increase in leisure enjoyed by young sportsmen, but also on the more favourable distribution of spare time made possible by the Act on working hours. Moreover, it cannot be denied that the systematic practice of sport, and especially training, demands considerable physical exertion, so that there can be no doubt that the statutory limitation of the working day has contributed much towards the promotion of sport by limiting daily physical exertion at work and leaving more energy for sport.[40]

It is of course true that trends in inter-war sport were inseperable from, *inter alia*, the demand for more autonomous leisure as a compensation for the rigours and monotony of work, the growth of purchasing power and paid holidays, public policy (especially in the fascist countries, where the Italian Dopolavoro and the Nazi office of the Reichssportführer sought to organise sport and leisure in order to boost production and reinforce totalitarian authority and ideology), and the continued search for means of social control. Yet above all, accepting the marginal setbacks of the later 1920s and 1930s, a crucial force behind the expansion of mass sport was the hours reduction of the 1918-20 period.

Of course, such trends also affected workers' sport. Even so, there can be few doubts that the fillip given to bourgeois sports organisations meant that they dwarfed their socialist counterparts. For instance, in 1926 the Dutch socialist youth's attempt to promote sports without competition foundered due to the counter-attractions of bourgeois sporting clubs.[41] No doubt the failure was also related to the penetration of Dutch commerce into the leisure domain, represented by the growth of broadcasting, cinema, reading and spectator sport.[42] Indeed, commercialised entertainment such as film-going – at their peak in 1937 the leading European countries had 66,320 cinemas, 24,759 of them wired for sound – were attractive alternatives to workers' sport. True, the French left's sporting initiative, the Fédération Sportive et Gymnique du Travail (FSGT), was strong in the mid-1930s, no doubt inspired by the election of a Popular Front Government in 1936 with a commitment to a radical sports policy. Yet even this initiative was a minnow compared to the much larger Catholic youth clubs with 200,000 members, and such central sporting bodies as the Fédération Nationale de Boulistes, with 150,000 licensed players.[43] On the other hand, with 250,000 members in 1929, the Norwegian Arbeiderness Idrettsforbund was the largest organisation for working-class youth in the country, whilst the Finnish workers' sports movement, with an active membership of 40,000 in 1938, reached a similar position of national prominence.[44] And as already stated, the German, Czechoslovakian and Austrian movements had particularly strong sections before fascist repression. After the Nazi seizure of power the membership of the SWSI, bereft of its core, fell from its peak of about two million to 350,000, though there was also an underground movement. In sum, however, David Steinberg is right to conclude that 'the disparity between bourgeois organizations and the workers' organizations was ... great; the bourgeois organizations had about four times as many members (at least half of whom were workers), as did the workers' sport movement, excluding the Soviet Union.'[45] To be sure, the fact that the socialist movement failed to displace bourgeois domination of sport was also related to the fact that sections of the labour leadership neglected this sphere, thinking that it diverted the working classes from more important political duties. It was only in 1929 that the German SDP officially recognised workers' sport, whilst in other countries support stretched little further than token recognition and small financial contributions. In other words, workers' sport faced both a lack of formal political support and a dearth of resources. Equally, it has to be added that the SWSI embraced the policy of political party neutrality. Despite links between the world of the working classes and the labour movement, there clearly was tension and competition between the habits and values of everyday life and leisure and the specific socialistic perspective. This is not to deny, however, that men and women could participate in workers' sport and still partake of bourgeois and consumer culture.

The British labour movement and international sport

Certainly one of the most interesting aspects of workers' sport in Britain was its links with the Continental movement. From its earliest days the CCC was informed by an ideology stressing solidarity and fraternity with workers from other countries. As the remaining sections of this chapter will show, the principle of internationalism flowed over into the sports arena. During the inter-war years a profusion of European working-class sport festivals and meetings were arranged, the Workers' Olympiads being the most well known of these. Moreover, British worker sportsmen and women supported and aided the struggles of Continental socialists, particularly against fascism.

It seems that initial contacts were made with the Continental sports movement on the eve of the First World War when the CCC received a letter from the French Socialist Sports and Athletic Federation, inviting them to attend an international conference.[46] As a result, the leading Clarion cyclist, Tom Groom, together with Fred Hagger, attended the inauguration of the socialist sports international in 1913. Groom later recalled:

> I, with my wife, cycled all the way; barring that bit across the Channel. Fred came by train and boat and we met in Ghent, where the conference was to take place. It was a gorgeous conference. The Tower of Babel was a fool to it. French, German, Italian . . . fired off their speeches in favour of the solidarity of the Workers of the World and the need for promoting Peace through Sport.[47]

On his return, Groom reported that the conference 'had been interesting', and, though no definite resolution had been passed, Clarion cyclists wished to be 'connected with an international movement'.[48] From then on the motto of the CCC was to be 'Peace through Sport'. Contacts were established with Continental groups such as the German Workers' Cyclist Federation, and affiliation was made with the new Socialist International for Physical Education, on which Groom was the British delegate.[49] Again after the war, Groom and other Clarion representatives attended conferences, firstly at Seraing (Belgium) and then at Lucerne which, as already stated, re-established the international workers' sports association.[50] Despite a certain degree of poor organisation and a lack of adequate translation facilities,[51] this signalled the beginnings of a more permanent relationship between Britain and the Continent. The newly-formed British Workers' Sports Federation (BWSF) agreed to the constitution of the SWSI and a quarter of the 2*d* individual membership fee was paid to the International.[52] Moreover, it should be recalled that in the early 1920s the British labour sports movement was guided by the ideas of the non-chauvinistic left as developed out of the Great War. This fitted in perfectly with the SWSI's rather naive assumption that contact on the sports field would unite workers from different countries and therefore break down international prejudice and rivalry, defuse national tensions, and undermine military ambitions.

As far as the British communist movement was concerned, it is perhaps unsurprising to find that contacts were made with Soviet Russia and the various Continental Marxist sport factions. Interestingly, two British Marxists – William Gallacher of the Scottish Shop Stewards and Scottish Workers' Committee, and Tom Quelch of the British Socialist Party – took part in a football match between a Russian team and foreign delegates at the second congress of the Third International in 1920.[53] In fact, by 1924, when even the *Times* was paying attention to the business of the RSI, Fritz Reussner, writing from Berlin, could suggest that contacts had been made in England and 'propaganda is being carried on by the R.S.I.'.[54] Links with the Continent were further demonstrated in 1926 when European worker sportsmen and women raised funds for locked-out British miners, and when a delegation of British youth to the Soviet Union enthused about the level of sports provision.[55] Yet it was not until the end of the twenties, after the BWSF had been 'captured' by British communists, that a role was found in the RSI. According to George Sinfield, when the Federation affiliated to the RSI in 1930 it 'helped to accelerate the rate of progress, and certainly consolidated the already existing clubs'.[56]

The new communist-inspired leadership of the BWSF repudiated the notion of 'Peace through Sport'. 'Peace will come', so it was claimed, 'only through Socialism, and not through sport alone'.[57] The ethical and idealistic principles of the social democrats were rejected in favour of the more scientific and materialistic principles of Marxism. Obviously, contacts with Marxist groups on the Continent were thought to facilitate the forward march to the socialist republic. Whereas the slogan of the social democrats was 'Peace through Sport', in the case of the communists it was 'All under the banner of the Red Sport International'.[58] After all, the RSI was said 'to gather together the sport-loving working masses of all countries on the basis of determined struggle against capitalism to educate them for the revolutionary struggle of the proletariat'.[59] This corresponded particularly well with the rhetoric of the British communist movement.

Provision and organisation of workers' sport

One of the points of contact between British labour and the Continental socialist movement was the sports arena. Delegates from European countries met and discussed common points of interest at the conferences of the SWSI and RSI. But perhaps more important as a force of unity was the actual sporting contest itself. This section will discuss the extent and significance of the sports field for the relationship between organised socialism in Britain and on the Continent.

If international peace was to be achieved 'by bringing together the workers of the world on the fields of sport',[60] then sports events had to be organised efficiently, in large numbers, and in such a way to develop political awareness as well as sporting progress. Certainly a very small minority of British workers were able to attend Continental sports meetings throughout the 1920s and 1930s, though there were obvious restrictions when foreign travel was both time-consuming and expensive. In 1922, for instance, the Clarion took part in competitions for football, running and swimming in Paris against six other nations.[61] By the end of the decade worker sportsmen and women had participated in events in Austria, Belgium, Czechoslovakia, France, Germany and Russia, as well as in informal cycling and hiking holidays. Interestingly enough, it seems that workers utilised the services of another socialist leisure organisation, the Workers' Travel Association (WTA), itself founded in 1921 by leading labour personalities as an outcome of the movement for international peace.[62] For instance, a party of fifty was catered for by the WTA during the 1931 Vienna Olympiad. For approximately £14 third-class or £17 10s second-class, a variety of services were laid on during the tour: 'travel, meals *en route*, services of leader, transport between station and hotel in Vienna, dinner, bed and breakfast in Vienna from arrival until departure, members' card for the Olympiad – entitling free admission to the Stadium, reduced fares on trams, etc.'.[63] In return, of course, Continental workers were invited to take part in British sport. Thus in 1923 a football match was staged in London between representative British and French sides; the visiting Fédération Sportive du Travail emerged as the winner.[64]

In the 1930s, the infant National Workers' Sports Association (NWSA) also participated in European sport. The first tour was made in 1931 when football and tennis sides accepted an invitation to meet the Dutch and German workers in Holland.[65] This was followed up in the years 1935 to 1939 with further trips by British athletes, boxers, footballers and tennis players to Belgium, France and Switzerland. There was again a willingness to reciprocate, for the Association organised sports meetings in England which attracted worker sportsmen and women from all over the world. In 1934, for instance, teams from Austria, Belgium, Palestine and Switzerland took part in athletics, cycling, football and lawn tennis at the Dorsetshire Labourers' Centenary Commemorations of the Tolpuddle Martyrs.[66] Later in the year Belgium, as the champion workers' team of Western Europe, were entertained by the London Labour Football Club, whilst two years later Belgian, Dutch and French tennis players were entertained at the Workers' Wimbledon.[67] All in all, in the eight years to 1934, 966 national and international sporting events were organised under the auspices of the SWSI.[68] Through such contacts, which even included an international chess competition by correspondence,[69] the NWSA was clearly committed to, and able to play a role in, the development of proletarian physical culture in Europe. Moreover, conclusions drawn from the Dorsetshire celebrations seemed to confirm the social democratic faith in 'Peace through Sport':

> The high standard of play and sportsmanship shown by the players, both Continental and English ... made me feel sorry that such matches are not held more frequently. It serves to show that the cause of Peace can be best achieved by the friendly rivalry between our Continental Brothers and ourselves on the Sports Field. When the Working Class of the World know one another better, and fraternise more freely, it will be much easier to talk Peace and infinitely harder for capitalists and Dictators to stir up nations to war against each other.[70]

The most glamorous event in the calendar of the workers' sports movement was the proletarian alternative to the Olympic Games, the so-called Workers' Olympiad.[71] Olympiads were held regularly in the inter-war period: officially at Frankfurt in 1925, Vienna in 1931 and Antwerp in 1937, as well as three unofficial Czechoslovakian Games staged at Prague in 1921, 1927 and 1934. A People's Olympiad was also due to take place in Barcelona in 1936, but was cancelled due to the outbreak of the Spanish Civil War. By all accounts, the Workers' Olympics stimulated a great deal of interest and mass support. It has been claimed, for example, that in 1931 over a quarter of a million attended the second Workers' Olympiad at Vienna with its new stadium built by the socialist Viennese Council – a pioneer of radical measures in child-care, education, housing, as well as recreation and culture. Spectators were attracted by a programme which included 220 contests in all athletic disciplines, a children's sports festival, artistic exhibitions, dramatic performances and even fireworks; 100,000 people watched the opening ceremony, 65,000 the football finals, and 12,000 the cycling finals. Significantly, some 1,000 worker athletes took part from twenty-six countries, compared to the 1,408 competitors from thirty-seven nations at the Los Angeles Olympics the following year.[72]

The British labour movement sent delegates and representative teams to each of the Olympiads. Again, the CCC pledged support because the 'Olympiad is in the nature of an International Demonstration in favour of Peace, through sport'.[73] The Labour Party expressed a similar view, and in

1927 the Party Chairman, Frederick Roberts, accepted an invitation to attend the Workers' Gymnastic Federation Olympiad at Prague.[74] Roberts returned to England in an exuberant mood; Prague had apparently 'left an ineffaceable impression'.[75] He enthused about the sports stadium which held 150,000 spectators, the 'magnificent sight' of thousands of young women gymnasts, 'the great army of processionists ... marching to inspiring music', even an agricultural exhibition and congress. But more important, Roberts stressed the political implications of the Prague gathering:

> The Olympiad was thus not only one of the greatest value on physical culture and educational grounds; it also furnished an opportunity for meeting together in a congenial atmosphere the Labour and Socialist representatives of other nations. This should help to maintain understanding and goodwill, and tend to strengthen the ties of comradeship which bind together the workers of the world.[76]

From then on Roberts became a passionate advocate of international workers' sport. He served as the Party representative on the executive committee of the NWSA, and attended 'the first dinner given to the competitors at the Vienna Olympiad'.[77] Further, the Labour Party retained interest in international sport to the end of the 1930s. It is apparent that the Party, as well as the TUC regarded the concept of a Workers' Olympiad as 'a greater significance than the mere attendance at a sports' gathering'.[78] Therefore in 1937 there was practical help with the campaign to reverse the ban imposed by the Amateur Athletic Association (AAA) on British participation in the Antwerp Workers' Olympiad.[79] And in fact the campaign was successful: British sportsmen and women joined workers from fourteen other countries – 50,000 in all – in what *Tribune* called 'a great sports meeting of exceptionally high standard'.[80]

The communist-backed BWSF also took part in international sports, mainly those under the control or influence of the RSI. Indeed as noted in chapter 3, the split in the British workers' sports movement had been caused by the decision of the London branch (supported by the CP) to organise a football tour of the Soviet Union in 1927. From the outset the BWSF was clearly most concerned about the political aspects of Continental tours, especially the social and economic position of the Soviet Union. Until its demise in 1935, the BWSF sent delegations of athletes, boxers, footballers, swimmers and netball players to the Soviet Union again, France, Germany, Holland, Norway and Switzerland, all in the hope of demonstrating and sustaining proletarian solidarity.

At the same time, delegations of worker sportsmen and women were received from Germany and France. Of particular note was the German football tour in Easter 1933. After a great deal of preparation,[81] a team from Westphalia played against working-class footballers in Dundee and the London district, including the militant Busmen's Rank and File Committee.[82] What is most interesting about the tour is that it took place on the eve of the Nazi seizure of power. It was therefore appropriate that Tom Mann, a father-figure in the British labour movement, should declare 'that the visit of the German workers' team had done much to reaffirm their support for the outlawed German workers' sports movement. In 1936, for example, an official protest against the imprisonment and non-trial of the German Communist Party leader (and a member of the workers' sports association), Ernst Thälmann, was forwarded to the German embassy.[84]

The Soviet equivalent of the social democratic Olympiad was the Spartakiade – seemingly a kind of ritualised Marxist demonstration against the hypocrisy of the bourgeois Olympics, with their apparent discrimination against working-class athletes – of which there were two in the inter-war years. In 1928, the Moscow Spartakiade attracted approximately one million spectators and participants from forty-one countries. Launched by a parade of 30,000 banner and torch-carrying athletes, there were twelve festival days in all with a comprehensive programme of twenty-one sports. Having claimed £400 from the Soviet Union for travel expenses – was this a form of 'Moscow gold' which contemporary anti-communist opinion claimed was finding its way into the British Party's coffers? – the BWSF sent a delegation of thirty-five athletes to Moscow.[85] On their return there was again enthusiasm about Russian economic and social life, and a clear awareness that the main aim of the Games was to 'strengthen the alliance of the working masses all over the world'.[86]

The second Spartakiade in 1932 was also held in Moscow, the BWSF sending a party of thirty-six athletes, partly financed by a £50 quota from the RSI.[87] From the frequent reports of the Russian tour which appeared in the communist *Daily Worker*, it is apparent that the British participants were mesmerised by their experience, in much the same way as the Webbs would be later in the thirties.[88] Even supposedly 'neutral' sportsmen, like Sidney Harris of the Dukinfield Cycling Club, were caught up in the Moscow syndrome, praising the way Soviet society was run – no unemployment, 'A.1' social and industrial conditions and good leisure facilities.[89] At the same time as forced collectivisation, food shortages and political repression, when serious criticism of the Soviet system was 'rendered impossible',[90] T. Flynn of the Glasgow BWSF wrote the following report about the workers of Yegoryevsk (a town about ninety miles from Moscow): 'one did not need to be a class conscious worker to feel that here was something different; happy faces, no signs of the starving children we have read so much about, a nation of people eager to shake you by the hand and call you comrade. Yes, this is something vastly different from the spirit we had left in England'.[91] Even though Clem Beckett had his new leather coat and half his motor-bike stolen by Soviet souvenir-hunters, and the BWSF delegation walked out of a restaurant because of slow service, the tourists' enthusiasm remained intact.[92] The statement that the life of the Soviet worker 'both culturally and industrially, stood high above that of the British working class'.[93] is of course highly questionable and requires no further comment here, but it shows that the BWSF courted Soviet sport because of wider economic and political sympathies. This internationalism was in fact based on a Soviet blueprint which, to say the least, was misrepresented by touring sportsmen and women.

Against fascist tyranny

It is appropriate to note here that by the 1920s sport was utilised in the highly-charged political arena of foreign affairs and international relations. This obviously had implications for the Empire, as well demonstrated during the English cricket tour of Australia in 1932–33. When the English captain, Douglas Jardine, applied the tactic of bodyline bowling or leg theory, seen by some as a cowardly form of intimidation, a strain was imposed on the imperial relationship and the British government intervened. On the team's return, the Dominions Minister, J. H. Thomas, summoned members of the MCC to Downing Street and, it is believed, urged them not to harm diplomatic relations any further.[94] Likewise, though for most of the inter-war years English football was cut-off from the European game, the Foreign Office evinced some interest in world soccer. In 1927, for instance, it inspired newspaper articles on the contribution of British sides in Germany, whilst in 1938 it was behind the decision of the Football Association to instruct the English national side to give the Nazi salute.[95] As Peter Beck has put it:

> during the 1930s the outcome of international football matches came to be interpreted by governments and the media as a reflection of the quality not only of a country's soccer skills but also of its socio-political system and overall

power. In this manner sport became an integral part of national propaganda machines. Although this was usually associated with totalitarian regimes, there is evidence of an increased awareness by the British government of the value of football as part of a wider programme of national advertisement, that is, of projecting a favourable image of Britain in the wider world.[96]

Furthermore, it is of particular interest to this study to discover that the Foreign Office (in collaboration with Scotland Yard and the Home Office) was perturbed about the political nature of the BWSF tour of the Soviet Union in 1927, as it was about the Federation's invitation to a Soviet miners' football team to tour Britain in 1930.[97] Indeed, on this second occasion, the Labour Home Secretary, J. R. Clynes, refused to grant entry visas to the Russian footballers, thus preventing the tour from taking place. Despite many protests, Clynes was not going to support 'these Communist sports organisations' who were to be used in strikes, pickets and 'for the military training of working class youth'; he considered the politics of the BWSF alien to the best traditions of 'genuine sport'.[98] But what else could be expected at a time of 'Class against Class'.

The hostile response of the state to certain socialist sporting initiatives did not stop the British labour movement from attempting to change official policy. This was true on international issues, as much as it was on domestic issues like access to the countryside. On a number of occasions in the 1930s British labour campaigned against the rise of fascism, and in turn fascist tendencies in sport. More than this, sport became a medium by which organised labour supported the rights and demands of the anti-fascist movement on the Continent.

Undoubtedly, organised labour in Britain expressed its repugnance of the Nazi seizure of power in no uncertain terms. As Brian Stoddart has discussed in an excellent paper, this was demonstrated in December 1935 when an international football match was staged at White Hart Lane, London, between England and Germany.[99] This provoked a sharp reaction and much antagonism from the London labour and progressive movement. A TUC delegation and floods of protest were received by the Home Office, and even Hitler and the Prince of Wales became embroiled in the controversy. The basis of Labour's objection to the match was well stated in Sir Walter Citrine's presentation to the Home Office. He stressed that the National Socialists directly controlled sport through a Reich Commissioner, who vetted the racial composition of teams, liquidated Jewish, socialist and even Catholic organisations, and basically saw to it that sport was under the direct auspices of the State.[100] In other words, calls for the prohibition and boycott of the match were based on labour's antipathy to Nazi repression and the fascist personality of German sport, especially its anti-Semitism. Although there were political divisions within the working class and a real failure to take advantage of Sir John Simon's intimation that cancellation was not out of the question – the match went ahead with a capacity crowd of 60,000 – many British socialists and progressives had, as history would show, quite rightly demonstrated their distaste of, and resistance to, Hitler's dictatorship. Indeed, for their protests twelve men were arrested – six outside the stadium itself and a further six outside Victoria Station when the German visitors were leaving – and a quantity of anti-Nazi literature and placards were seized by the Metropolitan Police.[101]

A similar pattern of activity can be discerned from the British labour movement's campaign against the Berlin Olympic Games of 1936. The call for a boycott first crystallised in the corridors and committee rooms of Transport House. In 1935, the NWSA, supported by the TUC General Council, Labour Party Executive and CCC, resolved that 'having carefully considered the racial attitude adopted by the German Government it is of the opinion that the British Sports Associations should not be connected in any way, either directly or indirectly, with the Berlin Olympiade'.[102] With such broad labour support, the workers' sports movement promoted the campaign in the upper echelons of the AAA. Once again, the socialist case was delineated from the premiss that sport was merely a tool of totalitarianism, a vehicle for fascist propaganda and tyranny. As the labour press put it, the Berlin Olympics were to be 'used for Fascist Propaganda', a 'Masquerade – in the Name of Sport', 'The Degradation of Sport'.[103] At a special meeting of the AAA, however, a motion calling for a boycott of the Olympics was defeated by 200 votes to eight, with twenty-seven abstentions – a few policy-makers, athletes, coaches and sportswriters were convinced that conditions in Germany necessitated such action.[104] The *Sporting Chronicle and Athletic News* spoke for many vested interests when it vilified the so-called Socialist Party's campaign and made the familiar protest that 'We will not tolerate any interference with our sport, or with our sense of fair play.'[105] Even Harold Abrahams – himself Jewish – as a typical representative of the English amateur elite, was very hostile to the boycott movement, remarking that he was not ashamed to shake hands with von Tschammer und Osten, the Nazi Sports Commissioner.[106]

Characteristically, the Foreign Office was reluctant to take up the issue, at least in the public domain. Nonetheless, discussions did take place behind the scenes. In late 1935, three Foreign Office officials, Orme

Sargent (deputy to the permanent under-secretary, Sir Robert Vansittart), J. V. Perowne and R. F. Wigram focused on the question of a boycott. Perhaps most importantly, for Sargent 'the importance of Herr Hitler's prestige and also German finances of a possible boycott of the Olympic Games must certainly be borne in mind'. On a more pragmatic plain, Perowne reminded his colleagues that at a time when they were 'damping down' adverse comment on the Anglo-German football match, it would be inconsistent to 'stir up hate' about the Games. In any case, he proceeded, there was no hard evidence that a British boycott would wreck the Games or improve the Jewish situation in Germany.[107] On the other hand, it is as well to remember that 'progressive' opinion within the Foreign Office was disturbed by Nazi expansionist policies. Vansittart himself advocated standing up to Germany. Consequently he expressed some doubts about the Games, and in this seems to have been championed by Wigram, who hinted that the British Government could get the Germans to modify their stance on the Jewish question by way of a bluff – that is, by threatening an Olympic boycott.[108] From a similar perspective, there was some interest in information that during the Winter Games Austrian visitors had been 'struck by the apparent waning enthusiasm of the people for Hitler and his régime'.[109] Now as a matter of course, the Foreign Office was perfectly aware that the Olympics were to be a means of National Socialist publicity; in the words of Sir Eric Phipps, British Ambassor in Berlin, an 'opportunity of impressing foreign countries with the capacity of solidity of the Nazi regime'.[110] No doubt all of this helped to absolve wider moral guilt. Yet, in the final analysis, the Foreign Office did not know what to do. In fact, it thereby went out of its way not to destabilise diplomatic relations with Germany, leaving the problem to be solved by 'private' functionaries of the Olympic Association and the AAA.

It must be added however, that support for a boycott also came from various progressive interests, including the British Non-Sectarian Anti Nazi Council, a few athletics clubs, the Association of Jewish Youth and even the main Oxford undergraduate body.[111] Sympathetic noises were also made by the liberal *Manchester Guardian*, believing that the Nazi system denied the Olympic spirit 'of complete equality between all contending nations and races'.[112] Further, the position of British labour was part of a wider oppositional movement led by the RSI and SWSI, and also taken up at the official level in various other countries, and at the unofficial, underground level in Germany itself – ninety former worker sportsmen were arrested by the Gestapo on the eve of the Games. Indeed. despite the hostility of the AAA, British worker sportsmen and women continued their campaign through global channels, being represented at a conference of adversaries of the Hitler Olympiad at Paris in June 1936 and in other international groupings.[113] Although the Nazi Games took place, glorified and romanticised in Rietenstahl's film, *Olympia 1936*, the morality and political judgement of the organised working class in Britain had been justified. In fact, by 1938 the AAA had changed course; on the prompting of the British Workers' Sports Association, they unanimously decided to boycott the 1940 Games, scheduled to take place in fascist Tokyo.[114]

As a protest against and substitute for the Berlin Games, a People's Olympiad was organised in Barcelona, in which Britain was to be represented by a team of forty-one athletes, including some champions. Significantly, British Labour's support of the Barcelona Games was not simply a sign of socialist and anti-fascist commitment; at least in the case of the social democrats it was also an appreciation of the so-called Olympic ideals of internationalism, unity and peace, albeit ideals which were invented in the late nineteenth century and sustained by the 1930s as powerful myths. Take the view of the co-operator, Arthur Logan Petch:

> The Barcelona Olympiad has not been out for record-breaking feats. It is merely a gesture to promote international co-operation and keeping sporting ideals - the spirit contained in Baron de Coubertin's circular forty-two years ago - to maintain the nobility and chivalry which have distinguished the Olympic Games of the past. It is the duty of every trade unionist, socialist, and Co-operator, who from the very ideals they have embraced must be liberty-loving citizens, to throw the whole weight into the idea to preserve the true Olympic spirit, which will bring the athletes of all countries together to do battle not in a wretched, cruel, maiming and devastating war, but in that place of freedom, fresh air, energy and exercise - the sports stadium.[115]

However, in view of the fact that the Spanish Civil War broke out on the eve of the Olympiad, it had to be abandoned. Nevertheless, British sportsmen and women - the girl athletes 'showed fine fortitude in the circumstances' - expressed their solidarity with the Spanish workers. Some members even wanted to take up arms on the side of the republican cause, 'and they were stopped only with the greatest difficulty'.[116] On their return home, the experiences of the athletes were given publicity in the national and local press, though one British observer in Barcelona believed that the workers' delegation did not contain a single sportsman and was simply 'some sort of Communist party stunt'. That said, George Elvin addressed many rallies and meetings in support of the republicans, from Hampstead to Harlesden, Ealing to Stepney.[117]

In fact, it is interesting to note that many worker sportsmen, especially from the old BWSF, joined the International Brigade and some, such as Sam Masters – claimed to be the first British volunteer in Spain – Clem Beckett, George Brown and Walter Tapsell, lost their lives on Spanish soil.[118] As the CCC affirmed, in supporting 'the Spanish people in their heroic fight for freedom against the forces of international Fascism', two members, Tom Darban and Ray Cox, died whilst fighting in the International Brigade in Madrid.[119] Understandably, Clarion cyclists pledged money to the funds of the Spanish Medical Aid Committee, the National Youth Food-ship Committee and the International Brigade.[120] By the same token, sections of the Woodcraft Folk such as the one in Sheffield supported the local Basque Children's Committee (Basil Rawson, a leading Folk member, serving as a vice-president), the Yorkshire Foodship Council and the rest.[121]

Sections of the British labour movement rallied to the defence of the Spanish working class 'in their fight against the menace of fascism and reaction'.[122] Not only was there political and financial assistance, but also continued sporting links. In September 1936, for instance, a British football side played in Paris against a Spanish eleven, 'most of whom had come direct from the firing lines in Spain, and who stated they obtained practice for the match during the lulls in the fighting'.[123] On other occasions, however, negative intervention by the National Government made it difficult to consolidate such contacts. The Foreign Office thus banned the proposed visit of a British football team to Catalonia – 'It really seems a most fantastic proposal' – on the grounds of the non-intervention pact, the difficult conditions prevailing in Spain, and seemingly the fear that British workers would provide military assistance to the republicans.[124] Even so, aid through sport continued. The CCC, in co-operation with the FSGT, organised a relay cycle ride from Glasgow to Barcelona which raised much needed funds and supplies.[125] Certainly, workers' sport contributed to the anti-fascist cause in the 1930s, albeit in a rather minor role.

Conclusion

Workers' sport in the special conjuncture of the inter-war years strengthened what was a rather weak internationalistic ethic. International contacts through sport, no matter how irregular, provided opportunities for the European working class to understand those factors which divided nation states, and in turn attempt to overcome them. It may be surmised that when workers of Britain, France, Germany and the Soviet Union came together in sport some form of international community, however muted, was in the making. The sources suggest that above all worker sportsmen and women were internationalists, ably demonstrated by the support for causes like anti-fascism, which circumvented national boundaries.

Yet it has to be stressed that internationalism through sport was limited, dependent upon broader initiatives on the economic and political front. Also, workers' sport may have professed internationalism and may even have achieved some progress in that direction, but this was very difficult in a European environment imbued with nationalist sentiment. In a world of shifting foreign policy objectives and the rise of totalitarianism, it can be argued that political isolationism and appeasement dominated, making the task of the working-class internationalist more difficult, if not impossible.

In examining the political activity of the British workers' sports bodies and their support for 'European' causes, three further points need to be stressed. The first point relates to the apparent bias of the British State. During the 1930s successive British governments intervened in international sport, yet this intervention was characterised by gross discrimination. Whilst on the one hand onerous conditions were placed on sporting relations with the Soviet Union and Republican Spain, on the other there was a much more flexible and favourable policy attitude shown towards Nazi Germany and Fascist Italy: Soviet footballers were not allowed into Britain in 1930 and British footballers were banned from visiting Spain seven years later, but the Italian national side was entertained by the British authorities in 1934 at the so-called 'Battle of Highbury', as was the German team in following year. Also in 1934, the Home Office banned the Austrian socialist and president of the SWSI, Dr Julius Deutsch, from presenting a lecture in London on the political situation in Austria.[126] Yet even as late as February 1939 the British Prime Minister, Neville Chamberlain, welcomed representatives from Germany and Italy to the London meeting of the International Advisory Committee of the World Congress for Leisure Time and Recreation.[127] All of this meant that the workers' sports movement faced official constraints in trying to build bridges between the British and Continental working class. One did not have to be a Marxist to agree with the remarks of George Sinfield that 'The Goverment allocates to itself the right to determine what is "right" and what is "safe" and what is "political".'[128]

Clearly there were many instances of overt political bias, yet there is still a need for at least one substantive amendment. It should be recalled that, as in domestic affairs, the approach of the British State to international relations was not simply an outcome of some kind of capitalist conspiracy. After all, presumably some of those mandarins with a brief for sport brought to the policy-making process a set of values learnt in public school and universities which failed to recognise the politicisation of modern games. Within the hierarchies of a conservative State, there had been no *conscious* decision to make sport a tool of official policy, but rather this happened due to wider changes in the role of government and Britain's international position. State policy towards sport rested upon a complex interaction of such variable conditions as the performance of overseas trade, strategic and military questions, the balance of power. In reality, civil servants and politicians may have been reluctant to acknowledge the social and political nature of sport, yet at a time when Britain was suffering from a depression in world trade and the possibility of military confrontation they had little alternative but to use sport as a prop for wider economic and diplomatic missions. This is why, when England was due to play Germany at soccer in Berlin in 1938 during a period of diplomatic sensitivity between the two countries, Sir Robert Vansittart, usually anti-German and not known for appeasement, urged Stanley Rous 'that it is really important for our prestige that the British team should put up a really first class performance'.[129] Further, the state was not, and is not, monolithic, having different interests and identities which, of course, changed over time. Thus, notwithstanding the apparent bureaucratic constraints which surrounded the England versus Germany football match of 1935, different positions were taken up by the various administrative interests, the Home Office in private discussions 'very anxious to get the match put off altogether', the Foreign Office 'very reluctant to intervene', believing 'It is a Home Office affair'.[130] Organised labour also had the opportunity to clarify official positions and act as a countervailing pressure, no matter how muted this may have been. At least the 'democratic' channels of the British state presented more opportunities for labour to influence issues than was the case in Fascist Italy or Nazi Germany, though perhaps this is not saying very much. In other words, despite the atavism of certain permanent civil servants, the State's approach to sport was structured by the economic, political and diplomatic realities of Britain's international position, but in such a way that outside agencies like the labour movement could not be ignored.

The second point relates to the relationship between the social democratic and communist wings of the sports movement. The position of the State may have hindered European contact, but this was of less significance than the disunity in the workers' sports movement itself. It is true that the BWSF was defunct by the mid-1930s, and that in light of the unity campaign communists were willing to arrive at a more harmonious relationship with Labour Party members and other progressives. However, as already mentioned, social democrats remained reluctant to co-operate, if not intransigent. The NWSA opposed fusion of the RSI and SWSI, whilst the TUC General Council remained rabidly anti-communist. Strong hostility to the Communist Party and its offshoots made it difficult for the sports movement to reach any kind of agreement. Indeed, though the Labour Party National Executive agreed that the Soviet Union should participate in the Antwerp Olympiad of 1937, British communists had already been at least formally barred from joining the Association's team for the Barcelona Olympiad.[131] Under such antagonistic conditions, the professed aims of internationalism and working-class solidarity were compromised on occasions, though it must be recalled that there were counter-moves to reconciliation. Elements in the CCC argued for the principle of unity, whilst there is unsubstantiated evidence that former members of the RSI in England moved closer to the position of the SWSI. Notwithstanding such signs of unity, for most of the period proletarian internationalism was no more than a veneer when the European working class was so vehemently divided between Marxism and reformism. Needless to say, the changing ideological and political priorities of the Soviet Union were crucial. As the home of the revolution and the first fully fledged 'socialist' order, Soviet Russia was able to impart a wide ranging influence on the strategy and development of the international working class. Thus as 'socialism in one country' emerged as the orthodoxy of the day, the communist demand for economic and social change through the common experiences and aspirations of the international proletarian faded into the background.

Third and finally, a study of the workers' sports movement may reveal a lot about the motives and purpose of labour activists, but may not say very much at all about the significance attached to labels like internationalism in everyday working-class life. As we have seen, though workers' sport may have been proletarian in composition and internationalist in aim, it was smaller than, and set apart from, non-socialist cultural and recreational groupings. In spite of the strength of workers' organisations in some countries, it is apparent that large sections of the working class were not aware of the workers' sports movement and its internationalism. This was perhaps more true in Britain where the labour movement as a whole was relatively quiescent about the sports question; certainly the majority of the British working class had little political understanding of notions such as 'Peace through Sport'. Indeed, sport was the site of competition between nations and could be a generator of nationalist passions. At least it is difficult to see in world football or the Olympic Games the embryo of some new internationalist ethic. Recent work has shown that the inter-war British working class was still chauvinistic, with a deep love of Empire,[132] and consequently the small workers' sports movement found it problematic to counter ingrained patriotic values. Indeed, the British movement failed to consider in any serious and theoretically sophisticated sense the intersection between sport and Empire, as raised at the beginning of this chapter. This said, the chapter should not end on a critical note, for, despite a collection of political difficulties, workers' sport helped to stimulate some form of common European ethos through sporting contact and in the struggle against tyranny.

Notes

1 J. Sugden, 'The power of gold: the source and currency of the political Olympics', *Physical Education Review*, vol. 4 (1981), p. 66. Cf. J-M. Brohm, *Sport – a Prison of Measured Time* (1978), pp. 45, 104, 122.
2 D. Triesman, 'The Olypmic Games as a political forum', in A. Tomlinson and G. Whannel (eds), *Five Ring Circus: Money, Power and Politics at the Olympic Games* (1984), p. 19.
3 T. Mason, 'Some Englishmen and Scotsmen abroad: the spread of world football', in A. Tomlinson and G. Whannel (eds), *Off the Ball: The Football World Cup* (1986).
4 B. Stoddart, 'Sport, cultural imperialism and colonial response in the British Empire: a framework for analysis', in D. Benning (ed.), *Sport and Imperialism* (1986).
5 C. L. R. James, *Beyond a Boundary* (1963). But see the critical comments of H. Tiffin, 'Cricket, literature and the politics of de-colonisation – the case of C. L. R. James', in R. Cashman and M. McKernan (eds), *Sport: Money, Morality and the Media* (New South Wales, n.d., 1982?).
6 R. D. E. Burton, 'Cricket, carnival and street culture in the Caribbean', *British Journal of Sports History*, vol. 2 (1985).
7 L. N. Constantine, *Cricket in the Sun* (n.d., 1948?).
8 R. Burns and W. van der Will, 'Organisation debate: working class organisation and the importance of cultural struggle. A critique of James Wickham', *Capital and Class*, vol. 10 (1980), p. 171.
9 M. Nolan, 'The Socialist Movement in Düsseldorf, 1890-1914', PhD, University of Columbia (1975), pp. 386-9.

10 R. F. Wheeler, 'Organised sport and organised labour: the workers' sports movement', *Journal of Contemporary History*, Vol. 13 (1978), p. 235

11 The most recent and comprehensive work on the workers' sports movement is A. Krüger and J. Riordan (eds), *Der Internationale Arbeitersport: Der Schlüssel zum Arbeitersport in 10 Ländern* (Köln, 1985).

12 D. A. Steinburg, 'The workers' Sport Internationals 1920-28', *Journal of Contemporary History*, vol. 13 (1978), p. 235.

13 Ibid., p. 236.

14 See J. Hoberman, *Sport and Political Ideology* (1984), pp. 178-89.

15 *Programme of the Young Communist International* (1929), p. 76.

16 CP, *The Young Communist International: Between the Fourth and Fifth Congresses 1924-1928* (1928), pp. 239-40.

17 *International of Youth*, Sept. 1922, March 1923.

18 F. Nitsch, 'Die internationalen Arbeitersportbewegungen', in Krüger and Riordan, *Der Internationale Arbeitersport*, pp. 185-6.

19 Quoted in D. Semotiuk, 'The sport system of the Union of Soviet Socialist Republics: an illustrated analysis', *North American Society for Sport History Proceedings* (1975), p. 50. For further details of Lenin and sport, see J. Riordan, 'Marx, Lenin and physical culture', *Journal of Sport History*, vol. 3 (1976). Hoberman, *Sport*, pp. 170-7.

20 J. Riordan, 'Sport in Soviet Society: Development and Problems', PhD, University of Birmingham (1975), p. 600.

21 *Labour Year Book*, 1927, p. 422.

22 D. Steinberg, 'Sport Under Red Flags: The Relations Between the Red Sport International and the Socialist Workers' Sport International 1920-1939', D.Phil, University of Wisconsin-Madison (1979), pp. 96-7, 112.

23 G. Roth, *The Social Democrats in Imperial Germany: A Study in Working Class Isolation and National Integration* (Totowa, 1963).

24 V. L. Lidtke, *The Alternative Culture: Socialist Labor in Imperial Germany* (Oxford, 1985), ch. 1. See also Nolan, 'Socialist movement in Düsseldorf', pp. 348-9. W. L. Guttsman, *The German Social Democratic Party, 1875-1933* (1981).

25 R. J. Evans, 'Introduction: the sociological interpretation of German labour history', in R. J. Evans (ed.), *The German Working Class 1888-1933* (1982). See also G. A. Ritter, 'Workers' culture in Imperial Germany: problems and points of departure for research', *Journal of Contemporary History*, vol. 13 (1978).

26 R. A. Woeltz, 'Sport, culture and society in later Imperial and Weimar Germany: Some suggestions for future research', *Journal of Sport History*, vol. 4 (1977), p. 306.

27 See R. Lenman, 'Mass culture and the State in Germany, 1900-1926', in R. J. Bullen, H Pogge van Strandmann and A. B. Polonsky (eds), *Ideas into History: Aspects of European History 1880-1950* (1984).

28 *International Labour Review*, vol. 99 (1969), p. 38.

29 G. Cross, 'The quest for leisure: Reassessing the eight-hour day in France', *Journal of Social History*, vol. 18 (1984), p. 200.

30 Y. Barou and J Rigaudiat, *Les 35 heures et l'emploi* (Paris, 1982), p. 82. See also International Labour Office, *Hours of Labour in Industry: France* (Geneva, 1922).

31 See Cross, 'Quest for leisure'. G. Cross, 'Les Trois Huits: labor movements, international reform, and the origins of the eight-hour day, 1919-1924', *French*

Historical Studies, vol. 14 (1985).

32 *International Labour Review*, vol. 6 (1922), pp. 327-33.

33 E. Weber, 'Gymnastics and sports in fin-de-siècle France: opium of the classes?', *American Historical Review*, vol. 76 (1971), p. 95.

34 R. Holt, *Sport and Society in Modern France* (1981), pp. 10, 188.

35 T. Zeldin, *France 1848-1945 II Intellect, Taste and Anxiety* (Oxford, 1977), p. 688. It must be stated, however, that Zeldin has a different interpretation for the rise of sport: 'One should see the growth of sport for the masses not as the cult of more free time but as a reaction against the lack of it' (p. 681).

36 International Labour Office, *Development of Facilities for the utilization of workers' leisure* (Geneva, 1923), pp. 16-17.

37 Woeltz, 'Sport, culture and society', p. 305.

38 Ritter, 'Workers' culture', pp. 176-7.

39 *International Labour Review*, vol. 9 (1924), pp. 227, 239, 581-2. L. Heerma van Voss, 'The use of leisure time by male workers after the introduction of the eight-hour day', paper presented to the fifth Anglo-Dutch Labour History Conference, 1986, pp. 5, 31.

40 *International Labour Review*, vol. 9 (1924), p. 853.

41 H. Diederiks, 'Looking for the true labourer: some introductory remarks on working class culture in the Netherlands 1920-1940', paper presented to the fifth Anglo-Dutch Labour History Conference, 1986, p. 6.

42 See Heerman van Voss, 'Use of leisure time'.

43 Holt, *Sport and Society*, pp. 156, 188, 205. Cf. W. J. Murray, 'The French workers' sports movement and the victory of the popular front in 1936', *International Journal of the History of Sport*, vol. 4 (1987).

44 Steinberg, 'Sport Under Red Flags', pp. 158-9, 299.

45 *Ibid.*, p. 112.

46 Manchester Central Library Archives Department (hereafter MAD), 016/i/3, CCC Mins, 12 Jan. 1913.

47 T. Groom, *National Clarion Cycling Club 1894-1944: The Fifty-Year Story of the Club* (Halifax, 1944). See also MAD, 016/i/12, Programme of the 1st International Congress of the Socialist Physical Education Groups, Ghent, 10 May 1913.

48 MAD, 016/i/3, CCC Mins, 15 June 1913.

49 MAD, 016/i/11, A. Zibell to T. Groom, 24 May 1913; Mins of 1st meeting of the International Committee from the Socialist Federations of Physical Education at the People's House, Brussels, 11 Jan. 1914; 016/i/3, CCC Mins, 25 Jan. 1914.

50 Groom, *Clarion Cycling Club*.

51 MAD, 016/i/8, Report of delegates to the Prague Olympiad and Conference of the International Federation for Socialist Sport. Cf. CCC, *Annual Conference Report*, 1922, p. 4.

52 BWSF Mins, 26 Nov. 1924. *Clarion*, 12 Nov. 1924.

53 J. Riordan, *Sport in Soviet Society: Development of Sport and Physical Education in Russia and the U.S.S.R.* (Cambridge, 1977), pp. 79-81.

54 *Times*, 15 and 22 Sept. 1924. *International Press Correspondence*, 18 Dec. 1924.

55 *Weekly Young Worker*, 13 Nov. 1926. *Labour's Northern Voice*, 3 Dec. 1926. YCL, *Report of Second British Youth Delegation to the USSR* (n.d., 1927?), p. 10.

56 *Labour Monthly*, March 1930. BWSF Committee Report to the National

Congress, 6-7 Dec. 1930.
57 *Young Worker*, 25 Feb. 1928.
58 *Labour Monthly*, April 1931.
59 *Daily Worker*, 23 July 1931.
60 *Clarion*, Jan. 1931.
61 MAD, 016/i/8, Report on the Clarion International Sports Tour, 1922.
62 See F. Williams, *Journey into Adventure: The Story of the Workers Travel Association* (1960).
63 British Library of Political and Economic Science, George Elvin Papers (hereafter Elvin Papers), COLL MISC 685/1, *Travel Log*, May and Sept. 1931.
64 *New Leader*, 30 March 1923. *Daily Herald*, 3 April 1923.
65 TUC, *Annual Report*, 1932, p. 101.
66 By all accounts the celebrations were a success. See TUC GC Mins, 26 April 1934. TUC, *Annual Report*, 1935, p. 113.
67 Elvin Papers, COLL MISC 685/1,2, *Hendon Times*, 7 Sept. 1934; *Tennis Illustrated*, June 1936.
68 NWSA, *5th Annual Report*, 1935, p. 4.
69 The NWSA inaugurated a chess section in 1932 which participated in the first international workers' chess tournament. *New Clarion*, 15 Oct. 1932. Labour Party, *Annual Conference Report*, 1932, p. 70.
70 NWSA, *5th Annual Report*, 1935, p. 7.
71 See J. Riordan, 'The workers' Olympics - a socialist alternative', in Tomlinson and Whannel, *Five Ring Circus*.
72 *Ibid.*, p. 106. Wheeler, 'Organised sport', p. 201. Cf. *ILO Year Book*, 1931, p. 465.
73 CCC, *Annual Conference Report*, 1925, p. 3.
74 Labour Party Organisation Sub-committee Minutes, 25 April 1927.
75 *Daily Herald*, 21 July 1927.
76 *Labour Magazine*, Aug. 1927. *Labour Woman*, 1 Aug. 1927. See also MAD, 016/ii/71, Souvenir of the 1927 Workers' Olympiad in Prague, 1927.
77 Labour Executive Mins, 16 Dec. 1931, 27 April 1932.
78 Labour Party Finance and General Purposes Sub-Committee Minutes, 14 May 1934.
79 See *Daily Worker*, 10 May and 5 June 1937. Labour Executive Mins, 26 May and 23 June 1937. TUC GC Mins, 26 May and 23 June 1937.
80 *Tribune*, 6 Aug. 1937.
81 BWSF Mins, 26 Oct., 11 and 25 Nov., and 2 Dec. 1932, 17 and 24 March 1933.
82 University of Warwick Modern Records Centre, George Renshaw Papers Mss 104, *Busman's Punch*, April and May 1933.
83 *Daily Worker*, 2 May 1933.
84 *Daily Worker*, 22 April 1936.
85 BWSF Mins, 3 and 29 June 1928.
86 *Worker*, 24 Aug. 1928. *Young Worker*, 8 Sept. 1928.
87 BWSF Mins, 7 June 1931. *Daily Worker*, 20 April 1932. *Worker Sportsman*, 1 May 1932.
88 See S. and B. Webb, *Soviet Communism: A New Civilisation* (1941).
89 *Ashton-Under-Lyne Reporter*, 30 July 1932. *Manchester Evening News*, 1 Aug. 1932.
90 A. Nove, *An Economic History of the U.S.S.R.* (Harmondsworth, 1982), p. 160.
91 *Worker Sportsman*, July 1932.

92 B. Rothman, interview with the author, 3 Aug. 1981. J. Norman, letter to the author, 15 Oct. 1981.
93 *Daily Worker*, 11 July 1932.
94 See R. Sissons and B. Stoddart, *Cricket and Empire: the 1932-33 Bodyline Tour of Australia* (1982).
95 P. McIntosh, *Fair Play: Ethics in Sport and Education* (1979), p. 143.
96 P. Beck, 'England v Germany, 1938', *History Today*, vol. 32 (June 1982), p. 29.
97 PRO FO 371/12606/3771/38-41; FO 371/14883/N2923/38.
98 House of Commons Debates, 1 May 1930, cols 349-50. See also *Daily Worker*, April to May 1930, *passim*.
99 B. Stoddart, 'Sport, cultural politics and international relations: England versus Germany, 1935', in N. Müller and J. K. Rühl (eds), *Sport History* (Niedernhausen, 1985). See also PRO FO 371/18884/5184, file on the Anglo-German football match at Tottenham, 4 Dec. 1935.
100 PRO HO 45/16425, Notes of a deputation from the TUC to the Home Secretary, 2 Dec. 1935. See also W. Citrine, *Under the Heel of Hitler* (1936).
101 PRO MEPO 2/3084.
102 Communist Party Archives, NWSA Mins, 8 May 1935. TUC GC Mins, 22 Oct. 1935. Labour Executive Mins, 23 Oct. 1935. MAD, 016/i/2, CCC AGM Mins, 12 April 1936.
103 *Bristol Labour Weekly*, 18 Jan. 1936. *Daily Herald*, 21 Jan. 1936. *Railway Review*, 14 Feb. 1936.
104 *Daily Worker*, 23 March and 25 May 1936.
105 *Sporting Chronicle and Athletic News*, 30 Dec. 1935.
106 *Jewish Chronicle*, 27 March 1936.
107 PRO FO 371/18863/C7600.
108 PRO FO 371/18865/C4966; FO 371/18863/C7600.
109 PRO 371/19922, Sir W. Selby to O. Sargent, 29 Feb. 1936.
110 PRO 371/19940, Eric Phipps to Anthony Eden, 13 Feb. 1936.
111 See PRO FO 371/19940 and newspaper cuttings in Elvin Papers, COLL MISC 685/2.
112 *Manchester Guardian*, 7 Dec. 1935, 23 Jan. 1936. Even so, the paper felt that sport and politics should be separate spheres, and as such opposed participation in the 1937 Antwerp Olympiad – characterised as 'political propaganda direct and undisguised'. *Manchester Guardian*, 3 May 1937.
113 Communist Party Archives, Minutes of the International Conference of Adversaries of the Hitler Olympiad and Friends of the Olympic Movement, 6 June 1936. See also *Daily Worker*, 8 June 1936. *Clarion Cyclist*, July 1936. *Labour*, July 1936.
114 *Tribune*, 18 Feb. 1938.
115 *Millgate*, Aug. 1936.
116 *Daily Herald*, 27 July 1936. *Daily Worker*, 27 July 1936. *Labour*, Aug. 1936. *Clarion Cyclist*, Sept. 1936.
117 See newspaper cuttings and leaflets in Elvin Papers, COLL MISC 685/2.
118 J. Jacobs, *Out of the Ghetto: My Youth in the East End, Communism and Fascism, 1913-1939* (1978), pp. 113, 278.
119 MAD, 016/i/2, CCC Mins, 28 March 1937.
120 *Ibid.*; CCC Mins, 12/13 Sept. 1936. *Daily Worker*, 30 Jan. and 30 March 1937.

121 British Library of Political and Economic Science, YMA/WF/204.
122 *Clarion Cyclist*, Oct. 1936, March 1937.
123 *Labour*, Oct. 1936.
124 PRO FO 371/21394/5467/246-8. *Daily Herald*, 19 March 1937. *Labour*, April 1937.
125 MAD, 016/i/2, CCC Mins, 29/30 Jan., 7/8 May and 17/18 Sept. 1938. For accounts of the British stages of the relay, see *Challenge*, 14 April, 12, 19 and 26 May and 2 June 1938.
126 Elvin Papers, COLL MISC 685/1, *Daily Herald*, 3 Sept. 1934.
127 *Times*, 7 Feb. 1939. The World Congress was first organised in 1932 in conjunction with the Los Angeles Olympics.
128 *Daily Worker*, 19 March 1937.
129 PRO FO 395/568/P1718/28/150, R. Vansittart, to S. F. Rous, 6 May 1938.
130 PRO FO 371/18884/5184/352, 353, 371.
131 Labour Executive Mins, 22 Jan. 1936. Labour Party Archives, WG/SPA/111-95, file 4, W. Gillies to J. S. Middleton, 17 June 1936.
132 See J. MacKenzie (ed.), *Imperialism and Popular Culture* (Manchester, 1986).

Chapter 8

Conclusion

This study has focused on the role of the British labour movement in shaping the context for the development of sport in the 1920s and 1930s. There is much in the argument that sport has been contoured by subtle interaction of socio-economic structures and human agency. Of course, structure and agency are complementary categories of analysis and should not be placed in opposition to each other. After all, people as human agents reproduce the structures through which history is made. Yet having said this, it is 'stupifyingly difficult to resolve ... the problem of individual and society, of consciousness and being, action and structure'.[1] In order to reconcile this problem, there is a need to provide a dialogue between theory and narrative; to expose the place of sports in capitalist society to detailed historical investigation. By focusing on the policies and actions of inter-war labour it has been demonstrated in at least one instance that the contradictions and tensions of capitalist society imposed limits on, yet offered 'real' possibilities for change in, and through, sport.

To be sure, the British working class faced a number of structural limitations as they increasingly participated in sport. Not only were there fundamental class and gender divisions, but also bourgeois male control at the top of many sports and games. However, the working class's contribution to the making and re-making of sport was an active process in which gains were made. It has been well described in the following extract:

> Examples from recreational and professional sport reaffirm the idea that the meanings and social practices which hegemony contours and defines favour, within the prevailing structures of power, dominant rather than subordinate groups. Yet, they serve to remind us that while hegemony turns history to the advantage of the dominant, this advantage must be continuously pressed against subordinate corporate cultures and the oppositional practices contained within them. Whether one deals with the conformity norms of recreational sport, one must be sensitive to the ways in which subordinate groups negotiate with the dominant and to the changes which occur in the practises of both the dominant and subordinate as a result of this, albeit asymmetrical, negotiation process.[2]

196

Though constrained by the economic and political 'realities' of capitalist structures, the inter-war labour movement was clearly and successfully involved in this negotiation process.

The workers' sports movement was never in a position to overhaul the dominant traditions of professionalism and bourgeois amateurism. It could never compete on equal terms with commodity sport or the thousands of voluntary organisations affiliated to the Amateur Athletic Association, Amateur Boxing Association, Football Association and the rest. At least this is the conclusion to be drawn from any simple quantative analysis. Sources suggest that both the British Workers' Sports Federation, with about 6,000 members in 1931 and the National Workers' Sports Association, with 9,000 members in 1935 were proletarian in composition with bases in the main industrial areas. However, by the mid-thirties non-socialist organisations catering for outdoor recreation were far more popular – by 1934 the Co-operative Holidays Association had 26,259 members, the Cyclists Touring Club 25,720 and the Youth Hostels Association 37,285. In addition, there were some 750,000 players linked to the Football Association. Similarly, the Woodcraft Folk estimated that in the same year, whilst membership of the imperialist, uniformed youth movement – Boy Scouts, Boys' Brigades, Girl Guides, etc. – was about 1.3 million, the combined membership of progressive organisations like the Folk, Labour Party League of Youth and Young Communist League was only 46,000.[3] Of course, the people also spent their hard-earned money on sports equipment and marketed forms of leisure, the cinema, as the most addictive of cultural institutions, pulling in 963 million film-goers also in 1934. When committed socialists were spending some of their spare time in the recreational associations of the movement, the mass of workers were at the football ground, the pictures, the pub or simply relaxing at home.

To add yet a further point, the BWSF and NWSA were small in comparison with the Continental workers' sports movement, a fact stressed by Heinrich Müller of the Workers' Gymnastic and Sports Alliance of America: 'In England, the classical land of sport, we find surprisingly a weak workers' sports movement.'[4] But, by way of speculation, perhaps the workers' sports movement did not need to be as strong in Britain as on the Continent due to the more direct colonisation of popular sports by the working class themselves. The British proletariat, as suggested in chapter 2, were particularly adept at using commercialised and even bourgeois-controlled amateur sports for their own ends. Put simply, workers' sport failed to replace those numerous proletarian sports based on club, public house, street or workplace. Indeed, what is needed now is further research on the relationship between the non-political institutions of the working class and the wider perspectives of the labour movement itself.

Sociological and historical approaches to sport are a relatively new development. There are many issues raised in this study which need to be further investigated from both theoretical and empirical perspectives. We need to know more about the way in which changes in sport were received by different social groups. Crucially, the historian should study the particular role of women and ethnic minorities in sport, and the role of supporters in modifying sport. And what about the intersection between work, the community and sport? Hopefully, a generation from now we will be more confident in our assessment of inter-war sport.

Yet having acknowledged these points, it is still far too simplistic for John Hargreaves to claim that 'the British working-class movement, and the Left as a whole continued to ignore the growing significance of sport in working-class people's lives, tacitly allowing this terrain to be hegemonized by forces unsympathetic to the Left'.[5] Despite the apathy of certain labour leaders, the evidence plainly suggests that socialists were involved in sporting activities and questions. First of all, given that Labour was preoccupied with such issues as unemployment, poverty and general attacks on workers' wages, living standards and industrial organisations, it is important to reiterate the point that the very emergence of a workers' sports movement is in itself creditable. But, notwithstanding this, if we add to the BWSF and NWSA the myriad of associations from the Labour League of Youth through to the ordinary co-operative society and trade union branch, sports and recreation were more widely supported than a simple investigation of the two main sports bodies would suggest.

Above all, a legitimate workers' sports movement did develop in Britain. Having its origins in the late nineteenth century with the religion of socialism and the Clarion Movement, workers' sport emerged in the 1920s on a more politically and strategically defined basis, and included all strands of socialist thought and organisation. Whereas the communist-inspired BWSF was primarily a political grouping which utilised sport to further the class struggle, the labour socialist NWSA placed greater emphasis on sports activity, though it too had a political side to its work. Hence in the 1930s, the BWSF approached sport with a fairly comprehensive Marxist critique of capitalist civilisation, whilst the NWSA viewed sport from a labour socialist or social democratic perspective which, though at times critical of capitalism, accommodated the established order. Nonetheless, with the advent of the 'united front', communists and Labour Party supporters interested in sport began to collaborate. Indeed, beneath all the rhetoric there were similarities between the two main agencies of workers' sport, the articulation of some form of socialist alternative being one of many. As part of a wider socialist recreational formation, which also included drama, film, literature and music, the workers' sports movement provided organised labour with limited means to oppose dominant capitalist structures. And as such it approximated to what Antonio Gramsci meant by cultural struggle – 'the "exploitation" of the cultural factor, of cultural activity, of a cultural front which is as necessary as the merely economic and merely political ones'.[6] In brief, Labour's intervention in the politics of sport at local, national and even international level meant that sections of the working class had the opportunity to challenge orthodox views about the relationship between sport and society.

Yet it must be added that workers' sport was not simply an alternative or oppositional cultural activity, for in complex ways it was connected to the established order in sport. We must approach socialist culture 'not as an autonomous practice but as a complicated series of practices, most of which were related to the dominant culture in unique ways'.[7] There were important similarities between the socialist critique of commercialised sport and that provided by middle-class moralists and rational recreationists. Also, both the BWSF and NWSA were affiliated to the bourgeois Amateur Athletic Association and had contacts with similar organisations, whilst worker sportsmen and women were not immune to the attractions of Cup Finals, test matches and the like. By the same token, labour's demand for improvements in existing sports provision cannot be divorced from the reproduction of the existing patterns of domination between State and society. Even so, the reforms advanced by the workers' sports movement were perhaps its main claim to success.

As far as this last point is concerned, organised labour played a part in changing perceptions about the need for access to the countryside, improved sports facilities and opposition to fascism on the Continent. As in the case of the American Play Movement, gains in the recreational sphere have not simply been imposed from above by upper and middle-class reform groups, but have also been linked to the activities of the subordinate classes. This study complements the work on American cities by Hardy and Ingham insomuch as primary material – central and local government records, the minutes and reports of labour organisations, newspapers – 'uncovers the petitions, lobbies and debates representing the agency of subordinate groups who were as vocal as the elite reformers they sometimes joined and sometimes battled. Their subsequent silence has stemmed from the limits of historical research, not from their own impotence in historical reality.'[8] Indeed, in reality, over a long period of time the working class has campaigned vigorously for sporting reforms. Sport is but one of the many sites of struggle which involve socialist intervention. The instruments of persuasion and change in capitalist society may be framed against the backdrop of profound economic and social inequalities, but this should not lead us to believe that the working class has been unable to gain access to the decision-making structures. In fact, as those theorists of 'pluralist Marxism' would recognise, organised interests drawn from the working class have influenced the way in which sport is perceived by rulers and ruled alike, and in turn extracted reforms and concessions. Arguably, through organised representation in trade unions, political parties and pressure groups, the working class has been able to modify ideas, policies and action on sport, a feature of the development of sport which continues to this day.

Notes

1 P. Abrams, 'History, sociology, historical sociology', *Past and Present*, no. 87 (1980), pp. 7-8.
2 A. Ingham and S. Hardy, 'Sport: structuration, subjugation and hegemony', *Theory, Culture and Society*, vol. 2 (1984), p. 100.
3 British Library of Political and Economic Science, YMA/WF/3, 333.
4 *Proletarian Sports*, April 1935. In a previous number, Herbert Elvin also suggested that in workers' sports circles, England and America were 'probably regarded as the backward countries'. *Proletarian Sports*, Feb. 1934.
5 J. Hargreaves, *Sport, Power and Culture: A Social and Historical Analysis of Popular Sports in Britain* (Cambridge, 1986), pp. 92-3.
6 Quoted in A. Showstack Sassoon, *Gramsci's Politics* (1980), p. 111.
7 C. Waters, 'Socialism and the Politics of Popular Culture in Britain, 1884-1914', PhD, University of Harvard (1985), p. 526.
8 S. Hardy and A. G. Ingham, 'Games, structures and agency: historians on the American play movement', *Journal of Social History*, vol. 17 (1983-84).

Select bibliography

This bibliography is composed of material cited in the notes.

1 Archival material

(a) British Library of Political and Economic Science (BLPES), London
George Elvin Papers.
Woodcraft Folk Records.
(b) Communist Party Archives (CPA), London
George Sinfield Papers, including records of the British Workers' Sports Federation.
(c) EP Microform Collection
Cambridge Trades Council and Labour Party Minutes.
Colne Valley Divisional Labour Party Records.
G. H. B. Ward Correspondence.
Sheffield Trades and Labour Council Minutes.
(d) Greater London Record Office (GLRO)
London County Council (LCC) Papers and Minutes.
(e) Harvester Microfilm Collection
Fabian Society Minute Books and Records, 1884-1918.
Independent Labour Party (ILP) National Administrative Council Minutes and Related Records, 1894-1950.
(f) Labour Party Archives (LPA), London
Labour Party Records.
(g) Leeds Archives Department
Leeds Labour Party League of Youth Records.
(h) Manchester Central Library Archives Department (MAD)
Clarion Cycling Club (CCC) Records.
(i) Public Record Office (PRO), Kew
Papers in the Records of the Board of Education, Foreign Office, Home Office, Metropolitan Police, Miners Welfare Committee, Ministry of Health, Ministry of Labour, Ministry of Transport, and Office of Works.
James Ramsay MacDonald Papers.
(j) Stockport Archives Centre.
Stockport Labour Fellowship Records
(k) Trades Union Congress (TUC) Archives, London
TUC General Council Minutes
(l) Union of Shop, Distributive and Allied Workers' Library, Manchester
National Amalgamated Union of Shop Assistants, Warehousemen and Clerks Records.
(m) University of Warwick Modern Records Centre (MRC)

George Renshaw Papers.
Transport and General Workers' Union Records.
(n) World Microfilms Collection
London Trades Council Minutes.

2 Reports, offical inquiries and yearbooks

A Congress of Young Fighters: A Report of the 4th Congress of the Y.C.L. of G.B., Dec. 1926.
Amalgamated Engineering Union (AEU), *National Committee Reports*.
Census of England and Wales 1931. Industry Tables (1934).
Central Council of Recreative Physical Training, *Annual Reports*.
Clarion Cycling Club (CCC), *Annual Conference Reports*.
Communist Party, *Report on Organisation presented by the Party Commission to the Annual Conference of the C.P.G.B.*, 7 Oct. 1922.
Communist Party, *Reports, Theses and Resolutions of the 9th Congress*, 1927.
Communist Party, *The New Line: Documents of the 10th Congress*, Jan. 1929.
Fifth Census of Production, 1935, Part III (1940).
ILO Year Books.
Independent Labour Party (ILP), *Annual Conference Reports*.
Labour Party, *Annual Conference Reports*.
Labour Year Book.
London Trade Union Handbook (1930).
Ministry of Health, *Annual Reports*.
Ministry of Town and Country Planning, *National Parks in England and Wales. Report by John Dower* (1945), cmd. 6628.
Minutes of Evidence taken before the Committee on Industry and Trade (1925).
Minutes of Evidence taken before the Royal Commission on Licensing (England and Wales) (1930).
Minutes of Evidence taken before the Royal Commission on Lotteries and Betting (1932).
National Playing Fields Association, *Annual Reports*.
National Trade Councils, *Annual Conference Reports*.
National Union of Labour and Socialist Clubs, *Annual Bulletins*.
National Workers' Sports Association (NWSA), *Annual Reports*.
People's Year Book.
Programme of the Young Communist International (1929).
Report of Comrade M. Woolf, 'The Day is ours!' 6th World Congress Young Communist International (1935).
Reports of the Commissioner for the Special Areas in England and Wales.
Report of the Committee on Football (1968).
Report of the Committee on Land Utilisation in Rural Areas (1942), cmd. 6378.
Report of the Departmental Committee on Crowds (1924), cmd. 2088.
Report of the 5th National Congress of the Y.C.L., 1928.
Report of the Departmental Committee of Inquiry into the Miners' Welfare Fund (1931), cmd. 4236.
Report of the Executive Committee to the 4th National Congress of the Y.C.L. of G.B., 1926.
Report of the National Parks Committee (1931), cmd. 3851.
Resolutions adopted at the 4th Congress of the Young Communist International (1924).
Royal Commission on the Distribution of the Industrial Population: Report (1940), cmd. 6153.
The Tasks of the United Front of the Youth: Resolutions adopted at the Sixth Congress (1935).

Select bibliography

Trades Union Congress (TUC), *Annual Reports.*
Transport and General Workers' Union, *Delegate Conference Reports.*
Workers' Film Association, *Annual Reports.*
Youth Hostels Association, *Annual Reports.*

3 Contemporary newspapers and periodicals

AEU *Monthly Report, Ashton-Under-Lyne Reporter, Blackshirt, Bolton Citizen, Boost, Bristol Labour Weekly, Busman's Punch, Challenge, Clarion, Clarion Cyclist, Communist, Communist Review, Contemporary Review, Co-operative News, Cotton Factory Times, Daily Express, Daily Herald, Daily Mail, Daily Mirror, Daily Worker, The Economist, Fabian News, Fan, Fight Like Hell, Forward,* (Glasgow) *Daily Record and Mail, Hendon Times, Hornsey Star, House of Commons Debates, House of Lords Debates, Industrial Review, Industrial Welfare, International Labour Review, International of Youth, International Press Correspondence, Jewish Chronicle, Journal of the Commons, Open Spaces and Footpaths Preservation Society, Justice, Labour, Labour Magazine, Labour Monthly,* Labour Party League of Youth *Monthly Bulletin, Labour Woman, Labour's Northern Voice, Lansbury's Labour Weekly, Leeds Weekly Citizen, Liberal Magazine, Listener, Locomotive Journal, London Citizen, London News,* (Manchester) *Evening Chronicle, Manchester Evening News, Manchester Guardian, Millgate, Morning Star, Nation and Athenaeum, New Clarion, New Dawn, New Leader, New Nation, Nineteenth Century, North Tottenham Citizen, Northern Rambler, Oldham Chronicle, Oldham Labour Gazette, Our Youth, Out-O'-Doors, Post, Proletarian Sports, Railway Review, Railway Service Journal, Record, Red Stage, Rochdale Labour News, Rochester, Chatham and Gillingham Journal, Russia Today, St Helens Newspaper and Advertiser, Shop Assistant, Socialist Leaguer, Spectator, Sport and Games, Sporting Chronicle, Sporting Chronicle and Athletic News, Sunday Worker, Tennis Ilustrated, Textile Weekly, The Times, Trade Union Propaganda and Cultural Work, Trade Unionist, Travel Log, Tribune, Weekly Young Worker, Worker, Worker Sportsman, Workers' Dreadnought, Workers' Illustrated News, Workers' Union Record, Workers' Weekly, Young Worker.*

4 Books, pamphlets and articles

All are published in London unless otherwise stated
Abrams, P., 'History, sociology, historical sociology', *Past and Present,* no. 87 (1980).
Aldcroft, D. H., *The Inter-War Economy: Britain 1919-1939* (1970).
Allison, L., 'Sport and politics', in Allison, L. (ed.), *The Politics of Sport* (Manchester, 1986).
Althusser, L., 'Ideology and ideological state apparatuses (notes towards an investigation)', in *Lenin and Philosophy and other essays* (1971).
Anderson, P., 'The origins of the present crisis', *New Left Review,* no. 23 (1964).
Anon., *Baden-Powell Exposed* (n.d.).
Arnold, M., *Culture and Anarchy* (1869).
Attfield, J., *With Light of Knowledge: A Hundred Years of Education in the Royal Arsenal Co-operative Society 1877-1977* (1981).
Bailey, P., *Leisure and Class in Victorian England: Rational recreation and the contest for control* (1978).
Barou, Y., and Rigaudiat, J., *Les 35 heures et l'emploi* (Paris, 1982).

Select bibliography

Beamish, R., 'Sport and the logic of capitalism', in Cantelon, H., and Gruneau, R. (eds), *Sport, Culture and the Modern State* (Toronto, 1982).

Beck, P., 'England v Germany, 1938', *History Today*, vol. 32 (1982).

Benson, J., *The Penny Capitalists: a study of nineteenth-century working-class entrepreneurs* (Dublin, 1983).

Birley, D., 'Sportsmen and the deadly game', *British Journal of Sports History*, vol. 3 (1986).

Blatchford, R., *Merrie England* (1895).

Booth, A., 'Essay in bibliography: the Labour Party and economics between the wars', *Bulletin of the Society for the Study of Labour History*, no. 47 (1983).

Britain, I., *Fabianism and Culture: A Study of British Socialism and the arts c 1884-1918* (Cambridge, 1982).

British Workers' Sports Association, *Sport – Drug or Tonic?* (1939).

Brockway, F., *Bermondsey Story: The Life of Alfred Salter* (1949).

Brohm, J-M., *Sport – a Prison of Measured Time* (1978).

Brown, G., *Sabotage: A Study in Industrial Conflict* (Nottingham, 1977).

Brownlie, J. T., *The Engineers' Case for an Eight-Hour Day* (n.d., 1914?).

Burgess, K., *The Challenge of Labour* (1980).

Burns, R., and van der Will, W., 'Organisation debate: working-class organisation and the importance of cultural struggle. A critique of James Wickham', *Capital and Class*, no. 10 (1980).

Burton, R. D. E., 'Cricket, carnival and street culture in the Caribbean', *British Journal of Sports History*, vol. 2 (1985).

Butsch, R., 'The commodification of leisure: the case of the model airplane hobby and industry', *Qualitative Sociology*, vol. 7 (1984).

Cairns, J., Jennett, N., and Sloane, P. J., 'The economics of professional team sports: a survey of theory and evidence', *Journal of Economic Studies*, vol. 13 (1986).

Cantelon, H., and Gruneau, R. (eds), *Sport, Culture and the Modern State* (Toronto, 1982).

Citrine, W., *Under the Heel of Hitler* (1936).

Clark, D., *Colne Valley. Radicalism to Socialism* (1981).

Clark, G. L., and Dear, M., *State Apparatus: Structures and Language of Legitimacy* (1984).

Clarke, J., and Critcher, C., *The Devil Makes Work: Leisure in Capitalist Britain* (1985).

Clinton, A., *The Trade Union Rank and File: Trades Councils in Britain 1900-40* (Manchester, 1977).

Colledge, D., and Field, J., '"To recondition human material ...": an account of a British labour camp in the 1930s. An interview with William Heard', *History Workshop Journal*, no. 15 (1983).

Communist Party, *The Young Communist International: Between the Fourth and Fifth Congresses 1924-1928* (1928).

Communist Party, *For Soviet Britain* (1935).

Condon, T. M., *The Fight For the Workers' Playing Fields* (n.d., 1931?).

Condon, T. M., *The Case For Organised Sunday Football* (1933).

Constantine, L. N., *Cricket in the Sun* (n.d., 1948?).

Cook, D., 'The battle for Kinder Scout', *Marxism Today*, vol. 21 (1977).

Cousins, G., *Golf in Britain: A Social history from the beginnings to the present* (1975).

Cox, D., 'The Labour Party in Leicester: a study of branch development', *International Review of Social History*, vol. 6 (1961).

Select bibliography

Cronin, J. E., 'Coping with Labour, 1918-26', in Cronin, J. E., and Schneer, J. (eds), *Social Conflict and the Political Order in Modern Britain* (1982).

Cronin, J. E., *Labour and Society in Britain 1918-1979* (1984).

Cross, G., 'The quest for leisure: reassesing the eight-hour day in France', *Journal of Social History*, vol. 18 (1984).

Cross, G., 'Les Trois huits: labor movements, international reform, and the origins of the eight-hour day, 1919-1924', *French Historical Studies*, vol. 14 (1985).

Cross, G., 'The political economy of leisure in retrospect: Britain, France, and the origins of the eight-hour day', *Leisure Studies*, vol. 5 (1986).

Crump, J., 'Recreation in Coventry between the wars', in Lancaster, B., and Mason, T. (eds), *Life and Labour in a 20th Century City: The Experience of Coventry* (Coventry, n.d., 1986?).

Cunningham, H., *Leisure in the Industrial Revolution, 1780-1880* (1980).

Cunningham, H., 'Leisure', in Benson, J. (ed.), *The Working Class in England* (1985).

Dabscheck, '"Defensive Manchester": a history of the Professional Footballers Association', in Cashman, R., and McKernan, M. (eds), *Sport in History: the Making of Modern Sporting History* (Queensland, 1979).

Dalton, H., *The Fateful Years: Memoirs 1931-1945* (1957).

Dawson, D., 'Leisure and social class: some neglected theoretical considerations', *Leisure Sciences*, vol. 8 (1986).

Deem, R., *All Work and No Play? The Sociology of Women and Leisure* (Milton Keynes, 1986).

de Grazia, V., *The Culture of Consent: Mass organisation of leisure in fascist Italy* (Cambridge, 1981).

Dellheim, C., 'The creation of a company culture: *Cadburys*, 1861-1931', *American Historical Review*, vol. 92 (1987).

Delves, A., 'Popular recreation and social conflict in Derby 1800-1850', in Yeo, E. and S. (eds), *Popular Culture and Class Conflict 1590-1914: Explorations in the History of Labour and Leisure* (Brighton, 1981).

Donoughue, B., and Jones, G. W., *Herbert Morrison: Portrait of a Politician* (1973).

Douglas, J. L., *"Be Prepared" For War!* (n.d.).

Downham, C. M., 'The problem of Millwall Football Club: an historical and sociological approach', in Benning, D. (ed.), *Sport and Imperialism* (1986).

Dunlop Rubber Company, *50 Years of Growth* (1938).

Dunning, E., Murphy, P., Williams, J., and Maguire, J., 'Football hooliganism in Britain before the first world war', *International Review of Sport Sociology*, vol. 19 (1984).

Dunning, E. and Sheard, K., *Barbarians, Gentlemen and Players: A Sociological Study of the Development of Rugby Football* (Oxford, 1979).

Durbin, E., *New Jerusalems: The Labour Party and the Economics of Democratic Socialism* (1985).

Elias, N., and Dunning, E., *Quest For Excitement: Sport and Leisure in the Civilizing Process* (Oxford, 1986).

Evans, H. Justin, *Service to Sport: The Story of the CCPR 1935 to 1972* (1974).

Evans, R., and Boyd, A., *The Use of Leisure in Hull* (Hull, 1933).

Evans, R. J., 'Introduction: the sociological interpretation of German labour history', in Evans, R. J. (ed.), *The German Working Class 1888-1933* (1982).

Featherstone, M., 'Lifestyle and consumer culture', *Theory, Culture and Society*, vol. 4 (1987).

Select bibliography

Fletcher, S., *Women First: The Female Tradition in English Physical Education 1880-1980* (1984).

Francis, H., and Smith, D., *The Fed: A History of the South Wales Miners in the Twentieth Century* (1980).

Frow, E. and R., *Clem Beckett and the Oldham Men Who Fought in Spain: 1936-1938* (Manchester, n.d., 1980?).

Goldman, R., '"We make weekends": leisure and the commodity form', *Social Text*, vol. 8 (1984).

Gosling, H., *Up and Down Stream* (1927).

Graves, R., and Hodge, A., *The Long Week-end: A Social History of Great Britain 1918-1939* (1940).

Green, G., *The History of the Football Association* (1953).

Griffen, C., *et al*, 'Women and leisure', in Hargreaves, Jennifer (ed), *Sport, culture and ideology* (1982).

Groom, T., *National Clarion Cycling Club 1894-1944: The Fifty-Year Story of the Club* (Halifax, 1944).

Gruneau, R., 'Sport and the debate on the state', in Cantelon, H., and Gruneau, R. (eds), *Sport, Culture and the Modern State* (Toronto, 1982).

Gruneau, R., *Class, Sports and Social Development* (Amherst, 1983).

Guttmann, A., *Sports Spectators* (New York, 1986).

Guttsman, W. L., *The German Social Democratic Party, 1875-1933* (1981).

Hall, S., 'Notes on deconstructing "the popular"', in Samuel, R., (ed.) *People's History and Socialist Theory* (1981).

Hall, S., 'Cultural studies: two paradigms', in Collins, R. *et al.* (eds), *Media, Culture and Society: A Critical Reader* (1986).

Hall, S., 'Popular culture and the state', in Bennett, T., Mercer, C., and Woollacott, J. (eds), *Popular Culture and Social Relations* (Milton Keynes, 1986).

Hall, S., and Schwarz, B., 'State and society, 1880-1930', in Langan, M., and Schwarz, B. (eds), *Crises in the British State, 1880-1930* (1985).

Hannington, W., *The Problem of the Distressed Areas* (1937).

Hardy, S., and Ingham, A.G., 'Games, structures and agency: historians on the American play movement', *Journal of Social History*, vol. 17 (1983-84).

Hargreaves, J., *Sport, Power and Culture: A Social and Historical Analysis of Popular Sports in Britain* (1986).

Hargreaves, J., 'The State and sport: Programmed and non-programmed intervention in Britain', in Allison, L. (ed.), *The politics of Sport* (Manchester, 1986).

Hargreaves, J. A., (ed.), *Sport, culture and ideology* (1982).

Hay, R., 'Soccer and social control in Scotland 1873-1978', in Cashman, R., and McKernan, M. (eds), *Sport: Money, Morality and the Media* (New South Wales, n.d., 1982?).

Haywood, L., 'Hegemony – another blind alley for the study of sport', in Mangan, J. A., and Small, R. B., (eds), *Sports, Culture and Society: International historical and sociological perspectives* (1986).

Henery, M., 'The Y.C.L. and the 1930s', *Scottish Marxist*, no. 21 (1981).

Hewitt, A. W., *The Ramblers Federation: Nineteen Years of Progress in Manchester* (Manchester, 1938).

Hill, H., *Freedom to Roam: The Struggle for Access to Britain's Moors and Mountains* (Ashbourne, 1980).

Hill, J., 'The development of professionalism in English league cricket, *c.* 1900 to 1940', in Mangan, J. A., and Small, R. B., (eds), *Sport, Culture and Society: International historical and sociological perspectives* (1986).

Hill, M., *George Sinfield – his pen a sword* (n.d., 1986?).

Hoare, Q., and Nowell Smith, G. (eds), *Selection from the Prison Notebooks of Antonio Gramsci* (1971).

Hoberman, J. M., *Sport and Political Ideology* (1984).

Hobsbawm, E., 'Mass-producing traditions: Europe, 1870-1914', in Hobsbawm, E., and Ranger, T. (eds), *The Invention of Tradition* (Cambridge, 1983).

Hobsbawm, E., 'The foundation of British working-class culture', in *Worlds of Labour: further studies in the history of labour* (1984).

Holt, A., 'Hikers and ramblers: surviving a thirties' fashion', *International Journal of the History of Sport*, vol. 4 (1987).

Holt, R., *Sport and Society in Modern France* (1981).

Holt, R., 'Working-class football and the city: the problem of continuity', *British Journal of Sports History*, vol. 3 (1986).

Hopcraft, A., *The Football Man: People and Passions in Soccer* (1968).

Horne, J., Jary, D., and Tomlinson, A. (eds), *Sports, Leisure and Social Relations* (1987).

Howkins, A., 'Class against class: the political culture of the Communist Party of Great Britain, 1930-35', in Gloversmith, F. (ed.), *Class, Culture and Social Change: A New View of the 1930s* (Brighton, 1980).

Howkins, A., and Lowerson, J., *Trends in Leisure 1919-1939* (1979).

Howkins, A., and Saville, J., 'The 1930s: a revisionist history', *Socialist Register* (1979).

Humphries, S., *Hooligans or Rebels? An Oral History of Working-Class Childhood and Youth 1889-1939* (Oxford, 1981).

Hunt, K., 'Women and the Social Democratic Federation: some notes on Lancashire', *North West Labour History Society Bulletin*, no. 7 (1980-81).

Hutt, A., *The Condition of the Working Class in Britain* (1933).

Ingham, A., and Hardy, S., 'Sport: structuration, subjugation and hegemony', *Theory, Culture and Society*, vol. 2 (1984).

Inglis, K. S., 'The Labour Church Movement', *International Review of Social History*, vol. 3 (1958).

Inglis, S., *Soccer in the Dock: A History of British Football Scandals 1900 to 1965* (1985).

International Labour Office, *Hours of Labour in Industry: France* (Geneva, 1922).

International Labour Office, *Development of Facilities for the utilization of workers' leisure* (Geneva, 1923).

International Labour Office, *Recreation and Education* (1936).

Jacobs, J., *Out of the Ghetto: My Youth in the East End, Communism and Fascism 1913-1939* (1978).

James, C. L. R., *Beyond a Boundary* (1963).

Jeffreys, J. B., *Retail Trading in Britain 1850-1950* (Cambridge, 1954).

Jenkins, M., 'Early days in the Y.C.L.' *Marxism Today*, vol. 16 (1972).

Jeremy, D. J., 'Critchley, Alfred Cecil (1890-1963): greyhound racing promoter and industrialist', in Jeremy, D. J. (ed.), *Dictionary of Business Biography*, vol. 1 (1984).

Jessop, B., *The Capitalist State: Marxist Theories and Methods* (Oxford, 1982).

Joad, C. E. M., *The Horrors of the Countryside* (1931).

Joad, C. E. M., *The Untutored Townsman's Invasion of the Country* (1946).

Johnson, P., *Saving and Spending: The Working-Class Economy 1870-1939* (Oxford, 1985).

Select bibliography

Johnston, F. (ed.) *The Football Who's Who* (1935).

Johnston, L., *Marxism, Class Analysis and Socialist Pluralism* (1986).

Jones, D. Caradog (ed.), *The Social Survey of Merseyside*, vol. 3 (Liverpool, 1934).

Jones, G. Stedman, 'Working-class culture and working-class politics in London, 1870-1900; notes on the remaking of a working class', *Journal of Social History*, vol. 7 (1974).

Jones, G. Stedman, 'Class expression versus social control? A critique of recent trends in the social history of "leisure"', *History Workshop Journal*, no. 4 (1977).

Jones, S. G., 'The economic aspects of association football in England, 1918-1939', *British Journal of Sports History*, vol. 1 (1984).

Jones, S. G., *Workers at Play: A Social and Economic History of Lesiure, 1918-1939* (1986).

Jones, S. G., *The British Labour Movement and Film, 1918-1939* (1987).

Jones, S. G., 'Labour, society and the drink question in Britain, 1918-1939', *Historical Journal*, vol. 30 (1987).

Jones, S. G., 'State intervention in sport and leisure in Britain between the wars', *Journal of Contemporary History*, vol. 22 (1987).

Jones, S. G., 'The survival of industrial paternalism in the cotton districts: a view from the 1920s', *Journal of Regional and Local Studies*, vol. 7 (1987).

Jones, S. G., 'Work, leisure and the political economy of the cotton districts between the wars', *Textile History*, vol. 18 (1987).

Jupp, J., *The Radical Left in Britain 1931-1941* (1982).

Kipnis, L., '"Refunctioning" reconsidered: towards a left popular culture', in MacCabe, C. (ed.), *High Theory/Low Culture: Analysing popular television and film* (Manchester, 1986).

Korr, C., *West Ham United: the Making of a Football Club* (1986).

Krüger, A., 'The influence of the state sport of fascist Italy on Nazi Germany 1928-1936', in Mangan, J. A., and Small, R. B (eds), *Sport, Culture and Society: International historical and sociological perspectives* (1986).

Krüger, A., and Riordan, J. (eds), *Der Internationale Arbeitersport: Der Schlüssei zum Arbeitersport in 10 Ländern* (Köln, 1985).

La Capra, D., *Rethinking Intellectual History: Texts, Contexts, Language* (Ithaca, 1983).

Labour Party, *Labour and the New Social Order: A Report on Reconstruction* (1918).

Labour Party, *Labour's Immediate Programme* (1937).

Lenman, R., 'Mass culture and the state in Germany, 1900-1926', in Bellen, R. J., Pogge van Strandmann, H., and Polonsky, A. B. (eds), *Ideas into History: Aspects of European History 1880-1950* (1984).

Liddell, B., *My Soccer Story* (1960).

Lidtke, V. L., *The Alternative Culture: Socialist Labor in Imperial Germany* (Oxford, 1985).

Llewellyn Smith, H. (ed.), *The New Survey of London Life and Labour. vol. 9 Life and Leisure* (1935).

Lowe, R., *Adjusting to Democracy: The Role of the Ministry of Labour in British Politics 1916-1939* (Oxford, 1986).

Lowerson, J., 'Battles for the countryside', in Gloversmith, F. (ed.) *Class, Culture and Social Change: A New View of the 1930s* (Brighton, 1980).

Lowerson, J., 'Studying inter-war leisure: the context and some problems', in Tomlinson, A. (ed.) *Leisure and Social Control* (Brighton, 1981).

Lowerson, J., 'Sport and the Victorian Sunday: the beginning of middle-class apostasy', *British Journal of Sports History*, vol. 1 (1984).

Select bibliography

Lowerson, J., 'Brothers of the Angle: Match Fishing, 1850-1914', *Bulletin of the Society for the Study of Labour History*, no. 50 (1985).

MacDougall, I. (ed.), *Militant Miners* (Edinburgh, 1981).

McIntosh, P., *Sport in Society* (1963).

McIntosh, P., *Fair Play: Ethics in Sport and Education* (1979).

Macintyre, S., *A Proletarian Science: Marxism in Britain 1917-1933* (Cambridge 1980).

Macintyre, S., *Little Moscows: Communism and Working-Class Militancy in Inter-war Britain* (1980).

MacKenzie, J., *Propaganda and Empire: The manipulation of British public opinion 1880-1960* (Manchester, 1984).

MacKenzie, J. (ed.), *Imperialism and Popular Culture* (Manchester, 1986).

McKibbin, R., 'Working-class gambling in Britain 1880-1939', *Past and Present*, no. 82 (1979).

McKibbin, R., 'Work and hobbies in Britain 1880-1950', in Winter, J. (ed.) *The Working Class in Modern British History* (Cambridge, 1983).

Macklin, K., *The History of Rugby League Football* (1974).

McLennan, G., 'Capitalist state or democratic polity? Recent developments in Marxist and pluralist theory', in McLennan, G., Held, D., and Hall, S., (eds), *The Idea of the Modern State* (Milton Keynes, 1984).

Magarey, S., 'That hoary old chestnut, free will and determinism: culture vs. structure, or history vs. theory in Britain', *Comparative Studies in Society and History*, vol. 29 (1987).

Mahon, J., *Harry Pollitt: A Biography* (1976).

Malcolmson, R., *Popular Recreations in English Society 1700-1850* (Cambridge, 1973).

Malcolmson, R. W., 'Sports in Society: A Historical Perspective', *British Journal of Sports History*, vol. 1 (1984).

Mandel, E., *Late Capitalism* (1978).

Mandell, R. D., *A Cultural history of sport* (Irvington, 1984).

Mangan, J. A., *Athleticism in the Victorian and Edwardian Public School: The Emergence and Consolidation of an Educational Ideology* (Cambridge, 1981).

Mann, T., *What a compulsory 8 Hour Working Day Means to the Workers* (1886).

Mann, T., *The eight hours movement* (1889).

Mann, T., *The Regulation of Working Hours: as submitted to the Royal Commission on Labour* (1891).

Marquis, F. J., and Ogden, S. E. F., 'The recreation of the poorest', *Town Planning Review*, vol. 3 (1913).

Martin, R. M., *TUC: The Growth of a Pressure Group 1868-1976* (Oxford, 1980).

Marwick, A., 'British Life and leisure and the First World War', *History Today*, vol. 15 (1965).

Marwick, A., *The Deluge: British Scoiety and the First World War* (1965).

Marwick, A., 'The Labour Party and the welfare state in Britain 1900-48', *American History Review* vol. 73 (1967-68).

Mason, T., *Association Football and English Society 1863-1915* (Brighton, 1980).

Mason, T., 'The Blues and the Reds', *Transactions of the Historic Society of Lancashire and Cheshire*, vol. 134 (1984).

Mason, T., 'Some Englishmen and Scotsmen abroad: the spread of world football', in Tomlinson, A., and Whannel, G. (eds), *Off the Ball: The Football World Cup* (1986).

Select bibliography

Middlemas, K., *Politics in Industrial Society: The Experience of the British System since 1911* (1979).

Middleton, R., *Towards the Managed Economy: Keynes, the Treasury and the fiscal policy debate of the 1930s* (1985).

Miliband, R., *The State in Capitalist Society* (1969).

Miliband, R., *Marxism and Politics* (Oxford, 1977).

Moorhouse, H. F., 'Professional football and working class culture: English theories and Scottish evidence'. *Sociological Review*, vol. 32 (1984).

Moorhouse, H. F., 'Scotland against England: football and popular culture', *International Journal of the History of Sport*, vol. 4 (1987).

Mott, J., 'Miners, weavers and pigeon racing', in Smith, M. A., Parker, S., and Smith, C. S. (eds), *Leisure and Society in Britain* (1973).

Murray, B., *The Old Firm: Sectarianism, Sport and Society in Scotland* (Edinburgh, 1984).

Murray, W. J., 'The French workers' sports movement and the victory of the popular front in 1936', *International Journal of the History of Sport*, vol. 4 (1987).

Nairn, T., 'The English working class', in Blackburn, R. (ed.), *Ideology in Social Science: Reading in critical social theory* (1979).

Naison, M., 'Lefties and Righties: the Communist Party and sports during the Great Depression', *Radical America*, vol. 13 (July–Aug. 1979).

National Council of British Socialist Sunday Schools Union, *The Young Socialist Crusaders: Aims, Objects and Method of Organisation* (Glasgow, 1920).

National Minority Movement, *On Strike: A Word to all Workers in Dispute*, (1929).

National Minority Movement, *Trades Union Congress and the Workers* (n.d., 1932?).

National Workers' Sports Association, *Labour and Sport* (1934).

Neale, R. S., 'Cultural materialism: a critique', *Social History*, vol. 9 (1984).

Newton, K., *The Sociology of British Communism* (1969).

Nicholas, K., *The Social Effects of Unemployment on Teeside, 1919-39* (Manchester, 1986).

Nield, B., 'Elvin, Herbert Henry (1874-1949)', in Bellamy, J. M., and Saville, J. (eds), *Dictionary of Labour Biography*, vol. 6 (1982).

Nitsch, F., 'Die internationalen Arbeitersportbewegungen', in Krüger, A., and Riordan, J. (eds), *Der Internationale Arbeitersport: Der Schlüssel zum Arbeiersport in 10 Ländern* (Köln, 1985).

Nove, A., *An Economic History of the U.S.S.R.* (Harmondsworth, 1982).

O'Brien, P. K., 'Britain's economy between the wars: a survey of counter-revolution in economic history', *Past and Present*, no. 115 (1987).

Pearson, G., *Hooligan: A History of Respectable Fears* (1983).

Pegg, M., *Broadcasting and Society 1918-1939* (1983).

Pierson, S., *British Socialists: The Journey from Fantasy to Politics* (Cambridge, Mass., 1979).

Pimlott, B., *Labour and the Left in the 1930s* (Cambridge, 1977).

Pollard, S., 'Trade union reactions to the economic crisis', *Journal of Contemporary History*, vol. 4 (1969).

Pollitt, H., *The Workers' Charter* (n.d., 1930?).

Prynn, D., 'The Clarion Clubs, rambling and the holiday associations in Britain since the 1890s', *Journal of Contemporary History*, vol. 11 (1976).

Prynn, D., 'The Woodcraft Folk and the Labour Movement 1925-70', *Journal of Contempory History*, vol. 18 (1983).

Pye, D., 'Fellowship is life: Bolton Clarion Cycling Club and the Clarion Movement

1894-1914', in North West Labour History Society, *Labour's Turning Point in the North West 1880-1914* (1984).

Redfern, A., 'Crewe: leisure in a railway town', in Walton, J. K., and Walvin, J. (eds), *Leisure in Britain 1780-1939* (Manchester, 1983).

Reid, A., 'Class and organisation', *Historical Journal*, vol. 30 (1987).

Reid, D., 'The decline of Saint Monday 1776-1876', *Past and Present*, no. 71 (1976).

Reid, D., 'Leisure and recreation', *History*, vol. 65 (1980).

Reid, F., 'Socialist Sunday Schools in Britain, 1892-1939', *International Review of Social History*, vol. 11 (1966).

Reid, J., *Reflections of a Clyde-Built Man* (1977).

Riordan, J., 'Marx, Lenin and physical culture', *Journal of Sport History*, vol. 3 (1976).

Riordan, J., *Sport in Soviet Society: Development of Sport and Physical Education in Russia and the U.S.S.R.* (Cambridge, 1977).

Riordan, J., 'The Workers' Olympics – a socialist alternative', in Tomlinson, A., and Whannel, G. (eds), *Five Ring Circus: Money, Power and Politics at the Olympic Games* (1984).

Ritter, G. A., 'Workers' culture in Imperial Germany: problems and points of departure for research', *Journal of Contemporary History*, vol. 13 (1978).

Robertson, A., *The bleak midwinter* (Manchester, 1987).

Rooff, M., *Youth and Leisure: A Survey of Girls' Organisations in England and Wales* (Edinburgh, 1935).

Roth, G., *The Social Democrats in Imperial Germany: A Study in Working Class Isolation and National Integration* (Totowa, 1963).

Rothman, B., *The 1932 Kinder Trespass: A Personal View of the Kinder Scout Mass Trespass* (Timperley, 1982).

Rowbotham, S., and Weeks, J., *Socialism and the New Life: The Personal and Sexual Politics of Edward Carpenter and Havelock Ellis* (1977).

Rubinstein, D., 'An interview with Tom Stephenson', *Bulletin of the Society for the Study of Labour History*, no. 25 (1972).

Rubinstein, D., 'Cycling in the 1880s', *Victorian Studies*, vol. 21 (1977).

Rust, W., *The Case For The Y.C.L.* (n.d.).

Rust, W., *Clem Beckett and the Oldham Men Who Fought in Spain 1936-1938* (n.d., 1938?).

Salter, A., *What Socialism Means* (Manchester, n.d.).

Sandbach, F. R., 'The early campaign for a National Park in the Lake District', *Transactions Institute of British Geographers*, vol. 3 (1978).

Sandiford, K. A. P., 'Victorian cricket technique and industrial technology', *British Journal of Sports History*, vol. 1 (1984).

Saville, J., 'The ideology of labourism', in Benewick, R., Berki, R. N., and Parekh, B. (eds), *Knowledge and Belief in Politics: The Problem of Ideology* (1973).

Saville, J., 'May Day 1937', in Briggs, A., and Saville, J. (eds), *Essays in Labour History 1920-1939* (1977).

Semotiuk, D., 'The sport system of the Union of Soviet Socialist Republics: an illustrated analysis', *North American Society for Sport History Proceedings*, (1975).

Shankly, B., *Shankly* (St Albans, 1977).

Sheail, J., *Rural Conservation in Inter-War Britain* (Oxford, 1981).

Shipley, S., *Club Life and Socialism in Mid-Victorian London* (1983).

Shipley, S., 'Tom Causer of Bermondsey: a boxer hero of the 1890s', *History Workshop Journal*, no. 15 (1983).

Showstack Sassoon, A., *Gramsci's Politics* (1980).

Sinclair, R., *Metropolitan Man: The Future of the English* (1937).

Sinfield, G., *The Workers' Sports Movement* (n.d., 1927?).

Sissons, R., and Stoddart, B., *Cricket and Empire: the 1932–33 Bodyline Tour of Australia* (1984).

Smith, D., and Williams, G., *Fields of Praise: The Official History of the Welsh Rugby Union 1881-1981* (Cardiff, 1980).

Snell, H., *The Case for Sunday Games, Against Sabbatarian Prejudice* (1923).

Southall Communist Party, *Communist Plan for Southall* (n.d., 1937?).

Spinghall, J., *Youth, Empire and Society: British Youth Movements, 1883-1940* (1977).

Steinberg, D. A., 'The Workers' Sports Internationals 1920-28', *Journal of Contemporary History*, vol. 13 (1978).

Steinberg, D., 'Workers' sport and the united front, 1934-1936', *Arena Review*, Feb. 1980.

Stevenson, J., *British Society 1914-45* (Harmondsworth, 1984).

Stevenson, J., and Cook C., *The Slump: Society and Politics During the Depression* (1977).

Stoddart, B., 'Sport, cultural politics and international relations: England versus Germany, 1935', in Müller, N., and Rühl, J. K. (eds). *Sport History* (Niedernhausen, 1985).

Stoddart, B., 'Sport, cultural imperialism and colonial response in the British Empire: a framework for analysis', in Benning, D. (ed.), *Sport and Imperialism* (1986).

Storch, R. (ed.), *Popular Culture and Custom in Nineteenth Century England* (1982).

Storch, R. D., 'The problem of working-class leisure. Some roots of middle-class moral reform in the industrial North: 1825-50', in Donajgrodzki, A. P. (ed.), *Social Control in Nineteenth Century Britain* (1977).

Studd, S., *Herbert Chapman, Football Emperor: A Study in the Origins of Modern Soccer* (1981).

Sugden, J., 'The power of gold: the source and currency of the political Olympics', *Physical Education Review*, vol. 4 (1981).

Taylor, I., 'Class, violence and sport: the case of soccer hooliganism in Britain', in Cantelon, H., and Gruneau, R. (eds), *Sport, Culture and the Modern State* (Toronto, 1982).

Taylor, J., *From Self-Help to Glamour: the Working Men's Club, 1860-1972* (1972).

Theberge, N., 'A critique of critiques: radical and feminist writings on sport', *Social Forces*, vol. 60 (1981).

Thompson, E. P., 'Time, work-discipline, and industrial capitalism', *Past and Present*, no. 38 (1967).

Thompson, E. P., *The Poverty of Theory and other Essays* (1978).

Thompson, F. M. L., 'Social control in Victorian Britain', *Economic History Review*, vol. 34 (1981)

Thompson, P., *The Edwardians: The Remaking of British Society* (1976).

Tiffen, H., 'Cricket, literature and the politics of de-colonisation – the case of C. L. R. James', in Cashman, R., and McKernan, M. (eds), *Sport: Money, Morality and the Media* (New South Wales, n.d., 1982?).

Tischler, S., *Footballers and Businessmen: The Origins of Professional Soccer in England* (New York, 1981).

Trevelyan, G. M., *Illustrated English Social History: 4* (Harmondsworth, 1964 edition).

Select bibliography

Triesman, D., 'The Olympic Games as a political forum', in Tomlinson A., and Whannel, G. (eds). *Five Ring Circus: Money, Power and Politics at the Olympic Games* (1984).

Trotsky, L., 'Where is Britain going?', in Chappel, R., and Clinton. A. (eds), Leon Trotsky, *Collected Writings and speeches on Britain*, vol. 2 (1974).

Vamplew, W., *The Turf: A Social and Economic History of Horse Racing* (1976).

Vamplew, W., 'Ungentlemanly conduct: the control of soccer crowd behaviour in England, 1888-1914', in Smout, T. C. (ed.), *The Search for Wealth and Stability* (1979).

Vamplew, W., 'Sports crowd disorder in Britain, 1870-1914: causes and controls', *Journal of Sport History*, vol. 7 (1980).

Vamplew, W., 'The economics of a sports industry: Scottish gate-money, 1890-1914', *Economic History Review*, vol. 35 (1982).

Vamplew, W., 'Not playing the game: unionism in British professional sport, 1870-1914', *British Journal of Sports History*, vol. 2 (1985).

Vamplew, W., *Pay Up and Play the Game: Professional Sport in Britain 1875-1914* (forthcoming).

Veblen, T., *The Theory of the Leisure Class* (1925).

Veitch, C., 'Play Up! Play Up! and win the war: Football, the nation and the First World War', *Journal of Contemporary History*, vol. 20 (1985).

Wagg, S., *The Football World: A contemporary Social History* (Brighton 1984).

Walker, H., 'The popularisation of the outdoor movement, 1900-1940', *British Journal of Sports History*, vol. 2 (1985).

Walton, J. K., and Walvin, J., 'Introduction', in Walton, J. K., and Walvin, J. (eds), *Leisure in Britain 1780-1939* (Manchester, 1983).

Walvin, J., *The People's Game. A Social History of British Football* (1975).

Walvin, J., *Leisure and Society, 1830-1950* (1978).

Walvin, J., 'Sport, social history and the historian', *British Journal of Sports History*, vol. 1 (1984).

Walvin, J., *Football, and the Decline of Britain* (1986).

Waters, C., 'Social reformers, socialists, and the opposition to the commericalisation of leisure in late Victorian England', in Vamplew, W. (ed.), *The Economic History of Leisure* (1982).

Watling, H. R., 'The cycle and motor-cycle industry', in Schofield, H. J. (ed.), *The Book of British Industries* (1933).

Webb, S. and B., *Soviet Communism: A New Civilization* (1941).

Weber, E., 'Gymnastics and sports in *fin-de-siècle* France: opium of the classes?', *American History Review*, vol. 76 (1971).

Weiner, M. J., *English Culture and the Decline of the Industrial Spirit 1850-1980* (1981).

West, B., 'Moores, Sir John (1896-): football pool promoter and retailer'. in Jeremy, D. J. (ed.), *Dictionary of Business Biography*, vol. 4 (1985).

Whannel, G., *Blowing the Whistle: The politics of sport* (1983).

Wheeler, R. F., 'Organised sport and organised labour: the workers' sports movement', *Journal of Contemporary History*, vol. 13 (1978).

Whipp, R., '"A time to every purpose": an essay on time and work', in Joyce, P. (ed.), *The historical meanings of work* (Cambridge, 1987).

White, J., *The Worst Street in North London: Campbell Bunk, Islington, Between the Wars* (1986).

Select bibliography

Whiting, R. C., *The View from Cowley: The Impact of Industrialisation upon Oxford 1918-1939* (Oxford, 1983).
Whitson, D. J., 'Sport and hegemony: on the construction of the dominant culture', *Sociology of Sport Journal*, vol. 1 (1984).
Williams, F., *Journey into Adventure: The Story of the Workers Travel Association* (1960).
Williams, F., 'From grand slam to great slump: economy, society and rugby football in Wales during the Depression', *Welsh History Review*, vol. 11 (1983).
Williams, G., 'How amateur was my valley: professional sport and national indentity in Wales 1890-1914', *British Journal of Sports History*, vol. 2 (1985).
Williams, P., *Hugh Gaitskell* (1979).
Williams, R., *Marxism and Literature* (Oxford, 1977).
Woodforde, J., *The Story of the Bicycle* (1970).
Yeo, E., 'Culture and constraint in working-class movements, 1830-1950', in Yeo, E. and S. (eds), *Popular Culture and Class Conflict 1590-1914: Explorations in the History of Labour and Leisure* (Brighton, 1981).
Yeo, E. and S., 'Perceived patterns: competition and licence versus class and struggle', in Yeo, E. and S. (eds), *Popular Culture and Class Conflict 1590-1914: Explorations in the History of Labour and Leisure* (Brighton, 1981).
Yeo, E. and S., 'Ways of seeing: control and leisure versus class and struggle', in Yeo, E. and S. (eds), *Popular Culture and Class Conflict 1590-1914: Explorations in the History of Labour and Leisure* (Brighton, 1981).
Yeo, S., 'A new life: the religion of socialism in Britain, 1883-1896', *History Workshop Journal*, no. 3 (1977).
Yeo, S., 'State and anti-state: reflections on social forms and struggles from 1850', in Corrigan, P. (ed.), *Capitalism, State Formation and Marxist Theory: Historical Investigations* (1980).
Yeo, S., 'Towards "making form of more moment than spirit": further thoughts on Labour, socialism and the new life from the late 1890s to the present', in Jowitt, J. A., and Taylor, R. K. S., (eds), *Bradford 1890-1914: The Cradle of the Independent Labour Party* (Bradford, 1980).
Young Communist League, *Report of the British Youth Delegation to the USSR* (n.d., 1927?).
Young, P. M., *Bolton Wanderers* (1961).
Zeldin, T., *France 1848-1945 II Intellect, Taste and Anxiety* (Oxford, 1977).

5 Unpublished work

Arnold, J., 'The Influence of Pilkington Brothers in the growth of sport and community recreation in St Helens', MEd, University of Liverpool (1977).
Diederiks, H., 'Looking for the true labourer: some introductory remarks on working class culture in the Netherlands 1920-1940', paper presented to the fifth Anglo-Dutch Labour History Conference, 1986.
Ferris, J., 'The Labour Party League of Youth 1924-1940', MA, University of Warwick (1977).
Fincher, J. A., 'The Clarion Movement: A Study of a Socialist Attempt to Implement the Co-operative Commonwealth in England 1891-1914', MA, University of Manchester (1971).

214

Select bibliography

Fishwick, N. B. F., 'Association Football and English Social Life 1910–1950', DPhil, University of Oxford (1984).

Hayburn, R. H., 'The Responses to Unemployment in the 1930s, with particular reference to South-East Lancashire', PhD, University of Hull, (1970).

Heerma van Voss, L., 'The use of leisure time by male workers after the introduction of the eight-hour day', paper presented to the fifth Anglo-Dutch Labour History Conference, 1986.

Jacques, M., 'The Emergence of "Responsible" Trade Unionism, A Study of the "New Direction" in T.U.C. Policy 1926-1935', PhD, University of Cambridge (1976).

Marlow, L., 'The Working Men's Club Movement, 1862-1912: A Study of the Evolution of a Working Class Institution', PhD, University of Warwick (1980).

Nolan, M., 'The Socialist Movement in Düsseldorf, 1890-1914', PhD, University of Columbia (1975).

Nottingham, C. J., 'More important than life or death: football, the British working class and the social order', paper presented to the fifth Anglo-Dutch Labour History Conference, 1986.

Power, J., 'Aspects of Working Class Leisure During the Depression Years: Bolton in the 1930s', MA, University of Warwick (1980).

Prynn, D. L., 'The Socialist Sunday Schools, the Woodcraft Folk and Allied Movements: Their Moral Influence on the British Labour Movement since the 1890s', MA University of Sheffield (1971).

Riordan, J., 'Sport in Soviet Society: Development and Problems', PhD, University of Birmingham (1975).

Rushton, J. I., 'Charles Rowley and the Ancoats Recreation Movement', MEd, University of Manchester (1959).

Salveson, P., 'Working-class culture and leisure in Lancashire in the late nineteenth century', paper presented to the North West Group for the Study of Labour History (1982).

Shaw, S., 'The Attitude of the Trades Union Congress Towards Unemployment in the Inter-War Period', PhD, University of Kent (1979).

Steinberg, D., 'Sport Under Red Flags: The Relations Between the Red Sport International and the Socialist Workers' Sport International 1920-1939', DPhil, University of Wisconsin-Madison (1979).

Stevenson, A. L., 'The Development of Physical Education in the State Schools of Scotland 1900-1960', MLitt, University of Aberdeen (1978).

Waters, C., 'Socialism and the Politics of Popular Culture in Britain, 1884-1914', PhD, University of Harvard (1985).

Whiting, R., 'The Working Class in the "New Industry" Towns Between the Wars: the case of Oxford', DPhil, University of Oxford (1978).

215

Index

Abrahams, Harold, 183
Acton Labour Party Netball Club, 108
Acts of Parliament:
  Access to Mountains (1939), 132, 146
  Ancient Monuments (1931), 146
  Bank Holidays (1871, 1875) 19
  Cruelty to Animals (1835), 17
  Education (1918), 132
  National Parks and Access to
    Countryside (1949), 146
  Physical Training and Recreation
    (1937), 132
  Public Health (1931), 147
  Public Health (1936), 132
  Public Order (1936), 116
  Right of Way (1932), 132
  Street Betting (1906), 137
  Trade Disputes and Trade Unions
    (1927), 104
Alden, Percy, 147
Allison, Lincoln, 129
Althusser, Louis, 10, 143
Amateur Athletic Association (AAA),
  21, 63, 64, 84, 179, 183, 184, 185,
  197, 199
Amateur Boxing Association, 21, 197
Amateur Metropolitan Swimming
  Association, 21
Amateur Rowing Association, 22
Amalgamated Cotton Mills Trust, 62
Amalgamated Engineering Union, 76,
  111
A.E.U. Journal, 74
Amalgamated Society of Carpenters,
  74
Amalgamated Union of Upholsterers,
  111
American Play Movement, 199

Ancoats Recreation Movement, 30
Angler's News, 50
angling, 26, 50, 63, 64
Anslow, Harry, 123 n. 121
Anti-Waste Party, 133
Arbeiter-Tunerbund (Workers'
  Gymnastic Federation), 171
Arbreiderness Idrettsforbund, 174
Arsenal F. C., 47, 48, 69 n. 35, 83
Artisan Golfers' Association, 63
Ashbourne, Derbyshire, 32
Ashton Brothers, 62
Aspin, David, 4
Association Football Players' and
  Trainers' Union, 49
Association of Cine-Technicians, 111
Association of Jewish Youth, 184
Association of Women Clerks and
  Secretaries, 111
Aston Villa F. C., 45, 46
Athlete, The, 21
athleticism, 22
athletics, 20, 22, 28, 30, 45, 49, 63, 76,
  106, 134, 177, see also Amateur
  Athletic Association
Audenshaw, Manchester, 88
Australia, 181
Austria, 167, 170, 172, 174, 177
Auto-Cycle Union, 88
Avonmouth, Bristol, 112

Baden-Powell, Robert, 84
badminton, 23
Badminton Association, 21
Baker, P. J. Noel, 148
Barcelona Olympiad (1936), 185, 189
Barrow, Lancashire, 78
Barson, Frank, 57

Bath, 107
Batley, Yorkshire, 112
Belgium, 167, 177
Beamish, Rob, 53
Beck, Peter, 181–2
Beckett, Clem, 88, 181, 186
Belle Vue, Manchester, 47
Bell's Life in London and Sporting Chronicle,
  20
Bennett, George, 77
Berlin Olympic Games (1936), 183–4
Bermondsey, London, 26, 116
Bethnal Green, London, 78, 95
Bevan, Aneurin, 101 n. 79, 157
Bevin, Ernest, 91, 105, 119
bicycle polo, 108
Bicycle Union, 22
Bicycling News, 50
billiards, 113
Birmingham, 33, 62, 81, 107, 110, 112
Birmingham City FC, 59
Birmingham Labour Church, 31–2
Blackburn, Lancashire, 33
Blackburn Rovers FC, 19
Blackpool, Lancashire, 142
Blatchford, Robert, 29, 31, 32–3
blood sports, 17, 136, 139
Bobker, Martin, 87
Bolton, Lancashire, 31, 33, 155
Bolton Wanderers FC, 46, 60
Booth, Alan, 105
botanical clubs, 139
bowling, 63, 113, 174
boxing, 20, 21, 26, 29, 45, 49, 50, 54,
  57, 58, 65, 76, 77, 83, 93, 106, 134,
  168
Boy Scouts, 61–2, 79, 84, 115, 116, 197
Boyd, Johnny, 57
Boys' Brigades, 197
Bradford City FC, 46
Bramley, Fred, 76
Brighton, Sussex, 81
Bristol, Gloucester, 33, 107
British Broadcasting Corporation
  (BBC), 83, 135–6
British Co-operative Employees'
  Sports Association, 112
British Cycle and Motor

Manufacturers' and Traders' Union,
  51
British Federation of Co-operative
  Youth, 116
British Field Sports Society, 140
British Journal of Sports History, 2
British Non-Sectarian Anti-Nazi
  Council, 184
British Socialist Party, 33, 176
Britsh Workers's Sports Federation
  (BWSF): 75–98, 106, 108, 110, 114,
  119, 120, 121, 142–3, 144, 149–54,
  175–6, 179–81, 182, 189, 197, 198–9
  ideology of, 75–6, 78, 82–9, 94–5
  membership, 92, 197
  and Soviet Union, 80, 94–5
  and women, 92–3, 97
Brown, A. C., 152
Brown, George, 89, 186
Brownlie, J. T., 27–8
Buchan, Charlie, 57
Burton, Richard, 165
Buxton, Derbyshire, 32

Cadburys Co. Ltd., 63
Calico Printers' Association, 62
Cambridge, 111
Campbell Bunk, Islington, 137
camping, 64, 134, 139, 146
Camping Club of Great Britain, 141
capital investment in sports industry,
  20, 47–8, 50–2
Carlisle FC, 60
Carnegie United Kingdom Trust, 22
Carpenter, Edward, 115
Carpenters, Amalgamated Society of,
  74
Challenge, 122
Chamberlain, Neville, 187
Champion, H. H., 27
Chatham, Kent, 115
Chelmsford, Viscount, 65
Chemical Workers' Union, 111
chess, 108
Chester Committee on Football (1968),
  46
Chopwell Communist Club, 30
Churchill, Winston S., 148

cinema, 45, 171, 173, 197
Citrine, Sir Walter, 182
Clarion, The, 29, 31, 32
Clarion Cycling Club (CCC), 31–4, 75, 81, 82, 91, 107–8, 109, 117, 118–9,121, 122, 149, 174–5, 183, 186, 189
Clarion Cyclists's Journal, 32, 108, 119
Clarion movement, 31–4, 35, 115, 141, 142, 166, 177, 178, 198
Clark, David, 36
Clark, G. L., 133
Clarke, Alllen, 30–1
class, *see* middle class; sport; working class
'Class against Class', 90–2, 96, 114, 144, 149, 170, 182
Clynes, J. R., 30, 182
Cohen, Jack, 76, 87
Cole, G. D. H., 74
Collyhurst, Manchester, 93
Colne Valley, Yorkshire, 36
Colne Valley Labour Union, 30
commercialisation of sport, 19–20, 43–61, 119, 199
commodification of sport, 29, 42, 53–4, 66, 74, 158, 197
Commons, Open Spaces and Footpaths Preservation Society, 141, 143
Communist International, 169, 170
Communist Party (CP) (Britain), 74, 77, 78–98, 154, 175–6 *see also* British Workers' Sports Federation; Young Communist League Communist Party (Soviet Union), 78–9, 81, 88, 94–5, 121, 169–70, 176, 179–80, 184, 189 *see also* Red Sports International
company sports *see* factory sports
Condon, Michael, 87, 89, 96, 151, 152–3
Constantine, Learie, 165–6
Cook, Chris, 53
Co-operative Holidays Association, 197
Co-operative movement, 11, 27, 30, 34, 75, 112, 141, 198
Co-operative Party, 109

Co-operative Wholesale Society, 110, 112
Co-operative Women's Guild, 112
Coppock, Richard, 153
Cotton, Henry, 51
cotton industry, 59, 62, 63
Council for the Preservation of Rural England, 141
Council of Recreative Physical Training, 135
countryside: access to, 64, 94, 130, 138–46, 155, 199
Coventry, Warwickshire, 62, 88
Cox, Harold, 27
Cox, Montague, 151
Cox, Ray, 186
Crane, Walter, 113
Crewe, Cheshire, 26, 33
Crewe Amalgamated Society of Railway Servants, 30
cricket, 18, 20, 21, 26, 29, 31, 32, 45, 49, 50, 58, 67, 74, 79, 83, 93, 106, 108, 134, 151, 165, 181
Cripps, Sir Stafford, 116
Critchley, Alfred, 47
Cronin, James, 73
Crooks, Will, 30
croquet, 165
cross country running, 134, 168
Cross, Gary, 172
crowd disorder, 25, 59, 61, 67
Crowds, Departmental Committee on (1924), 136
Croydon, 78
Crystal Palace, London, 110
culturalism, 10–11
Cunningham, Hugh, 17–18
cycle paths, 149
Cycle, The, 32
Cycling, 32
cycling, 20, 21, 22, 28, 30, 31–4, 51–2, 64, 76, 77, 93, 134, 139 *see also* Clarion Cycling Club
Cyclist, The, 21
Cyclists' Touring Club, 33, 84, 197
Czechoslovakia, 167, 170, 174, 177

Daily Citizen, 86

Daily Herald, 46, 47, 52, 77, 120, 144, 157
Daily Mail, 78
Daily Mirror, 157
Daily Worker, 80, 82–4, 86, 89, 91, 95, 121, 153, 154, 180
Dalton, Hugh, 117
Darban, Tom, 186
darts, 113
Darwen FC, 19
Dawson, Julia, 33
Deacon, George, 177
Dean, 'Dixie', 57
Deaner, Clara, 93
Dear, M., 133
Delves, Anthony, 17
Derby, 17th Earl of, 114
Derby, 17, 20, 91, 93, 143
Deutsche Turnerschaft (German Gymnastic League), 171
Dirt Track Riders' Association, 88
Douglas, Johnny, 96
Dover, Kent, 108
Dower, John, 144
drinking, 59, 139, 197
Dukinfield Cycling Club, 180
Dundee, 47, 180
Dunfermline, 22
Dunlop Rubber Co., 50–1
Dunnico, Herbert, 107
Dunning, Eric, 5–6, 24–5
Durham, 60
Dusseldorf, Germany, 166–7
Dutt, Ranjani Palme, 86–7

Ealing, London, 109
Economic Advisory Council, 131
economic change: (1870–1914) 18–19; (1918–39) 42–3
Economist, The, 48
Edinburgh, 78
Education, Board of, 134–5, 156
Edwardes, Charles, 25
eight-hour day, 27, 171–3
Elias, Norbert, 5, 6
Elvin, George, 111, 120, 121, 185–6
Elvin, Herbert, 111, 113, 115

Engineers, Amalgamated Union of, 76, 111
English Sewing Cotton Company, 62
Ensor, Ernest, 25
entertainment tax, 135
Erith, Kent, 78
ethnic minorities, 8–9, 49, 60, 63, 184, 198
Evans, Richard, 171
Everton FC, 45

Fabian News, 29
Fabian Society, 27, 28–9
Falkirk Trades Council, 127 n. 117
fascism: opposition to, 181–6, 187, 199
factory sports, 62–3, 84–5, 88, 119
Fancier's Guide and Homing World, 21
Farrant, Vic, 89
Fay, Jimmy, 49
Featherstone, Mike, 56
Fédération Nationale de Boulistes, 174
Fédération Sportive et Gymnique du Travail (FSGT), 173–4, 186
Ferris, John, 114–15
field sports, 139, 146
Fife, 88
figurational sociology, 5–6, 8, 25
Fincher, Judith, 32, 33, 35, 107–8
Fine Cotton Spinners' and Doublers' Association (FCSDA), 62, 63
Finland, 172, 174
Finsbury, London, 151
First World War, 42
Fisher, Sir Warren, 133
Fishwick, N. B., 54, 57
Flynn, T., 181
football: 2, 6, 9, 10, 15, 18, 19, 20, 22, 25, 26, 42, 45–7, 48, 49, 52, 54–5, 56, 57–60, 74, 76, 79, 83, 89–90, 93, 106, 108, 109, 134, 164–5, 168, 172, 177
international matches, 180–2, 187, 188
and socialist attitudes, 28–9, 32
on Sundays, 64, 92, 121, 150, 151–4
Tour to Soviet Union (1927), 80, 94–5, 179, 182
Football Annual, 21

Football Association, 21, 46–7, 109, 153, 197
Football Pictorial, 50
football pools, 52, 54
Ford, Percy, 155
Foreign Office and sport, 183–4, 186
Forestry Commission, 145
Forward, 120
Fox, Ralph, 86
France, 167, 172, 173–4, 177, 179
French Trade Union Confederation (CGT), 172
Friars, Austin, 47
Friends of Soviet Russia, 89
Fulham FC, 94

Gaitskell, Hugh, 115
Gallacher, William, 176
Gallatown, Scotland, 57
gambling, 20, 52, 56–7, 59, 60–1, 85–7, 106, 139
Geddes axe, 133
General Strike (1926), 43, 58, 73, 79, 104, 176
German Gymnasts' Association, 166
German Social Democratic Party, 106
German Soccer Association, 172
German Workers' Cyclist Federation, 175
German Workers' Sports and Gymnastic League, 166
Germany, 132, 166–7, 170, 171, 172, 174, 177, 179
Gillett, George, 133
Girl Guides, 61, 197
Glasgow, 47, 63, 93, 97, 120, 137, 150, 155, 181, 186
Glasgow Celtic FC, 45, 58
Glasgow Rangers FC, 45
Glasgow Socialist Rambling Club, 30
Glasier, Bruce, 28, 31
Goldman, Rebecca, 84
Gollan, John, 87
golf, 23, 48, 50–1, 63, 151, 164, 165
Golf Illustrated, 50
Gorton, Manchester, 77
Gould, Gerald, 120

Gramsci, Antonio, 7, 21–2, 199
Greenwood, Arthur, 148
Greyhound Express, 50
Greyhound Outlook and Sports Pictures, 50
greyhound racing, 29, 45, 47–8, 52, 57, 58, 59, 85, 101 n. 79, 106
Groom, Tom, 32, 75, 77, 80–1, 118, 122, 127 n. 101, 175
Gruneau, Richard, 9–10, 12, 34, 130
Guildford, Surrey, 75
gymnastics, 76, 93, 168, 171, 173

Hackney, London, 93
Hagger, Fred, 175
Halifax, Yorkshire, 31, 47
Hardie, J. Keir, 28
Hardy, Stephen, 26, 61, 196, 199
Hargreaves, Jennifer, 1–2
Hargreaves, John, 5, 7–8, 11, 24, 44–5, 132, 198
Harris, Sydney, 180
Hay, Roy, 55
Hayfield, Derbyshire, 143
Headley, George, 165
Hebden Bridge, Yorkshire, 112
hegemony, 7–8, 196
Henery, Marion, 97
Herne Hill, London, 108
Hexham, Northumberland, 108
Hiker and Camper, 144
Hill, Howard, 140, 146
History Workshop Journal, 11
Hitler, Adolph, 182
Hobbs, Jack, 58
Hobsbawm, Eric J., 21, 23, 24
hockey, 23, 32, 93, 135, 151, 165
Hockey, 21
Hockey World, 50
Hoggart, Richard, 1
Holiday Fellowship, 141
holidays, 17
Holland, 172, 173, 177, 179
Holt, Richard, 26
horse racing, 2, 18, 19–20, 29, 42, 45, 48, 52, 54, 57, 60, 65, 136, 165
Hoskins, John, 48
Howkins, Alun, 97

Hughes, Albert, 46
Hull, Yorkshire, 47, 62
hunting, 139
Hutt, Allen, 150–1
Hyde Park, London, 148

ice-hockey, 45
Ice-Hockey, 50
imperialism, 22, 164–6, 190
Ingham, Alan, 26, 61, 196
Independent Labour Party (ILP): 27,
 28, 29, 31, 34, 76, 77, 107, 120, 141,
 144,
 Guild of Youth, 116
International Class War Prisoners' Aid,
 89
International Journal of the History of Sport, 2
International Labour Organisation,
 171
international sport, 164–90; and
 British labour movement 174–6,
 182–6
International Union for Physical
 Education and Workers' Sport, 167
internationalism and sport, 75, 118–19,
 167, 174, 185, 186–7, 189–90
Investors' Chronicle, 48
Irlam, Lancashire, 112
Islington, London, 48, 151
Italy, 132

Jacob, William, 114
Jacobs, Joe, 97
Jacques, Martin, 73
James, Alex, 57
James, C. L. R., 165
Jardine, Douglas, 181
Jenkins, Mick, 97
Jessop, Bob, 155–6
Joad, Cyril, 141
Johnson, Len, 49
Jones, Arthur Creech, 145
Jones, Gareth Stedman, 24
Jones, Jack, 147
ju-jitsu, 93
Justice, 28, 29
juvenile delinquency, 131

Juvenile Instructional Centres,
 Ministry of Labour, 134

Keable, Gladys, 93
Keep Fit, 135
Keep-Fit Movement, 64
Kempton Park, 20
Kentish Town, London, 78
Keynes, John Maynard, 131
Kinder Scout trespass, 143
King of the Road, 32
King's Lynn, Norfolk, 75
Kirkcaldy, 78
Korr, Charles, 70 n. 64

Labour Annual, 28
Labour Church, 31–2
Labour Club, 30, 36
Labour Leader, 28
Labour Monthly, 86
Labour movement and sport; 26–34,
 74, 112–14, 123, 138–58, 181–7 *see also*
 British Workers' Sports Federation;
 Clarion Movement; Labour Party;
 League of Youth; National Workers'
 Sports Association; Trades Union
 Congress
Labour Party and Sport: 74, 81, 82, 86,
 104–23, 131, 199
 provision of sports facilities, 146–9,
 154, 155, 157
 support of international workers'
 sport, 178–9
Labour Representation Committee, 27
La Capra, Dominick, 11
Lansbury, George, 113, 148, 155
Larwood, Harold, 55, 58
Lawn Tennis and Badminton, 50
Lawton, Tommy, 57
League Against Cruel Sports, 140
League Against Imperialism, 89
League of Young Labour, 114
League of Youth, 114–15, 116, 123,
 197, 198
Leeds, 117, 142
Left Book Club, 122
Leicester, 31, 75, 112

Leicester City FC, 59
Leicester Co-operative Society, 75
Leigh, Lancashire, 114
leisure during industrialisation, 16–18
Lenin, V. I., 169
Leyton Orient FC, 87
Liddell, Billy, 57
Liddell, Eric, 151
Lidtke, Vernon, 171
Ling (Physical Education) Association, 135
'Little Moscows', 98
Liverpool, 22, 62, 112, 122–3
Liverpool FC, 45, 47
Lloyd, Geoffrey, 146
local authorities: provision of sports and leisure facilities, 29, 65, 133, 147, 150, 155, 157
London, 32, 45, 47, 54, 62, 64, 75, 76, 93, 94, 106–7, 113, 133, 148, 150, 151–4, 155, 180 *see also individual districts*
London Citizen, 74
London County Council, 150–4, 156
London Labour Football Club, 108
London Labour Party Sports Association, 106–7
London Workers' Football Council, 152
London Workers' Sunday League, 152, 154
Longsight, Manchester, 112
Lord's Day Observance Society, 151
Lowe, Rodney, 105
Lowerson, John, 143
Lucerne, Switzerland, 167, 175
Lyons Co. Ltd., 63

Macdonald, James Murray, 27
Macdonald, James Ramsay, 85, 104, 106, 113, 142
McGovern, John, 101 n. 79, 137
McLennan, Gregor, 129
MacLeod, Alec, 106–7
Macmillan Committee, 131
Magarey, Susan, 10
Manchester, 30, 32, 33, 54, 78, 81, 88, 89, 91, 94, 96, 97, 112, 121, 142, 144, 146, 150, 156

Manchester City FC, 46, 47
Manchester Guardian, 184
Manchester Ramblers' Rights Movement, 142, 150
Manchester and District Ramblers' Federation, 142
Mandell, R. D., 21
Mangan, J. A., 2, 22
Mann, Tom, 27, 30
Marshall, Fred, 146
Marshall, Howard, 49–50
Martin, R. M., 105
Marxism and sport, theoretical approaches, 7–12, 42, 53–67, 129–30, 154
Mason, Tony, 20
mass trespass, 143
Masters, Sam, 186
Matthews, Stanley, 57
Maud, Philip, 152
Maxwell, John, 156
Maynard, H. R., 157
Merthyr Town FC, 94
Meyer, Sir Frank, 56
middle-class sports, 23
Middlemass, Keith, 105
Middlesborough, Yorkshire, 108, 137
Miliband, Ralph, 137
Millwall FC, 60
miners' institutes, 65
Miners' Welfare Committee, 65, 134
Ministry of Health, 133
Ministry of Labour, 133–4, 156
Mirror of Life, 21
mondism, 81
Moores, John, 52
Moorhouse, H. F., 8, 60
Morris, John, 96
Morris, William R. (Lord Nuffield), 59
Morrison, Herbert, 106
Moscow, Spartkiades, 180–1
motor-cycle racing, 45
mountains; access to, 140, 142, 145
Müller, Heinrich, 197
municipal provision of leisure, 29, 65, 133, 147, 150, 155, 157
Murray, Bill, 60

Index

Nairn, Tom, 24
National Clarion Swimming Club, 32
National Council of Ramblers'
  Federations, 141, 142
National Council of Social Service,
  113, 134
National Cyclists' Union, 33
National Emergency Committee of
  Christian Citizens, 86
National Federation of Swedish
  Gymnastic and Sports Societies, 173
National Fitness Council, 135, 156
National Greyhound Society, 101 n. 79
National Liberal Federation, 56
National Minority Movement (NMM),
  88, 113, 149
national parks, 142, 145, 146
National Playing Fields Association
  (NPFA), 113, 134, 147-8
National Society of Operative Printers
  and Assistants, 110, 111
National Sunday Football Association,
  153
National Unemployed Workers'
  Movement (NUWM), 89, 104, 113
National Union of Boxers, 49
National Union of Clerks, 111
National Union of Commercial
  Travellers, 111
National Union of Labour and Socialist
  Clubs, 112-13
National Union of Railwaymen, 111
National Workers' Football and Sports
  Ground Ltd., 109-10
National Workers' Sports Association
  (NWSA):, 81, 90-1, 95, 105, 106-23,
  144, 197-9, 183, 189, 198-91
  ideology of, 117-22; and Labour
  movement, 110-11
  membership, 107, 110, 197
  and politics, 110-13, 117
  and women, 110
National Workers' Sports Association Bulletin,
  122
National Young Labour League, 114
Neale, R. S., 10
netball, 93, 106, 108, 110
Newcastle-upon-Tyne, 54, 81, 93, 112

Newcastle Socialist Society, 30
New Clarion, 122
New Leader, 141
New Life Fellowship, 115
Nicholas, Kate, 137
Nield, Ada, 33
Nineteenth Century, 27
Northern Weekly, 30
Norway, 174, 179
Nottingham, 32, 142
Nottingham, Christopher, 54

Oldham, Lancashire, 77, 93
Oldham Chronicle, 143
Olympic Games, 164, 166, 183-5 *see
  also* Spartakiade; Workers' Olympiads
Oxford, 109, 111

pacifism, 76, 116, 167 *see also* 'Peace
  Through Sport'
Palestine, 177
parks, 132, 133, 148, 151-4
Patterson, J. G., 62
Paul, Leslie, 115
'Peace Through Sport', 75, 118, 168,
  175, 176, 178-9, 190
Pearson, Geoffrey, 34
pedestrianism, 57
Pelling, Henry, 34
People's League for Economy, 133
People's Year Book, 77
Perowne, J. V., 184
Perry, Fred, 108-9
Perry, Samuel F., 109
Petch, Arthur Logan, 185
Phipps, Sir Eric, 184
physical education, 134-5
Physical Training and Recreation
  Advisory Council, 157
Physical Training and Recreation Bill
  (1937), 157
Pickford, William, 64
Pierson, Stanley, 35
pigeon racing, 21, 65, 67
Pilkington Brothers, 85
Pimlott, Ben, 105
Pink 'Un, 50
Pleasant Sunday Afternoon

Brotherhood, 35
pluralist Marxism, 9–12, 129–30, 154, 200
police, control of sports, 17, 60, 132, 136–7, 156
Pollard, Sidney, 104
Pollitt, Harry, 87
Pontyridd, Glamorgan, 155
Poole, Philip, 144
Portsmouth, Hampshire, 108
Prague (Workers' Olympiad), 77
press, sporting; 20–1, 49–50 *see also under individual titles*
Preston, Lancashire, 23
Preston North End FC, 19
Prince of Wales (later Edward VIII), 84, 182
professionalism in sport, 49, 55, 83, 197
Progressive Rambling Club, 144
prostitution, 131, 137
Proudfoot, David, 80
Prynn, David, 115
Pye, Dennis, 33

Queens Park FC, 60
Quelch, Tom, 176
Quinn, C. A., 121

Racecourse Betting Control Board, 135
Racing, 50
Racing Pigeon, 50
racism, 49, 182–3, 184
Railway Review, 74, 85
Raleigh Cycle Company, 52
Ramblers' Association, 143
Ramblers' Rights Movement, 142–3, 150
rambling, 29, 30, 31, 32, 64, 77, 93, 134, 139, 141–6, 168
Rambling Federation, 84
Rawson, Basil, 186
Reading, Berkshire, 107, 111
Reading Labour Rowing Club, 108
Red International of Labour Unions, 88
Red Sports International (RSI), 78, 79,

81, 121, 169–70, 176, 179, 180, 184, 189 *see also* Communist Party (Soviet Union)
Reddish, Lancashire, 112
Reeves, Joseph, 115–16
Reid, Jimmy, 158
'religion of socialism', 27, 34, 74, 77, 82
Reussner, Fritz, 176
Richardson, Robert, 147
Ritter, Gerhard, 172
Roberts, Frederick, 107, 179
Roberts, Kenneth, 1
Rochdale, Lancashire, 47, 88
Rochester, Kent, 85
Rojek, Chris, 5
Roth, Gunter, 170–1
Rothman, Benny, 143
Rothermere, Viscount (Alfred Harmsworth), 133
Rottingdean, Brighton, 116
Rous, Stanley, 188
Rowbotham, Sheila, 30
rowing, 4, 29, 108
Royal Arsenal Co-operative Society, 115
Royal Commission on Distribution of the Industrial Population (1940), 157
Rugby Football Union, 21
rugby league, 47, 56, 58, 85, 134
rugby union, 2, 5–6, 20, 24–5, 47, 56, 60, 134
Rugby Union Football Annual, 21
Russia, 80, 94, 132, 174, 177, 182, 189

Sabbatarianism, 150–4
St Helens, 85
St Monday, 17
Salford, Lancashire, 109
Salter, Alfred, 28
Sandown Park, 20
Sargent, Orme, 183–4
Saville, John, 105
Scout, 32
Seraing, Belgium, 175
Shankly, Bill, 57–8
Shaw, Stephen, 104
Sheail, John, 145
Sheard, Kenneth, 5–6, 24–5

Shipley, Yorkshire, 78, 145
Sheffield, 26, 31, 32, 62, 76, 78, 88, 111, 115, 137, 142, 146, 186
Sheffield Clarion Ramblers, 31, 142
Sheffield Socialist Society, 30
Sheffield Trades and Labour Council, 81
Silvertown, London, 110, 112
Simm, Matt, 28
Simon, Sir John, 183
Sinclair, Robert, 47
Sinfield, George, 49, 79–81, 87, 91, 95, 153, 176, 187
skiing, 173
Slazenger, 50
Slough, 109
Smith, W. F., 52
Snowden, Philip, 30
soccer, *see*, football
social control and sport, 7, 17–18, 25–6, 53–61, 66, 173
Social Democratic Federation (SDF), 27, 28, 30, 34
social formalism, 4–5, 6, 8, 9
socialism and sport: 26–36, 73–98 *see also* British Workers' Sports Federation; Clarion Cycling Club; Independent Labour Party; Labour Party; National Workers' Sports' Association
Socialistic International for Physical Education (1913), 34
Socialist International for Physical Education, 167, 175
Socialist League, 27
Socialist Sunday Schools, 31
Socialist Workers' Sports International (SWSI), 75, 167–70, 174, 175, 176, 178, 184, 189
Society for Cultural Relations with the USSR, 89
sociology of sport, 3–12
Southall, Middlesex, 150
Southampton, Hampshire, 75, 110
Southsea, Hampshire, 109
Southwark, London, 151
Spalding Company Ltd, 50
Spartakiade, 180–1
Spanish Civil War, 185–6

Special Areas Office, 133–4
Spectator, The, 52
speedway, 45, 48, 58, 59, 88, 106, 165
Springhall, John, 62
sport: bourgeois attitudes to, 17–18, 21–2, 34, 54–6, 59, 66, 132
and disorderliness, 58–61, 66
historical approaches, 1–3
historical developments, 15–26, 43–61
and industrial efficiency, 62–3
and media, 20–1, 49–50, 54
non-commercial activities, 61–5, 67, 84
and socialism, 26–36, 73–98
and state, 129–58
theoretical approaches to, 3–12
and working class, 11–12, 22–6, 54–61
see also commercialisation; commodification *and individual sports*
Sports and Games, 96
Sport and Play, 32
Sporting Chronicle, 50, 60, 183
Sporting Gazette, 20
Sporting Life, 20, 50
Sporting Opinion, 20
Sporting Times, 20
sports facilities; provision of in urban areas, 130, 146–54, 199
Sports Fellowship, 58
sports goods, manufacture of, 20, 50–3, 55, 58, 67, 141, 197
sports industry, numbers employed, 48
sports stadiums, 20, 45, 47, 67, 101
Stacey Enid, 33
Stafford, 32
State: theories of, 129–30, 137, 154–5
and sport, 129–58
provision of sport, 132–4, 146–7
regulation of sport, 134–7
and international sport, 187–9
Steinberg, David, 171, 174
Stephenson, Tom, 33, 144–5
Stepney, London, 78, 97
Stepney Workers' Sports Club, 87
Stevenson, John, 43
Stockport, Cheshire, 94
Stoddart, Brian, 56, 165, 182

Storch, Robert, 17
Stratton, H., 29
street football, 136-7, 156
street games, 65, 136-7, 151, 156
structuralism, 10-11
Sunday football, 64, 150, 151-4
Sunday League Football Campaign
  Committee, 154
Sunday Sport, 94, 151-4
Sunday Worker, 79
Sunderland FC, 28
Sutcliffe, Herbert, 58
Sweden, 172-3
Swindon, 107
Swinton, Lancashire, 47
swimming, 29, 31, 32, 45, 64, 76, 93,
  148, 177
swimming baths, 132
Switzerland, 167, 177, 179

table-tennis, 108
Tapsell, Walter, 79-80, 186
Taylor, John, 30
Teachers' Labour League, 89
temperance, 29-30, 111
tennis, 23, 63, 64, 106, 108-9, 110,
  151, 164, 165, *see also* Workers'
  Wimbledon
Thälmann, Ernst, 180
theatre, workers', 89, 122
Thomas, J. H., 47, 181
Thomas, Tom, 89
Thompson, E. P., 2, 10, 155
Thompson, P. Gilchrist, 142
Thurtle, Ernest, 148
Tillett, Ben, 26, 30, 49, 113
Times, The, 78, 148
Tischler, S., 37 n. 22
Tokyo, Japan, 185
Tolpuddle Martyrs Centenary (1934),
  177
Tootal Broadhurst Lee Company, 62
Tottenham, London, 109, 147, 152
Tottenham Labour Sports Association,
  106
Tooting, London, 78, 152
Trades Union Congress (TUC) and
  sport, 76, 81, 82, 104-6, 110, 111,
113, 121, 122, 134, 144, 147, 157,
  179, 182, 183, 189
trade unionism, 11, 18, 20, 26-7, 34,
  49, 73, 104-5, 198, *see also* Trade
  Union Congress *and individual unions*
traditions in sport, invention of, 21
Transport and General Workers'
  Union, 49, 105, 111, 119
transport and sport, 44
Trevelyan, C. P., 142
Trevelyan, G. M., 56
Tribune, 179
Triesman, D., 64
Trotsky, L. D., 82

Underhill, Reg, 117, 122
United Mineworkers of Scotland, 88
United Patternmakers' Association,
  111
United States of America, 197, 199
Upholsterers, Union of, 111

Vamplew, Wray, 18, 25
Vansittart, Sir Robert, 184, 188
Vienna Olympiad (1931), 177, 178, 179
voluntarism, 134

Walsall, Birmingham, 33
Walthamstow, London, 79, 151
Walvin, James, 2, 17, 19, 46
Ward, G. H. B., 142
Ware, Hertfordshire, 109
Warrington, Lancashire, 47
Waters, Chris, 35, 146
Watling, H. R., 51
Webb, Beatrice and Sidney, 180
Weber, Eugen, 172
Weekly Young Worker, 79
Weeks, Jeffrey, 30
Wembley Cup Final (1923), 60, 136
Wembley Empire arena, 45
West Bromwich Albion FC, 45
West Ham United FC, 47, 60, 83
Western Mail, 60
Weston-Super-Mare, Somerset, 120
Whannel, Gary, 62
Wheeler, R. F., 171
whippet coursing, 57

White, Graham, 142
White, Jerry, 137
Whitson, David, 7
Widnes, Lancashire, 47
Wildung, Fritz, 167–8
Wilkinson, Ellen, 142
Willesden, London, 110
Williams, Raymond, 1
Winter Hill demonstrations, Bolton (1896), 31
Wisden's Cricketers' Almanack, 21
women: participation in sport, 8–9, 16, 23, 43, 44, 61, 64–5, 75, 112, 135, 198; and British Workers' Sports Federation, 92–3, 97; and Clarion Movement, 32–3; and National Workers' Sports Association, 110
Women's Institutes, 61
Women's League of Health and Beauty, 61, 64
Wood, Sir Kingsley, 147, 148
Woodcraft Folk, 115–16, 123, 141, 186, 197
Woolley, Frank, 58
Woolwich, London, 109, 110
Wootton, Barbara, 144
Workers' Defence Force, 89
Workers' Football Advisory Board, 153
Workers' Gymnastic and Sports Alliance of America, 197
Worker Sportsman, 96
workers' sports movement: in Europe, 166–74
divisions in, 170
ideology of, 168
and labour culture, 170–4
see also British Workers' Sports Federation, National Workers' Sports Association

Workers' Olympiads, 77, 109, 122, 175, 177, 178–9, 185, 189
Workers' Temperance League, 111
Workers' Travel Association (WTA), 145, 177
Workers' Union Record, 74
Workers' 'Wimbledon', 108–9, 111, 178
working class: consciousness 23–4
culture, 23–6, 34–6, 66–7, 83, 90, 97, 169, 171
working hours, 19, 27–8, 44, 55, 58–61, 73, 171–3
Working Men's Club and Institute Union, 65, 112
working men's clubs, 18
World Congress for Leisure Time and Recreation, 187
wrestling, 93

Yegoryevsky, Russia, 181
Yeo, Eileen, 29
Yeo, Stephen, 11–12, 27, 29, 35–6
York, Duke of, 113
Young Communist International, 77, 78, 82, 169
Young Communist League (YCL), 78–80, 89, 91, 95, 116, 121, 122, 141, 150, 197
Youth Hostels Association, 64, 134, 141, 145, 197
Young Communist, 79
Young Pioneers, 89
Youth clubs, in France, 174
youth movements *see* Boy Scouts; League of Youth; Girl Guides, Woodcraft Folk, Young Communist League

Zeldin, T., 192 n. 35